Swedish Lessons

A *Memoir* of sects, love and indentured servitude. Sort of.

Natalie Burg

Swedish Lessons is a true story, told according to my own memory, journals and emails. Names of people, places and organizations have been changed to protect anonymity. Some dates, as well as the order of certain minor events have been altered to fit the flow of the narrative.

Cover Design by Alisa Bobzien

ISBN: 1490347356
ISBN-13: 978-1490347356

To Nancy & Tim
for letting me make all my own mistakes

To Alisa
for being a true friend through all of them

And to Mike
for being a maker of good decisions
and for being proof that I can make them too

Table of Contents

Natalie Burg

Michigan seems like a dream to me now…
I've gone to look for America

– Simon & Garfunkel, "America"

1
Avfärd
Departure

Saturday, August 17, 2005

Alisa,
I can't believe I've only been here a week. I've done and seen about 463 new things in the last seven days, including learning how to drive a stick shift, riding in a wooden boat on the Baltic Sea (the North Sea? some channel, maybe?), and finding out what it feels like to be "the American." It's like I am my own status symbol. The kids are awesome—totally cool and totally funny...this is the greatest job I've ever had...

The thing about a downward spiral is that you never know you're in one at the beginning. In fact, in my embarrassingly vast experience, they typically begin with unabashed enthusiasm. I should have recognized the pattern too, having just recently tumbled to the bottommost depths of my own personal barrel. But there I was, back on top, embarking on a thrilling adventure abroad. What was the fun in learning from your mistakes when you could just repeat them? On a much grander scale? On the other side of the Earth?

Hindsight, which wasn't an oft-used tool in the first twenty-three years of my human experience, now exposed my decision to skip off to Sweden for a year as more whimsical than it was, say, smart. Sitting on the plane ready to return home, I now knew that trading the pangs of a broken heart at home for the throes of a *Dateline*-worthy meltdown thousands of miles away was not an optimal exchange. But when choosing between a known variable that hurt, and the promise of unknown adventure, I'd made the same choice every recently single, underemployed young American with an

English degree would have made. I chose adventure!

At this moment, however, the only choice with which I was concerned was in-flight magazine versus in-flight movie.

Ding!

I let out an audible sigh of relief as the fasten-seatbelts light further reminded me that it was all over. I was buckling in; I was going home.

Where was my usual fear of flying? Nowhere in evidence. How was I not fretting over mid-air collisions? It was a mystery. Had I forgotten to count the on-board children? I always counted kids on my flights. It was my secret recipe of anxiety-induced OCD and superstition: The higher the number of children the better, because (obviously) God was less likely to allow a plane packed with his little angels to crash than one populated entirely with us crummy adults. Not this time. All of us crummy adults were headed home, and that was all I needed to know.

Was I apprehensive to be seated next to a traditionally dressed Muslim cleric on a tarmac in Copenhagen just days into a worldwide controversy over a cartoon of Mohammed running in a Danish newspaper? Nope. Not in the least. I was feeling too good for racial profiling, even. I gave my new plane buddy a smile.

"Is Detroit your home?" the gentleman asked.

"Yes," I said more affirmatively than necessary. "Michigan is anyway. I'm going back after being gone a long time. Do you live there too?"

"I do," he said, adjusting his dark tunic into a comfortable arrangement for the long ride. "I am looking forward to my return, as I can see you are." He gave me a smile.

Was I that obvious?

I rummaged under the seat ahead of me for my journal. Intermittent journaling and emailing my best friend had been the touchstone of my sanity for the duration of my time away. As I uncapped my pen to record the very end though, I wondered where I would start the whole story, were I to tell it in one fell swoop. I guess it started in the Waaras' basement (*VAR*-a, I'd carefully pronounce), where I woke up one morning and realized I'd just moved to Sweden. And I wasn't at all clear on why.

But no, I couldn't just start explaining things from Sweden, Day One. The story really began at the close of another, so to understand how I ended up in such a precarious situation, we'd have to start there: at the end of one story, just before the next was about to begin.

I'd just hit the cold, hard bottom of what had been my most dramatic, if clichéd, downward spiral to date. Greg and I had broken up. And for real this time. We'd tried breaking up twice before, but that passionate, unshakable love we shared (and/or our mutual insecurities, fear, and codependency) kept us coming back to one another—only to be completely shocked months later when we'd found nothing had changed, and he was screaming at me, and I was crying. Again.

But this time we'd called it quits in a way that at last felt final. (Fingers crossed!) Although it was a relief, it was also very traumatic for my twenty-three-year-old heart. There were months of tears, anger, binge-drinking, lengthy episodes of bitching about him, and over-analyzing every word he'd ever said to anyone who would listen—all the breakup classics. Maybe it wouldn't have been so difficult for me had I not been so sure about Greg. Our two-year relationship had begun so perfectly and fatefully and with such, well, unabashed enthusiasm.

And as luck would have it, just as I was skidding into the frosty denial stage of grieving—when any opportunity to move on prematurely would have looked as tempting as a stroll through the Candy Cane Forest—I went out to lunch with my mother's new husband's sister. I suppose that made her my step-aunt, though being an adult when your parents remarry allows one to invest significantly less in such hyphenated titles.

Mom was in Lansing to attend a folk festival of which Jane, her new sister-in-law, was an organizer. Of course, my mother being in town was a great opportunity to score the kind of meal I couldn't afford on my shop girl wages. Plus, I'd heard great things about Jane. She was supposedly the most relatable character in my freshly acquired troupe of hyper-extended family, and I was going to like her a lot. She was like me, my mom said: creative, down-to-earth, walked to her own drummer, etcetera. Jane had dedicated her career to helping refugee women integrate into society. Although I fully intended to do something meaningful with my life, I didn't have the first clue as to what that might be. Since I was beginning to worry it would never come to me, hanging around someone with Saving the World on her résumé sounded like a smart idea.

So it happened that my mother, Jane, and I decided to have lunch on the sunny rooftop patio of my favorite Mexican restaurant in East Lansing. Jane and I hit it off. We spent the August afternoon chatting it up over our topopo salads about being vegetarians, my writing, and her amazing career. I loved her long, flowing hippie dress, and she liked my new, short, sassy breakup hairdo. What a great day. And then I said something about not knowing what I was doing with my life.

"I like working at Ann Taylor," I said, "but I really just got the job because I had to stop working at this awful vet clinic where I'd been forever. I guess I'll just be working on getting more regular writing jobs until I can make ends meet. I don't have anything keeping me in Lansing except a weekly bar review gig and not knowing where else to go."

Jane paused for a moment, tortilla chip still in mouth, her eyes widening. "You'd be perfect!" she said. "I have just the thing for you! Have you ever considered working abroad?"

I had no idea what the answer to that question was. I couldn't even find a job with my English literature degree in the United States, (where, in theory, people read *literature* in *English*). What could I possibly have to offer an employer overseas? "Um…I don't know," I said. "What kind of work?"

"My friend, Inger, is looking for an au pair for her children," she explained. "She lives in Sweden and wants to find an educated American girl in her mid-twenties to come stay with her for a year. What do you think? Would you be interested?"

I was amazingly qualified for this position. I'd never been qualified for a job I wanted in my life. Was this a job I wanted? Not having any criteria against which to judge the question, except that living abroad sounded like fun, the only logical conclusion was yes. Yes, I did want to be an au pair. That's a nanny, right? I liked kids. And plus, there would be that whole running away from my feelings thing—that was a bonus. It was perfect timing for my chilly heart to freeze right where it was; who needs to go through depression and acceptance? Not me!

Six weeks later, I was on an international flight, leaving behind an apparently traumatized Greg (maybe he thought we still had round four left in us? Too late now!), and knowing exactly five facts about where I was going:

- I was to be a nanny/English tutor for three Swedish kids for a year.
- I'd be living on a farm where a bunch of people my age worked.
- I was going to be paid little, but would have all of my living expenses taken care of.
- The family was signing me up for Swedish classes in the city.
- I'd be going along on trips to the South of France with the family and could take all the day trips around Europe I wanted.

Honestly, it sounded like plenty of information to me.

2
Ankomst
Arrival

Saturday, August 10, 2005

I am in Sweden. Sweden looks like someone took my little hometown, cleared out all of the trailer parks and aluminum siding, and rebuilt it with a few scattered gingerbread houses and buildings made at IKEA. It feels really peaceful here. My main concern right now is fitting into this family, figuring out what I need to do for my job, and not letting them think I'm a lazy American. Wow. I'm so tired. This jetlag is nuts.

It's Saturday morning, my first in Sweden. So far I've spent the morning putting my room together, getting dressed, and wondering if I should be doing something. I also really have to pee. Where is the bathroom, again? It was so late when we got here! I should go look, but I'm just sitting here. Inexplicably.

This house is incredible. Inger gave me a brief tour last night when I got here and told me it was built in the 1830s. It is full of all sorts of rooms and hallways and staircases. The floor is all tile and hardwood. Everything is made of wood, plaster, or glass. There's no drywall, no carpeting. It's so...is "organic" the right word? Or just "old"?

"Natalie?" It was the tiniest voice I'd ever heard, and only barely audible through my door. Thank God! I'd been sitting in my new Swedish bedroom in the cold Swedish basement since I'd woken up thirty Swedish minutes earlier. It was my first morning here, and I was half-hazed over with jetlag, and half-terrified of the irrevocability of being here, both states rendering me completely motionless. Why didn't I know what time Swedes woke up in the morning? Did they eat breakfast? Of course they ate breakfast. Was I invited? Was I supposed to bring my own? What was the protocol? Why didn't I know this? Holy hell, I had to pee so badly. Was it possible that I'd committed myself to living in a foreign land for a year without doing the slightest bit of research? Even regarding bathroom etiquette? Good move, Natalie. Great job.

So Lisbeth's scarcely audible beckoning elated me. Yes! Maybe it's someone telling me what to do! I poked my head out from behind the heavy wooden door.

"Yes?"

"Would you have some food with us?" the thin, strawberry-blonde girl asked.

Lisbeth was a beautiful seventeen-year-old girl rendered plain by her painfully visible shyness, a slightly imperfect nose, and the shit-dumb luck of having a knockout of a younger sister. She was the kind of girl whose delicate insecurity made you want to compliment her to the point of seeming creepy, even though nothing you could say would ever sink in. She'd decided she was plain, and that was that.

At the moment, I was less concerned with her emotional wellbeing and more excited that she'd overcome her shyness long enough to offer me food. As I followed her up the stairs, I realized that I would never have made it out of my cellar without this assistance. Was I really so meek? I'd never thought so, but I'd never found myself completely alone and disoriented in a European basement before either. Besides, I had no idea how to even find the kitchen, and it really wasn't my style to wander through strangers' humongous homes, poking around for food. Or toilets. Would it be weird if I stopped in one now? Was the whole family waiting for me somewhere?

The house was amazing. It was a large colonial-style home (though, not having been colonized, I assume the Swedes have another name for rectangular houses) that served as the master house for the enormous surrounding farm, Ödmjuk Gård ("Humble Farm," in Swedish). This was no field-next-to-a-barn farm like most of those I'd grown up around in northern Michigan. This was a farm whose acres extended past the horizon and had its own worker houses—with workers living in them. It had multiple barns. It had a hostel on the premises. Why a Swedish farming family in the tiny town of Kassgården would need an empty hostel, I had no idea, but Inger had mentioned it as if it were an active part of the estate.

My stomach rumbled as we neared the top of the mammoth staircase.

I looked up at the little waif and her bunchy, scrunched-down woolen socks with increasing gratitude. She was sweet. I liked her already.

"Was your sleep nice?" she asked.

"It was," I said. I wanted to follow up with some politely reciprocal question, or a quick little joke to suggest I'd be a fun, older-sister figure for her. But I had nothing. My mind was as blank as it was swimming. Jetlag. I'd have to be charming later.

What was going on with those weird socks? I thought instead. Where I came from, brightly colored woolen scrunch socks had exited stage left with Zack Morris. What was it, 1993 over here? I looked down at my bright blue Puma sneakers, fresh from my suitcase. Now there was some fashion forward footwear. But then, I was in her country and her house. Maybe I should be taking cues from her attire, not expecting her to live up to my Midwest couture standards. Nah, those socks were ridiculous.

But as we rounded the top of the stairs and turned into the kitchen, my concern was validated. Before me stood a pale, wide-eyed family of five be-socked Swedes. Unbeknownst to me, one of rudest things a guest could do in a Swedish household was to wear shoes inside. This, apparently, was a sock culture. Whoops.

"Good morning," I stammered.

Inger, the red-haired mother who'd picked me up at the airport the night before, was the only one I'd said more than hello to before going to bed. I'd also spoken with her several times on the phone over the past few weeks, so she was beginning to feel a bit familiar, if only relative to everyone else in this hemisphere. She was poised at the head of the table, opposite the doorframe in which I was standing. The large, sunny dining room and attached kitchen were in perfect order, as was the breakfast spread before us. The family was lined up like Von Trapps around the dining room table: boys on the right, girls on the left, matron in the middle. Inger swiftly seized the hostess reins from her daughter as Lisbeth took her spot at her mother's right side. "Good morning [*god mawwwwwning*], Natalie! You are soooo welcome here! Please, sit down there at the end of the table across from me."

Inger had said that yesterday too, that I was "sooooo welcome here," when she picked me up at the airport. In fact, she'd said it several times during our first conversation, which had occurred over a quick meal at the terminal café. I'd taken its redundancy to be a reflection of her enthusiasm, or some cultural tic to which I wasn't yet accustomed. She'd also managed to tell me all about herself, her family history, her personal philosophy on several topics, but it wasn't until this moment that I realized she hadn't told me a thing about these people standing in front of me: her family.

These mystery beings were now incredibly present and staring right at me. In addition to Inger, the Waara tribe included Jan—the father and farmer—and three kids: Åke, Lisbeth, and Pia, ages seventeen, sixteen, and fourteen—boy, girl, girl. They all greeted me in timid, flawless English as we settled into our breakfast chairs. They were all taller than myself, which wasn't saying too much, and they all had large, round, bright eyes. Åke was a platinum blonde, while his sisters both had matching long, smooth, strawberry hair. Lisbeth and Pia also shared an attractive sprinkling of freckles on the bridges of their noses. All three were good-looking kids, but Pia was remarkably lovely. They all seemed adorably shy and instantly likable.

Why did these teenagers need an au pair again? Not for diaper changes, clearly, and not English lessons either, now that I'd heard them introduce themselves. Hm. I probably should have sorted that out before getting on the plane. I mean, Inger had sent me photos of them. She'd written something or other about them in emails. I think it's safe to confess at this point that I have never been much of a details person.

And why was Inger at the head of the table with me sitting at the other end? Did I take the dad's spot? Or did he usually sit so sheepishly at his wife's left hand, third in command behind the eldest daughter? Or am I taking this seating arrangement too seriously? They aren't Greek gods after all; they're Swedish farmers.

The six of us huddled around the table as the oddities around me compounded. Everything was maniacally still but the tinkling of utensils against plates. Why were they using their knives and forks simultaneously, gathering each bite like clumsy, two-fisted chopsticks? All of the scraping of metal and scooping of food sure was a noisy way to eat. Should I be eating that way? No, that would be weird, right? I should eat the way I eat.

Everyone seemed far too interested in two-fisting their food to be concerned with the foreigner sitting at the table. The teenage boy to my right—was his name pronounced *Aaa-ka*?—was eating exactly the way any American kid his age would eat. His plate was piled high with sausage patties, eggs, toast, some sort of crackers and cheese, and he was presently whispering something in Swedish to his father that seemed like a request to pass him even more food. So that seemed normal. Jan nodded at the murmur and reached across the table toward a box of cereal. His own plate resembled his son's, stacked high with nearly everything on the table, yet Jan had everything plopped on top of each other like a feed pile. Across the table, the girls had much more measured portions on their plates, particularly the younger. Pia was so slight it made sense that she ate very little, but dang. She was sure slothing her way through the world's tiniest serving of scrambled eggs. While the others made steady progress scraping and scooping away at their meal, putting bite after bite in their mouths, Pia spent a majority of the time timidly cutting her small bits of food into even smaller bits of food. Digestive issues? Did she have a tiny esophagus? No molars?

How my mind had wandered to food-consumption analysis, I had no idea. I was exhausted past the point of even pretending to be chatty, but I felt urgently compelled to say something to break the silence. To be entertaining. There was a stranger sitting in their kitchen; shouldn't they have been itching to do the same? Fortunately, Inger cut through my internal tangent with what I would soon recognize as her complete inability to ever shut her mouth.

"So how was your rest, darling? Did you sleep well in your new bed?"

To picture Inger properly, imagine Ronald McDonald's sister, sans the makeup job. She was tall and thin with a round head and even rounder red poof of hair. And her mouth—oh her mouth!—it was almost as crazy looking as the stuff that would later come out of it. It was broad and redder than her hair, and almost constantly poised in the largest smile you've ever seen.

Her unique features hadn't made such an impression the day before, when she was fetching me from the airport. Between the jetlag and listening to her life story for three hours, all details were a little blurry. I did recall noting her candidness as a good sign, however. I was going to be a part of the family, after all, so I appreciated her willingness to share on any topic that entered her head.

"We are a nation in transition," she'd said out of nowhere at the airport, briefing me on Sweden's national identity before diving right back into another personal narrative about her youth. She went on to describe her parents as stuffy, money-grubbing Swedes who spent their lives avoiding the true meaning of living.

"My mother—she never worked outside the home a day in her life, but would have not survived without a maid," she laughed. "Ha HA! Every inch of floor and window was scrubbed clean each day and never was a linen out of place!"

I nodded along, tearing hungrily through the dry baguette she'd ordered me from the café.

"But in Sweden, each generation finds itself so different to the past. We…we are a household in motion! I think of what my mother would say as I step over piles of clothes on the stairway or whatever the children have left behind. Life is too much, too important to worry about such details, correct?"

Excellent. I could not have been more pleased with this explanation, as regardless of having been hired to assist with domestic duties, I wasn't much of a housekeeper. It seemed we had this in common.

"I just want to tell you, you are sooo welcome here," she said again at the breakfast table, leaning forward, her forearms resting on the edge of the tabletop, grinning like she was eating shit, not eggs. "Sooooooo welcome!"

"Oh…ah…thank you. I…" I was so confused. Why was she still telling me this, like there should be some doubt about my state of welcome-ness? You told me to come, woman. Did someone here not feel I am "soooo welcome?" Again, why were these kids teenagers?

Inger's conversation glided past my panicked reaction. She leapt right into a debriefing of my new life with the Waaras.

"You'll feel free to come and go through the house as you'd like," she said. "Have whatever you'd like from the kitchen. We'd like you to be comfortable and eat whatever would make you happy. You might notice that we Swedes have different eating habits to the American diet."

"Oh?" Looking down at my plate of eggs and toast I was thus far unconvinced. This looked like breakfast to me. And there was Åke, pouring milk on his cereal—wait—what was that he was pouring on his cereal? It was coming from a carton, but it was way too thick to be milk. Was it yogurt? Liquidy yogurt? In place of milk? On cereal?

OK, Inger, I'll bite on your dietary differences story. Go on.

"Oh! When I lived in your state of Kansas as an exchange student so long ago, I remember eating pizza from restaurants at all hours of the night! It was amazing! It was the middle of the night, and there we would be, in the kitchen, eating pizza! But here, dear, we typically eat from home. Restaurants are so very expensive, and we tend to take our meals at home and make most of our foods from the kitchen."

"Really?" I was genuinely interested now. I wasn't much of a cook at twenty-three, but I did have a desire to be one. Would I learn to cook here? This and the promise of Swedish Chef jokes in my future made me excited about the prospect. Or was I supposed to know how to cook already?

"Oh yes, we don't have many of the processes you put into your foods there," she went on. "Many of your fast foods and your foods made with chemicals are much less consumed here. In fact, they are mostly not permitted by law."

"Oh, well I'm pretty picky about eating healthy—"

"Why when Sarah left—she was an au pair with us two years ago now—she said she lost ten pounds while she was here. Can you imagine? Just because we eat so differently! Ha ha! You may notice a difference too!"

Umm…thanks. Was I cranky from lack of sleep, or was she suggesting I might (or should?) lose weight because I clearly didn't know how to take care of myself at home? As a vegetarian who hadn't eaten fast food in years, I was a little unclear of what my reaction should be. Would defending my personal diet be offensive to her? Or worse, would it reveal that she had offended me? (I'm Midwestern, remember. Being offended is one of our worst offenses.)

Maybe she was just trying to gently warn me that there were no Big Macs in my future. As I didn't eat Big Macs, it didn't really matter how I responded. Clearly, no one would try to offend a new visitor to their home, let alone one that had just shipped herself thousands of miles to live with you for a year. Obviously, I was just sleepy and short-tempered. And yet, she was still patiently grinning at me, awaiting a response, as if I were naturally going to agree with her cheerfully demeaning assessment of my own eating habits, which she'd never witnessed.

I was still trying to think of some way to respond when Jan saved me. From his seat to my right he turned his head to speak to me for the first time. It was as if he'd been waiting patiently for his wife to run out of steam before attempting to say anything. He was clearly not the alpha dog of this pack. His mannerisms were so childlike and sweet that he disarmed my annoyance at his wife instantly.

In slow, unsteady English he said, "You like in the sailing? In the boat?" As he spoke he waved his fork up and down, like a tiny ship going over waves of air, and then grinned at me with bits of half-chewed bread bursting from behind his teeth. I've never felt so completely disgusted and charmed at the same time.

"Yes!" I said, with an empty mouth. "I do like sailing. Do you have a boat?"

Sunday, August 11, 2005

I'm going to have to start making lists of everything I see and do or I'll never remember it all. It's my first full day here and I'm already overwhelmed with activity. Here's today so far:

- Met a sea captain
- Took apart a sailboat (As I'm bailing water out of the bottom of the boat with a coffee can, I say to Åke, "Is this what I'm supposed to be doing?" He responded, "In Sweden?" Ha! I certainly hope he was planning on saying no!)
- Had coffee and muffins in a garden
- Learned four words:
    - *Moofin* = muffin
    - *Kaffe* = coffee

- *Stopp* = stop
- *Gård* = farm

The first weekend was like something from a travel memoir. The morning of our first breakfast, Jan, Åke and I went sailing. Kassgården, the village where Ödmjuk Gård was located, sat a short ride from the southern coast of Sweden. The three of us climbed into the oldest, reddest Volvo station wagon I'd ever seen and took off through miles and miles of flat farmland.

Jan and Åke had a great deal in common, primarily in how they were both unlike Inger. Whereas Inger was loud, verbose, and flowery, these men were subdued, fair, and simple. Or were they boys? Although father and son, they seemed like peers to me, and it wasn't obvious whose maturity was unaligned with his age. Perhaps they met somewhere in the middle. Regardless, besides Åke's height advantage on his father, and Jan's now gray towhead, they were a remarkably matched pair. They both had round, pale blue eyes and goofy but endearing smiles. Like the elder of his sisters, Åke was a perfect cross between attractive and painfully awkward. On the train from the airport the night before, Inger said that she would give me a wage increase if I could teach her son how to be comfortable around girls. I pointedly chose to take this as a joke. I may have been a young American woman on the rebound, but I did have some standards.

The point was taken, however. Åke was shy. Both he and his father possessed the quality of males who long ago learned that the humiliation of being submissive to a dominant female was better than losing the fight to her again and again. They were going to be easy to get along with, I thought.

Our first day together validated this assessment. The three of us clunked along in the Volvo in near silence. We traded pleasantries now and again, but between Jan's awful English, Åke's bashfulness, the jetlag and my fear of trying to pronounce "Åke," we were all content to watch the scenery go by. I was shocked how much the countryside looked just like northern Michigan. Foreign trees and landscapes were supposed to look different then their boring Midwestern counterparts, weren't they? Yet here were the same expansive fields of neatly organized green and brown squares I knew so well from home. There they were, surrounded by the same smatterings of maples, elms, birch, and evergreens, sometimes in thin lines around the farm perimeter, sometimes lumped into small forests, just like the town of Tawas where I was born and raised.

Except with castles, apparently.

Each time we passed a large stone house, Jan would point out the window. "You see castle?"

Really? That was a castle? It was an honest-to-goodness shock to me that European castles were a totally different breed than Cinderella's. They were beautiful; there was no denying that. But they were houses, mostly shaped like the Waaras' home: large rectangles with evenly spaced windows in two or three rows across the face, and a solid wooden door standing squarely in the center. Some were bigger than others. One or two might have had a regal-looking stone gate. But they were essentially big, old houses.

Don't be disappointed that that is what a real castle looks like, I told myself. *Don't be so American.*

It was not an ideal time to be an American overseas. It was 2005, and we were well into a war that was even less popular in Europe than it was at home. On top of that, we'd just managed to reelect the same guy who had gotten got us into it. Whatever amount of incredulity I felt toward this snafu in national judgment, believe me, Europeans were stunned tenfold. Liberal as I may have been personally, Americans of all creeds were looking like huge dumbasses abroad, and I was inescapably American.

I was well aware of this Stateside. My editor at the newspaper for which I'd written bar and entertainment reviews in Lansing called it the minute I told her my plan to leave.

"You know they are all going to think you love Bush and try to argue with you about how stupid Americans are, right?" she warned. Having read my recent Ted Nugent concert review (and editing out almost all of my verbal vomiting, as if *Lansing State Journal* readers *weren't* interested in a twenty-two-year-old freelance writer's political opinion), she knew that this was not a misunderstanding with which I would be comfortable. Also, she may have been trying to get me to stay. I was good with deadlines.

"OK, fine," she said when this didn't change my mind, "but be careful. For all you know, you could be signing yourself up to be a part of the underground European sex trade."

Ha! Sex trade. Like I would get myself into a situation where I was being exploited overseas. Like that would happen. No one could do to that to me; I was an American.

The point was, I was prepared to be perceived as what the band Green Day had just conveniently coined an "American Idiot." It was not by chance that this self-depreciating lyric had boosted their popularity worldwide; clearly, the rest of the planet was overwhelmed with relief that one of us had said it. I was prepared to say it too. I wanted to make it clear how I hated how our country was being run and how we should be so much more like Europe and how I loved international agreements and socialized medicine and sustainable growth and all that shit. I had a lot to say, and I was ready to say it.

But sailboat day was not the day for saying things, and I really doubted Åke or Jan cared in even the slightest way about my political convictions. If the car ride to the boat was a little quiet, the boat trip was silent. And long. For hours, the heavy lapping of the ocean against the wooden boat was all I heard. Once that became white noise, the remaining silence started to multiply. It seemed not one moment of my life had been so absolutely, deafeningly absent of sound. And now I was surrounded by hours of it. I could hardly stand it. Even when Jan needed to tell Åke to do things on the sailboat with the ropes and the sails and whatever, he whispered to him. When the afternoon sun finally charged me with enough serotonin to form sentences, I tried to ask questions about where we were and general Swedish things, but Jan's answers were brief and short on sense. So we sat. And sailed. Quietly.

I laid down on the boat's bench. If it was going to be quiet, I might as well try and get comfy. Why was this quiet making me feel so nervous? With a panicked leap my heart alerted me to something far more palpable than the absence of sound; it was the sound of absence. The numbness filling my ears felt like every inch between here and Michigan pressing against my brain. Would it always be this quiet, I wondered? This empty? Coming from a life lived at breakneck speed and high volume at home, I'd never been big on silence. Here, the lack of sound hit me as the lack of everything that had kept me afloat since Greg. No way was my great escape going to become an introspection-fest, I told myself. This was an adventure. A fun, crazy, loud adventure. Or at least it would be, eventually. Once I got off this boat.

At that moment, I realized with a terrifying ache that I had no way of knowing if that was true. I had no idea what I had just walked into. And yet there I was, somewhere in between Sweden and Denmark, as good as alone. In the quiet. Shit.

Trying to conceal my panic, I sat up to take some deep breaths. That's when I accidentally looked around and noticed that everything in every direction was breathtaking. There was trembling water on either side of the boat, glistening for miles. To the right was the coast of Sweden, spotted with colorful homes and rising hills. To the left was Denmark, with a port, a city, and what appeared to be a castle, a real one with spires and towers. And I was sailing in a little wooden boat between the two.

I am in the freaking Baltic Sea, I thought (or at least I was in some channel or canal or something that connected to it). *How could I possibly be concerned about quiet or boredom?* Two days ago I'd been in Detroit. I could have chewed on the contrast, it was so palpable. Even having grown up surrounded by the Great Lakes, the water here struck me as stunningly vast and impossibly blue. The air seemed cleaner than any I'd breathed before.

I was OK. I decided I could handle day one of my Swedish adventure being more peaceful than exhilarating. I had an entire year to thrill-seek. To run away. With the wild wind forcing crisp air into my lungs, relaxation finally settled in upon me. I closed my eyes and let the Swedish sun warm my eyelids as Jan, Åke, and I collectively rocked back and forth through the open water. It was quiet, but it was nice.

When we finally made it back to shore, the boat came with us. It had been the last sail of the season. Jan managed to explain to me that he'd be going back to farming in a week, as fall hurried along more quickly here than it did in Michigan. It was amazing to me that we'd been sailing in something so…wooden. I'd never seen such a boat, even growing up on Lake Huron. Our boats were aluminum or fiberglass, and we never let them age. We got new ones. But all the boats in this particular marina were the same: really old, and completely made of wood. Like the Waaras', the boats were all in various stages of wear, with scuffs and peeling paint. If we were in Pottery Barn, our boat could have been flipped upside-down, made into a coffee table, and sold as "shabby chic." Jan told me his had been in the family for eighty years. I wondered if the Waara men knew how fashionable their old boat was.

The process of tucking it away for the winter was also completely new to me, despite years of American boating. The three of us yanked the old, wooden sailboat ashore and emptied it of its water before disassembling it, covering it with a tarp, and tucking it into bed for the winter. It would just sit there for months in a public spot where anyone who wanted could apparently just stash their boat, with no doors or locks or measures to protect it, just a tarp. No one was going to take it, apparently, from the public boat abandonment spot. People don't steal here, I guess.

The whole process was all very one-with-the-land and salt-of-the-Earth—hyphenated phrases to which I'd never considered linking myself before. But after the mental and emotional upheaval of the last twenty-four hours, a little manual labor was a welcome diversion.

Way to go, Natalie, I told myself. *Way to get in touch with the land and the sea like these earthy Swedes.* That seemed to be how everything was here: organic. This was a step beyond buying produce from the hippie section of the grocery store; this was a way of life. For the first time since making the decision to live abroad, I had a tangible idea of how fundamentally altered life could be in another culture. I had a feeling that whatever amount of flower power I imagined was in my blood was about to get thicker. Yeah. I could be a Swede.

The pleasant afternoon only became more so when we stopped to visit Jan's parents' house in the little fishing village where we'd just laid the boat to rest. The five of us had coffee (*kaffe*) and muffins (*moofins*) in a charming

Swedish garden. By that point my jetlag was nearly out of control, making even these sharply new experiences blurry.

I was just aware enough to learn that Jan's father was a retired sea captain. He was a real-deal sea captain too. He told me stories of sailing to Asia and gave me tips on how to deal with Japanese traders versus Chinese ones (racist tips, but tips all the same). He'd once sailed to Bay City, Michigan where he was interviewed by a *Bay City Times* reporter—the same newspaper my family read back home. It felt like magic. Here I was, in Sweden, meeting an authentic sea captain and then finding that we had something so bizarre in common.

I listened, as enraptured as possible while being nearly asleep, while Åke and Jan sat quietly with us at the seaside garden table. They shared a delicate and timid presence that reminded me of the way Pia cut up her food. Åke was the quintessential awkward teenager, full of half-repressed smiles, mild acne, and unintentional facial expressions under his neat but fluffy blonde hair. Jan alternated speaking softly to me in terribly broken English, and to his parents in more confident but equally soft Swedish. He seemed far more at ease in their garden than in his own kitchen.

The visit was fun, chatty, but short, and we were soon on the way home again. I was thinking how happy I was that Jan's father was so cool, and how fortunate it was that they lived so close by. We'd probably see a lot of them. As the Volvo carried us back through the farm fields (the gårds, I'd just learned) I fought against my jetlag to stay awake as wooden boats, *moofins*, sea captains, and the Baltic cartwheeled through my mind. This had been a good day.

This, I thought, *is going to be a good adventure.*

3
Den Jobb
The Job

Monday, August 12, 2005

Work has just started. I'm wasting time in the kitchen right now while Inger's on the phone. It seems that I am more her personal assistant than the kids' au pair, and that's fine. I'm way more comfortable taking care of schedules and to-dos than being in charge of kids. And it doesn't seem like these kids need much tending to anyway.

I slept horribly last night. Scratch that. When I actually slept it was fine, but I didn't do that until I tossed for about three hours. My first insomniatic night here...

I'd never been particularly excited about being an au pair, but it seemed like a fair exchange for getting to spend an exotic year overseas. But the prospect of being a personal assistant improved the deal considerably. After years of veterinary reception work (a benefit of entering the workforce with an English degree), I had this gig down pat. Seated at the kitchen counter, Inger tossed out her appointment times and important dates to remember, and I jotted them down in my journal like it was my job. Was it my job? It must be, as she's telling them to me and not questioning why I'm writing them. OK. I must have this one right.

And what was her job? She had appointments with people—two of them on that day, and she made references to an upcoming retreat weekend, which sounded like a group of clients coming to stay on the farm. She called her appointments "processes," and she referred to herself as a counselor, so I figured it must be some sort of therapy. And on the side, she sold Tempur-Pedic products as an individual sales consultant, Avon lady-style, I guess. Her samples were kept in one of the old barns that she kept referring to as the "conference center." She'd already offered me a pillow that cost more than a month of my wages. In fact, she'd had me sleep on it for a night before putting a hard sell on me. I mean yeah, it was a sweet pillow and all, but do the math, lady.

"I'll be seeing Patrik at ten, and then I'll need to be taking a phone call from another client by 11:30," she was saying. I wondered if I was responsible for keeping her on track. What if Patrik's "process" was still going at 11:31? Should I knock and tell her to get her ass on the phone? I decided I'd have a better idea of how I was supposed to interact with her appointments if I knew what was happening during them.

"So what is it that you do exactly?" I asked.

"Ah!" Inger's perma-smile stretched even larger at my inquiry. "Well! That is a very long explanation, I believe," she said. "To begin with, I help people work through the pain of their past."

"So you're a therapist?"

"Quite, quite. But darling, perhaps in a different way than you might be aware of now. I facilitate the process of helping people realize their true potential and rise above the negative forces in this world. I also write books on the subject and make musical CDs."

She had me right up until "musical CDs." Even a solidly "details-schmetails" person like myself couldn't let that one go by unnoted. Still, I made the decision to not press her on it, silently acknowledging that Inger was Swedish, and there were a lot of Swedish things I didn't understand, so I'd ignore it and figure it out later.

"So Natalie," Inger said, abruptly switching gears. "Tell me why you are here."

"Oh. Well," I began, pen still poised above my notebook as if to take notes on myself, "I had to, I guess. The opportunity presented itself, and I had no reason to say no."

Inger's bright red eyebrows and mouth were poised high and wide in anticipation of my next words. I decided I'd better come up with some.

It sounded strange saying it now, in the quiet sunlight of the farmhouse kitchen, but it was absolutely true; I had to come. I'd felt bound to do this the moment it was presented to me. Now, as I glanced out the window at what looked like a historic reenactment of a bustling country farm, it was clear that this specific destination wasn't the requisite piece of the equation.

I had to leave, because otherwise I would have gone back to him.

Maybe not in a month, or even two, but eventually, I knew that I would. Greg was not someone easily left. Emotionally or physically. I thought of a night about a year earlier, when we were fighting and I tried to leave. Not the relationship, just the apartment. But he wouldn't let me go. I was racing down the stairs from our walkup duplex, in tears, frantically searching my purse for keys. I didn't know where I was going; I just needed to leave. I needed space. I needed the screaming to stop. As I fumbled down the stairs, however, he pushed past me, whipped around, and blocked my path.

"Let me go," I pleaded, my voice shaking.

"This is not happening," he said, leaning toward me with his arms extended to the walls of the compact stairwell. "You are not leaving."

So that was fairly terrifying. And I, I learned that day, was completely susceptible to terror. After some additional back-and-forth, I relented. We went back upstairs to finish the fight, and I never tried to leave before the end of an argument again.

What can I say? I come from a monumentally non-confrontational family. My parents never once fought in front of me. In fact, they'd recently divorced, and I'd still never witnessed an argument. When Greg would start with the screaming and the accusations and the name-calling, I had no idea what to do. I would do anything to make it stop. Except leave. That one had been struck from my list of options.

And once it had stopped for long enough, I'd forget about it. I would try harder to not anger him, and he'd shower me with praise and affection and gifts, and we'd be fine. Which was exactly what would have happened if I hadn't taken the first opportunity to get out of Lansing when it presented itself. He couldn't push past me and trap me on the stairs this time.

I sure wasn't about to tell Inger *that* on my first day of work.

"Well," I said carefully, "I just got out of a long relationship, and I guess I'd never tried to find the right job or the right place to live after I graduated. He was in Lansing, so that's where I stayed. So when we broke up, and Jane dropped this opportunity in my lap, I was excited to take it."

"Waaaaandafool!" Inger's unexpected approval of my generic explanation took me by surprise. "So you are not wondering if you have left something behind, and you are fully decided to be here with us now."

You can say that again, sister. Even though it was kind of weird thing to say.

"I just mean to say that we are so glad to have you here," she continued, "and I'm very glad to feel you are glad to be here too. You are just so polite and kind, and even more lovely than the pictures you sent."

This Inger woman was a bit nutty, but she sure had a way with the compliments. I was starting to warm up to her just fine. And I loved listening to her speak. I'd heard that Swedes spoke melodically, but I could never wrap my mind around what that meant. Now it was clear. Every sentence Inger spoke began in a strong, high-pitched tone and every word to follow would trickle down a musical scale. It was fascinating. Or, as Inger would say, FAAA-

AW-

-snay

-ting!

We quickly moved on to the tour portion of my work instructions. That was when we took the unexpected turn of locating and identifying several household-cleaning accessories. I mean, I assumed I would be helping around the house in some way, but Inger was traipsing around the large house, stringing together a rather rigorous agenda of household chores for me to complete. As we moved from room to room, she made such announcements as, "Here is where we keep the vacuum, in this cupboard under the stairs. The floors need no more than two vaccumings per week, upstairs and down. I'll show you how that works later." And then, "The windows are quite tall, dear, but if you're careful, the chairs and tables should help you reach sufficiently to clean them. And no more than once a week for each window, dear." And even, "We are all responsible for changing our own linens, of course, and here is the bureau where you can find all that you need for that. Oh, except for Jan. Would you mind terribly to just put that on your list of things to do in the morning? His linens only need to be changed once a week, but if you could make up his bed each morning, that would be delightful! He's terrible at remembering!"

It could have been my eagerness to please, the enthusiasm with which Inger explained this task, or learning her husband had his own linens, ergo, his own bed, but somehow the whole piling on of domestic duties wasn't really sinking in. Sure, I'll make your husband's bed every morning! Why not? How long can that take? I'm sure I'll have plenty of time between—what else had I already written down?—cleaning up the kids' breakfast, taking out the compost, doing the laundry, vacuuming, walking the dogs, and what was that about horses?

"How do you feel about them?" Inger asked, her red eyebrows practically scraping the ceiling.

"Oh," I said, wondering if she joking. "Honestly, I find horses to be a little intimidating. Why?"

"Well! Ah ha ha!" Inger took a moment to laugh and laugh and laugh at my answer.

Wow, I thought. *I do not have the same sense of humor as these people.*

"Well, that's just fine, dear," Inger said when she had finally collected herself. "Do you feel comfortable enough to try getting to know them?"

What else could my answer have been? "Of course!" I replied. "Throw it at me."

We hopped into the Volvo and went to investigate the horses. The short car ride took us down a smooth country road hugged by a cool grayness I'd soon recognize as the typical Swedish morning. We drove about a mile, passing mostly farmland and a small huddle of three tiny houses before turning right onto a dirt road that led to the horse barn. Apparently, the Waaras had horses. And they needed to be tended to each morning. And night. But why were we driving to them? It seemed to me that when you own a huge farm with multiple barns, it makes limited sense to keep your horses a mile away at another farm. However, I was finding it difficult to interject my questions into the tangent Inger had been on for nearly an hour.

"We've had this car for twenty years!" she was saying, while wildly manhandling the gearshift, "can you believe that? I don't think Americans have a habit of keeping cars that long, no? Well, we are far less disposable with our property. And you will learn to drive this in no time. They don't ever teach you how to drive a manual car when you take your training?"

"Oh, I guess not," I said. "It wasn't an option for me. And it's pretty rare to own a manual anymore in the US. You just don't see them."

"Well—ah ha ha!—no matter. You will learn very quickly! I can tell you will be a quick learner."

OK, I knew what I said wasn't funny that time. But in addition to thinking unfunny things were funny, I sensed another theme running through Inger's commentary. Nothing, it seemed, was a big deal. My lack of horse enthusiasm, my inability to drive a stick shift or bake bread—which was apparently something I was going to need to learn, ASAP—nothing was a problem, she kept saying. It should have been reassuring, but I was picking up something notably disingenuous in her tone. Oh well. I decided I would figure out how to do all of those things and then it wouldn't matter.

Inger drove me to the farm where the horses were located. She informed me as we were getting out of the clunky Volvo that I would be driving it home, and from then on I'd be driving here each morning to do whatever it was that we were about to do to the horses alone. Right. Because learning to drive a new kind of car and learning how to administer daily care for 3,000-pound hamsters are two lessons everyone should learn in the span of an hour.

After parking barely off center in the bend of a country road, we hiked up a rugged hill to the barn. My job each morning, Inger described, would be to walk up this hill to the barn, "prepare the horses for their day," and then walk them down the hill and into the pasture. Where they would stand all day, I guess, until Lisbeth and I came to get them in the evening, when they would walk back up to the barn, and require more maintenance.

"You won't be charged with clearing their waste from the barn, dear," said Inger reassuringly as we trudged up the hill. "That will be left for the evening when Lisbeth is here."

Well, thank goodness.

"And you will be helping her with that, of course."

Of course.

The primary job was walking up and down the hill, first with each of two horses. ("They're just dreadful to walk in a pair. They'll nip at each other and trod on you. You'll want to walk them separately.") And then with several wheelbarrows full of hay.

"And then there's Grölle's coat," said Inger with an eye roll and a smile.

"What does that mean?" I asked, praying her answer wouldn't involve a flea comb.

"Well, you see, daaarling, Lisbeth prefers to give her horse, Grölle, a coat to wear in the winter," Inger said. "This is rather silly, as horses grow their own coats against the cold, but once you start putting a coat on the horse of course, they'll never grow this coat. So we must put it on him now."

So, in addition to walking these gargantuan things down a treacherous hill each morning, and then following with several trips up and down the same hill with wheelbarrows full of hay, I would need to play dress up with this sissy-pants horse. Oh, and I should be careful, because horses don't like to be touched very much in the places where the coat fastens. Super.

After the equine-maintenance lesson, I slid into the front seat of a manual car for the first time. After a brief explanation of gears and clutches and several false starts, I got the car moving. Inger laughed all the way back to Ödmjuk Gård. Each grind of the transmission, every stall-out, each frustrated search for the next gear was, apparently, hilarious. She laughed incessantly, except during the time when her phone rang, and she took the call. While I was in between gears.

Arriving home after my first horse-tending lesson, with my brain still sloshing back and forth in my skull from the driving lesson, I started counting up my morning chores. There was feeding the horses and leading them out to the pasture, walking the dogs, making Jan's bed, and sometimes changing his linens, vacuuming the entire house two or three times a week, dusting at least twice weekly, occasionally watering plants, and doing the laundry at least once a day. Wow. And that was just morning tasks. Doesn't that sound more like what a maid does than an au pair? Or a personal assistant? There was definitely no way I'd be knocking on Inger's door if an appointment ran over. With everything on my plate, I'd have no way of knowing.

When Inger explained the remainder of my agenda to me at home, however, I decided perhaps I had been overly concerned. After completing this handful of mundane morning chores, I would have the afternoon to myself. I pictured trips into the nearby city of Helsingborg to explore, runs through the pleasant Swedish countryside, reading, writing, meeting friends, and basically soaking up the overseas experience. Yes! This was what it was all about! And my free afternoons were when it all would happen.

Then I would just have to be back when the kids were out of school to help Lisbeth with the horses and the kids with their homework, give Lisbeth piano lessons, or tend to whatever their needs were for the evening. The issue was that according to my calculations, I would only have about three and half hours per day of not working or sleeping, and we were a good hour's commute from the nearest city. That had to be wrong, right? Right. Math has never been my strong point. Whatever.

Sounds great! Let's get started!

* * *

I awoke the next morning well rested and optimistic. I had a list of things to do, and I was going to do them. Inger had commented that while my duties so far seemed quite mundane, I should just get started on what we'd talked about yesterday, and as time went by, my job would evolve. I would soon be enrolled in Swedish classes, and that would replace much of my afternoon duties, and I would be soon helping Inger more with her work, once I learned more about it. OK, I could live with that. Everything on my list thus far involved cleaning, true, but I knew how to clean, and I could do it well, even if it wasn't my idea of a good time. As two of my mad passions in life happened to be doing things impressively well and crossing items off lists, I was actually enthusiastic about getting started.

The kids were off at school already, and I enjoyed a breakfast of cereal (they had Special K! Yum!) while Inger briefed me on her busy day of taking a few appointments and spending the day writing in her office. Was I quite comfortable with my list? If not, please just knock on her office door, and she'd be soooooo happy to help. Oh, and by the way, she was so pleased that I found a cereal that I enjoyed in the cupboard, and I was welcome to the remainder of the box, but just so I was aware, it was purchased by accident and no one seemed to like it, and it's quite expensive, so we wouldn't be buying any more of it again. Ever. On with our day!

My first task was vacuuming. As the entire house was hardwood flooring, I assumed that this meant the twice-weekly vacuuming would include zipping through a few rugs and being done with it. Oh no, Inger explained that morning, the whole house would be vacuumed, wood floors, stairs, and all. Although the house had to be six thousand square feet and included two stairways, Inger exclaimed how easy it was to cover all that ground because of the convenient, vacuum-in-the-walls system with which this nineteenth-century farmhouse came inexplicably equipped.

This was how it worked. The cupboard under the stairs, in addition to housing the tiny bathroom next to my cellar-suite, contained a mass of tubing and a vacuum head. One would plug the end of this tubing into one of several sockets located in various places throughout the house and—voila!—you were vacuuming. This seemed practical, but as I learned that first day, the low ratio of wall holes to square footage in the large house made it quite the opposite. The result was the vacuumer bumbled up and down stairs and around the great house with yards and yards of tubing wrapped around her arms, over her head and tangled between her legs. If I had a *krona* (a Swedish dollar) for every brush the tubing and I had with a fatal tumble down the stairs—well, suffice it to say I'd have more *kronor* than I ever made vacuuming.

It had taken me the greater part of the morning to sort out this vacuum system fiasco and manage to run the thing throughout the entire house. I had just enough time to take Agda, the adorable and gargantuan Newfoundland, out for a walk (How long of a walk? How far do I take him? And where? Inger: Whatever you like, dear!) before it was time to join Inger and Jan for lunch.

"How was your morning, dear?!" Inger inquired as she fussed around the stove. Lunch smelled terrific. She was making potatoes, salad, and fish, and the absolutely wonderful aroma of a warm lemon sauce filled the kitchen. I was hungry.

"It was good," I said, finally feeling alert enough to interact normally with my new family. Jan was seated at the table, smilingly awaiting his lunch. "Is there anything I can do to help?"

"Oh no, darling," Inger said cheerfully. "Do take a seat. I'll teach you some of our basic cooking later, but you just enjoy yourself today. What we are about to eat is what we call *middag*."

Inger pronounced the Swedish word slowly and with the skill of someone who had taught her native tongue to a foreigner before: *meehed-daaawg*.

"Med dawg?" I said. "Is that lunch?"

"It is!" She was carrying pots full of food over to the table as Jan nodded, clearly very enthusiastic to hear me speak a word he genuinely understood.

"I'm so excited about learning Swedish," I said. "Please, throw all the words you can at me. In six months I want to be fluent."

"Ah! You are such a good girl!" Inger praised. "It's so nice you have an interest in our language. You know, most people assume learning Swedish is unnecessary because nearly all Swedes know English. Our last au pair absolutely refused to learn. She said it was pointless and wouldn't stand for Swedish being spoken around her."

"What?" I said, incredulously. Why anyone would choose to live overseas without relishing the opportunity to learn a new language was pure insanity to me.

"Well, we will get you into some Swedish—or *Svenska,* as we say—classes right away, Natalie," Inger promised as she placed the last dish on the table and took her seat with Jan and me. "I think you will have a nice time going to university to learn.

"And until then," she went on, gesturing at the table in front of us, "let's begin with our *middag.*"

She then pointed out to me that we were eating *fisk* (fish) with *citronsås* (lemon sauce), *potatis* (potatoes), and *sallad* (was that lettuce, or salad? Because that looked like a bowl of iceberg lettuce to me). This was going to be so much fun!

As we dug in, I noticed Jan and Inger do the same, strange thing. They transferred their small, round potatoes one at a time onto a salad plate and then used their knives to remove the skin before relocating the rest of the potato back to their dinner plate. The process was repeated with the next potato and the next. It seemed the sole purpose of the salad plate was to banish the potato skins as far from the rest of their food as possible.

Having just shoved an entire half of a potato in my mouth, skin and all, I was feeling a bit like I'd worn shoes to breakfast.

"You don't eat the skins?" I asked.

"Oh no!" Inger replied. "The skins are in the ground. They are dirty." Jan nodded along in agreement. To me, that sounded like, "Oh no! We burned her because she was a witch. She floated when we tossed her in the water."

"But the skins are my favorite part!" I laughed. "And you've just washed them and boiled them, so there's no chance they're dirty anymore. And—" I hesitated before challenging a farmer's knowledge of potato trivia, "—aren't all of the nutrients in the skin? Isn't it just starch on the inside?"

"No, no." Jan unexpectedly came to life to address this question of his own industry. These very potatoes, in fact, had come from Ödmjuk Gård. "Potato ees very…good faw you. No skin. The good ees een potato."

Oh. Well that mystery was solved. I wish I could say that I felt enlightened by this expert opinion, but instead I completely disregarded it. Worse, I knew I was just going to go on eating potatoes with the skins on and hope the conversation never happened again.

Despite the potato-skin controversy, it was an enjoyable lunch. We chatted about Swedish—or *Svenska*, rather, and about *Svensk* food and my life back home. Jan even chimed in a bit now and again. At the end of the *middag*, he said something to his wife in Swedish, and she rose, retrieved something from the kitchen, and returned with a square paper package, butter, and jam.

"*Knäckebröd*." Jan grinned at me, pulling a graham cracker-shaped sheet of square, crispy bread from the package.

Like most Swedish—*Svensk*—spoken to me by a native speaker at this point, the word sounded like a jumble of unrecognizable syllables to me.

"This is *ka-nick-ee-brud*," Inger explained. "It is a very Swedish food eaten with many meals. It is really just crisp bread, and that is what it means in English."

"Oh," I said. "It looks like a huge cracker."

Jan was still sitting poised, with the *knäckebröd* on display toward me, giddily waiting for his chance to speak again. While grinning from ear to ear he said, "You see?" and showed me both sides of the *knäckebröd*. Both were dimpled, though the bottom had shallower dimples scattered across the surface. He gestured toward this side of the cracker and began to speak.

"This side," Jan explained in his slow, measured English, "we say is, eh...home side." As he spoke he dipped his knife in butter—*smör*—and spread a bit along the hard, bumpy bread. I had no idea where he was going with this, but humoring Jan felt as fun as humoring an excited little kid, so I watched carefully as small bits of *smör* were left behind in the dimples.

He then flipped the *knäckebröd* over, exposing the top's deeper, wider indentations, as if someone had dotted the entire surface with a finger.

"This side is away side." Jan was beaming over this punch line, as he once again retrieved some *smör* for demonstration. And when he applied his knife to the bread, I understood. The *smör* sunk deep into dimpled surface, using far more than the "home side." It was a self-deprecating Swede joke, making fun of themselves for being cheap on *smör* at home and indulgent when away! And I got it! And it was funny! Jan and I laughed together for several minutes, delighting in both the joke and our landmark success at communicating. I felt I'd just earned a stinking Nobel Peace Prize.

Inger, who also had been eagerly awaiting the end of this story, was clearly not as pleased. "Jan!" she said sharply, "*Du förlägenhet! Jag ärden svennebanan.*"

Inger hadn't spoken any Svenska in front of me. From her tone, I could tell she was shutting her husband down, scolding him. Whatever she'd said worked. The conversation was over.

Later, after Jan was back out in the fields and I helped her clear the table, she apologized to me for Jan's behavior.

"I am sorry for Jan's crude joking," she began.

"Oh, I didn't find it crude at all," I said. This was what she considered crude? I made a mental note to keep 90 percent of my thoughts to myself.

"Jan is," she began cautiously, "a very true Swede. Which is wonderful in many ways, dear, but sometimes he says things that may be more what a farming Swede's view of things might be, not a typical, modern Swede."

Huh. Well, that explained separate bedrooms. She was embarrassed by Jan. She thought of her husband as a hick. Interesting. Honestly, I wasn't sure with whom to side. Being paranoid about appearing to be an "American idiot" made me know exactly what she meant by using "true Swede" as a pejorative term. Plus, Inger was my number one friend over here, and she was clearly the boss of this household. Self-preservation urged me to align myself with her.

However, Jan's joke was funny. And earnest. As helpful and friendly and English-speaking as Inger was, not a thing she'd said or done so far smacked even slightly of sincerity, something my Midwestern sensibilities could not ignore. Was Inger sort of a bitch? Or was Jan sort of an idiot? I decided it was an enigma that absolutely did not need to be solved on my second day of work.

Wednesday, August 14, 2005

> Thus far I have not done half the reading or half the writing I intended to do. It seems that by the time I do all that Inger wants me to, I have an hour to write emails and go to bed. Boo on that. It's a busy week though. I'm sure it will improve. I mean, I'm not complaining. I've loved it so far. I'm just tired and looking for something to whine about. I'm fine.

With the ratio of cleaning to free time bordering on outrageous for the first three days of my new job, I was indeed feeling the need to whine, but I was determined to be optimistic. I mean, what choice did I have? Would I tell Inger I was too educated and ambitious to accept quietly mopping and emptying the compost bucket as my existence for a year? I wanted to be working toward something. I needed to be learning something or writing something.

At twenty-three, I was as aspirational as a person can be without having any idea of what she wanted to aspire to. I wanted to be a writer, but I had no idea what to write about. I also wanted to make a difference, to be someone whose life mattered. I had no idea whose life I could impact, or what I could do that would be meaningful, but I felt deeply ambitious about it. As I pulled the sheets off of Jan's bed in the morning, careful to avoid the wad of pajamas he kept weirdly stuffed under his pillow, I thought, *maybe I'm supposed to figure out my destiny by process of elimination. Cross this off the list.*

But again, I had just completed my third day of working. I was overwhelmed now, but everything would be much easier once I got the hang of it. The first week in any job was always the hardest, I reminded myself. And I was sort of overexerting myself to try to make a good impression. Besides, I liked the kids. They would be my allies. And though they were all quiet, I knew they would start opening up soon.

"Natalie, are you ready to go for the horses?"

Lisbeth's soft, high-pitched request would become a part of my daily routine. Every evening after diner, we'd get on our grubby clothes and head out into the darkness to take care of those damn horses.

I had no idea what one did to maintain horses, besides the obvious removing of their shit from the place where they sleep. Which we did. The poo-shoveling and hay redistribution was incredibly time-consuming. I could not imagine owning a pet that required such an investment of time and gag-reflex control. When Greg and I lived together with his little-old-lady cat, I didn't so much as touch the litter box. Not my cat, not my poo. This, I could only assume, was the karmic response for being such a snot about it. And I was getting it ten-fold now; this "litter box" was the size of a small room, and each dump was as big as that ratty old cat had been.

After this fabulous chore, Lisbeth spent about a half an hour grooming Grölle, her horse. There wasn't much I could do to help with the brushing, brushing, and additional brushing, so I tried to use the opportunity to stand awkwardly next to her as she brushed and cultivate the best-girlfriends relationship I intended to form with her.

"So how was school today?"

"It was nice." Lisbeth's accent was adorable. Her version of a melodic Svensk accent included alternately smooth and staccato syllables. These people made my Midwestern accent sound downright crass. For example, though Lisbeth had said, "It was nice," it came out "Eeeeeeeet wass nice," with each word cascading down a musical scale from high to low.

"Did you do anything exciting?"

"No."

"So, tell me about some of your friends at school. Are there a lot of people you like there?"

"Mmm…Not really. I go to a very small school, and lots of girls are not so nice."

Yikes. Where do I go from here?

"That's too bad. What about the boys? Any nice guys there?"

"Not really."

Silence.

This was exhausting. As I'd already made the determination that of all noises in the universe, Swedes most loved complete silence, I thought I'd just let us wallow in that for the rest of the night. Mental note: continue pursuit of best-girlfriendship next time.

* * *

After three nights of horses and bonding attempts, I was saved by the needs of Pia. After all, I was there to be an au pair to all of the kids, right? Not just the oldest daughter and her stinky horses? I did like Lisbeth, but between helping her with the horses and giving her uncomfortable piano lessons, I was beginning to wonder if the other two kids wandering around the house were aware of the American living in their basement.

Pia, Inger explained to me on Thursday, would like to go to an exercise class at the gym. Would I like to go with her? Well of course! I loved exercise! And I hated horses! And I was absolutely giddy about seeing a Svensk version of a gym. I was brazenly being the American-jock-bully, just waiting to see what these pale, gentle nerds thought a workout facility should look like. Come on, cut me some slack; I'm much more nerd than jock at home. I was really soaking up the fleeting feeling of athletic superiority.

"Wonderful!" (Waaaandafool!) Inger said, handing me a completely mysterious wad of cash. "You will go the first time with Pia and see if you like it. If you wish to go again, you can pay for your own."

Wha—? I could pay to take Pia to a class? That didn't sound right, but whatever. I'd deal with that later. I would take this colorful bunch of however-much-money-I-was-holding and just be glad there was no horseshit involved.

Since I was such a skilled stick-shift driver three days following my ten-minute lesson, I only felt 98 percent terrified to be driving this fourteen-year-old girl into an actual city on actual Swedish roads with actual Swedish traffic signs. In the dark. Let's just say the "road" on which I'd been driving between Ödmjuk Gård and the horses wasn't exactly a high traffic zone. I had yet to encounter another car.

"You know there's a good chance that I'm going to kill us both, right?" I asked Pia as we buckled in.

She smiled sweetly. "I trust you," she said in a voice so close to a kitten mew I had to resist the urge to give her a gentle scratch behind the ears. Everything about Pia was precious. She was tiny, with perfect little features, glowing strawberry-blonde hair, and eyes so big and green they seemed like they should belong to someone much larger than herself. Even at fourteen she was stunning—nerve-wrackingly pretty.

Pia had no problem chatting with me as we lumbered along in the Volvo. Although she certainly wasn't interested in talking about anything as mundane as school, she told me all about her friends and the things they did together. We talked so easily it almost made me think for a moment that my best Svensk girlfriendship was destined to be with her instead of Lisbeth. But I instinctively knew that was wrong; Pia didn't need best friends; Lisbeth did. It made me wonder if being Lisbeth's friend wasn't an unwritten part of my job description. That, and loosening Åke up, apparently. It certainly didn't have anything to do with this beautiful, well-adjusted teenager in the passenger seat. She was getting along just fine without a life coach.

All serious thought flew from my mind, however, upon arriving at *Friskis & Svettis.* Yes, ladies and gentleman, the Svensk gym was named "Healthy & Sweaty." I couldn't even think of a joke that would make it any funnier than what it actually was. Except that next time you're all sweaty, think of yourself as *svetti*. That's a pretty good one.

And it only got better inside. If you've ever been in an exercise class, you know how ridiculous everyone looks to begin with. Well, let me assure you, when the class was full of tall, pale people of all ages very seriously following instructions yelled in Swedish, it was even more hilarious. The "general fitness" class was so large we took up an entire gymnasium with our semi-unison jumping, stretching, and running around in circles. Inger had described Swedes to me as people who "love to follow instruction," and have a particular passion for rules. This crowd wasn't just getting their svett on. They were following the rules.

"*Och trampa vänster! Vänster! Vänster! Vänster!*" the brutally athletic Svensk in the center of the circle would say, stepping her outrageously toned thighs to the left, left, left. With all her breathiness and spunk, she could have been the love child of Arnold Schwarzenegger and Björk. It occurred to me that this would be a perfect opportunity to pick up on some Swedish as her repetitions of words combined with the physical movements could have been a great learning tool. But it was confusing listening to the briskly shouted Svensk instructions with Madonna and N*Sync blasting from the sound system. Don't they listen to music with Svensk lyrics? It was difficult to comprehend the nonsense of a new language with the nonsense of American pop lyrics drowning it out. And this was no time for confusion. I had to concentrate on stepping right, right, right. Right?

Fortunately, my ignorance of Svenska was paired with a great number of my classmates' lack of coordination. Being a half step behind didn't even make me stick out that much. I bet they didn't even know how lost I was.

Ow!

I guess I'd *trampa*-ed right, not *vänster*, and got a Svensk elbow to my forehead. The older gentleman apologized (I assume) in Svenska. I smiled back and said, "It's OK!" As if it was completely normal to respond to gibberish in one language with what was likely gibberish to him in another. I hoped my smile had translated, at least.

All in all, it was pretty fun, and not a bad workout. *Not the greatest workout*, the American-jock-douchebag part of my consciousness commented, *but not bad*. As we were putting our street shoes back on in the gym lobby, Pia suggested that since I liked it so much, maybe I should buy a card now so we could keep coming back.

"Oh," I said, taken a bit off guard by this innocent sales pitch, "I don't have any money with me now, except what we used to pay for today, but let's find out how much it is for next time."

Pia disappeared to chat with the lady at the desk and returned to me with the information. "It is 200 *kronor* without a card for a class, but you can get a card of six for 750 and each class is only 125 *kronor*."

Great. So I'm paid a 3000 *kronor* a month—a measly $360—which was supposed to be over and above my "living expenses" and I was going to spend sixty bucks of that to take one of my charges to a workout class once a week. While on the clock, to boot. Wouldn't this count as a living expense? But Pia's big, hopeful eyes were too much for me.

"Sure," I said. "I'll get a punchcard next time."

I was going to have to talk to Inger about this. Had she asked me to come all the way around the world so she could get all cheap on me? No, that's silly. I was sure we'd work it out.

* * *

Then it was the weekend again. I wasn't exactly sure how to interact with the Waaras during the weekend. I mean, hanging out with the kids was kind of my job (right?), so hanging out with them on the weekend would be weird (right?). But then, I was on a farm that stretched as far as the eye could see, and I had yet to figure out if asking to borrow the car was an option. Nor did I have any idea where I would go if I could. I could get to the city by train, but what was there to do in the city? And how did the train work? I'm from Michigan, after all. We drive cars.

Then there were all of these rules. Trying to imagine what I would do for fun that wouldn't break any of the firmly established family rules was mind-boggling. Most of the rules were economic in nature. I couldn't be on the Internet or phone too long because it was expensive. I couldn't have any wine from the large, boxed wine supply in the cupboard unless Inger suggested I have some, and then only one glass, please. No one watched TV here. No one even discussed what activities might be going on outside of the house, say, in that city I'd heard of. Both driving cars and riding trains cost money, you know.

So I spent Friday night in my cellar hovel, reading a novel Inger had recommended to me (pretty good story, a little new-age for me, but a decent read) and becoming increasingly nervous about the next two days. What would I do? Stay in here and read? Go into the living room and read? I went to bed early. I had no idea what else to do.

The next two days were indeed quiet. Pia was spending the weekend at a friend's house, and Lisbeth had a riding lesson all day on Saturday. I went for a long and quiet bike ride with Jan and Åke that nearly mimicked the long and quiet boat ride we'd experienced the week before but with less water and more pedaling.

When we arrived home, I chatted with Inger as she prepared dinner. Surprise! We were eating boiled potatoes and iceberg lettuce with some sort of meat dish again. Wowzers, did these people love *potatis*. I'd go extra heavy on the *knäckebröd* and *smör*. Again.

"So where will these Swedish lessons take place?" I asked Inger, careful to sound more enthusiastic about learning the language than impatient to get the hell off the farm.

"Ah! I am so glad you are looking forward to them, dear!" Inger laughed as her long fingers, a kitchen knife, and shards of iceberg lettuce made a frenzied whirlwind on the counter in front of her. "I have checked at the university—that is *universitet på Svenska*—and they have you on a list. They were going to begin a class this week, but they did not have enough students signed on as yet. They hope to have more soon."

"Oh. No one in Sweden needs to learn Swedish, huh?"

"Ah—HA HA!" I was beginning to take Inger's sudden outbursts of laughter with a grain of salt. This was clearly either a cultural thing, or she simply found me outrageously hilarious. I would just have to learn to live with one or the other. "I suppose we have few visitors who are as eager as you to learn. Perhaps we could order your books in advance so you might begin to study them."

"Really?" I said. "That would be great!"

"Remind me on Monday dear, and I will find out more for you," she said, returning her gaze to the lettuce—excuse me—*sallad* chopping.

"Now tell me, Natalie," she continued, "more about your life in the United States. You said you worked both for an animal doctor and as a writer? You must have been a very busy girl!"

Oh, Inger. She certainly had a thirst for mundane facts about my life. But it did feel good to have her ask so many questions of me. Even though I hadn't really left the farm (with the exception of Friskis & Svettis, of course), I found that being so permanently in a foreign country felt incredibly…anonymysing, if such a concept exists. I couldn't quite place my finger on why yet, but I found Inger's questions comforting. She seemed genuinely interested in me.

Good thing too, as it was that glimpse of comfort, and the promise of incoming Svenska books, that got me through the weekend. I certainly hoped the weekends would pick up around there. Where I came from, weekends were for going out with friends, parties, crashing on couches, morning field trips to diners, napping, and then more fun. Where were all of these "young people" who lived on the farm, anyway? Nowhere I could find, and I looked when I took Agda on an hour-long stroll through the farm fields on Sunday. But no matter, I assured myself. I'd be getting into Svenska classes soon. I'd be going on the train to Helsingborg to get to the *universitet*, I'd meet other people from abroad studying Svenska too. We'd all be friends and go out on the town together. That would be the start of my adventure.

4
Den Metod
The Course

Two weeks later, the domestic routine was under my belt, and the monotony was getting under my skin. That's when I learned that Inger was a cult leader. Everything sort of went in a new direction from there. Oh come now, I'm kidding. It was more like a sect than a cult.

It took me much longer than it should have to piece this all together. Well, that's not entirely true either; I didn't piece anything together. It wasn't until she asked me to view a recruitment video that I realized her "therapy" business was something like a cross between Scientology and Amway. And here I'd thought selling Tempur-Pedic mattresses out of the barn was the sketchier of her two ventures.

In my defense, I think my excuse for not seeing this one coming was pretty sound. I really liked Inger—I had to, she was the closest thing I had to a friend in 10,000 miles. I needed her to be sane. So even though I'm sure red flags had been popping up whenever she talked about her *Metod,* I failed to see them. *"Metod,"* it turned out, was her Svensk pet name for her batshit "religion," the "Miraculous Process."

It was just an ordinary weekday morning when she interrupted my vacuuming to ask if I had time to watch a video. I was vacuuming her stinking living room, so the question was little moot, but I took the time to pretend to assess my to-do list before agreeing anyway. When she delighted at my responsiveness and told me the video was an introduction to Den Metod, *that's* when I started to feel as if something funny might be at play. For the very first time. Even I know that when someone tells you they have something "life-altering" to share with you via VHS, it's time to start asking questions.

"I don't want to make you feel that you have to accept it," Inger said as she grinned me into the living room. "I would just like to share it with you so you are familiar with what I do. And, of course, I would sooooo like to discuss it with you further if you choose."

On the other hand, I also felt grateful for the opportunity to better understand Inger's career, as it seemed like a pretty important element to whatever my role was supposed to be. She had, after all, told me that I would be helping with it somehow, and I was all about moving on to the next phase of my job here. Inger would be hosting one of her counseling retreats the very next weekend. There were going to be all sorts of people here. She'd already told me about all of the bread I was supposed to bake (mental note: it's really time to learn how to do that) and meals I was to prepare for their arrival.

So OK, I thought, *if I'm going to help with Inger's alternative counseling weekend, let's watch her alternative counseling video.*

I, being the biggest nerd I've met, brought my notebook and pen in case of a pop quiz later

The Miraculous Process Video

Based on: Love, forgiveness, and inner peace [OK. Can't argue with these things.]
Invented [?] by Carly-something, died in the nineties.
An atheist Jewess? [Do people use that word?] from New York
She experienced recurring childhood dreams involving bubbles of varying colors—disturbing; seemed to be telling her something.
1962—Carly has vivid dream sequences involving rocks and the phrase "He is Jesus"
The credo:
"No reality can be unreal
No unreality exists
Therefore, God is peace"
Jesus wrote a book through Carly's mind [Wait. What?]
He tells the world that there is no such thing as sin [Ooo...bet he's pissed about the crucifixion now.]
We are not created by God. [Do tell.]
What we think of as bodies are a mystical balance of anger and love. Anger is the enemy. God doesn't know about humans. [Shhh...maybe we can keep it that way.]

> Our bodies are not real. We imagine our illnesses and bodily existence through an imbalance of anger.
> Sex is a false attempt to join our souls, but our bodies are fake so it doesn't work. [...]
> Sex is our failed attempt to join Jesus. [Seriously, gross. And sort of blaspheme-ish. And gross.]

Well, at least that explained Inger and Jan's separate bedrooms. Clearly, Inger didn't bother to have sex because she just "joins Jesus' light" instead. Ick. Ick, ick, ick. In everything from her disparaging comments about Jan being a "true Swede," to the way she treated him like the youngest and dimmest of her children, I could see how this religion worked as an excellent excuse. There's a new solution to marriage issues. Not attracted to your husband anymore? Find a religion that gives you permission to never touch him. It was like the Mount Everest of passive aggression.

Apparently the "atheistic Jewess" in the video founded the Miraculous Process after dictating the "corrected Bible" for Jesus some time in the sixties. In some ways it followed the ideas of Christianity, with some clearly notable changes, not the least of which was that humans didn't actually exist. Although in no way a theologian, I was pretty sure humans played a fairly integral role in the Bible.

There's also a whole bit about our brains dividing in half multiple times into successively smaller parts that represent deeper and deeper places in our psyche, like Freudian Russian dolls. Den Metod explains in detail the identity and function of each piece of our split up brains, and how each split damages our soul, and why. You know, kind of like Voldemort splitting his soul to embed a piece of it into a horcrux. Like that. It's a flabbergasting amount of invented anatomy for a religion that does not believe in human bodies, the vessels in which, my limited knowledge of science could confirm, brains are actually located.

As soon as the video was done, while I was still sitting wide-eyed on the couch, the washing machine buzzed in the basement. Before Inger could come back into the living room to debrief, I retreated downstairs to debrief with myself.

How bad could being a housekeeper for a cult leader be? Maybe not overly so, I reasoned with myself amidst a sea of damp, unscented whites (no scented detergents here, of course). It's not like Inger's cult was a freaky, sign-over-to-us-your-wages-and-firstborn-daughters sort of cult. The prophet's name was *Carly*, for pity's sake. It occurred to me that I should probably not even call it a cult, which was probably unfair to Inger's...religion thingy. Which I could maybe learn to respect, and try hard to not insult. In front of her.

And it wasn't as if she was asking me to join her little religious club or camp or business or whatever it was. She'd just asked me to move to Sweden and spend a year of my twenties being her janitor while she ran the thing. Honestly, I totally understood why she didn't put all that in her first email.

I was no longer pretending to pull the freshly washed whites from their proper machine and the colors from the other (yes, there were two washing machines: one for whites, and another for colors), but was instead allowing my eyes to wander through the window, out and over the Swedish farmland beyond the backyard. Of course there was farmland, or *åkerjord* rather, through the windows in the front and either side of the house too. I was really in the middle of nowhere with these people. And their…religion or whatever.

At least there was relative peace here in the basement, my personal wing of the farmhouse, where both my sleeping quarters and the laundry room resided. I shook the weight of being lost in Den Metod from my shoulders, and began to pull damp clothes from the machine and pin them to one of several clotheslines running through the cement laundry room. Inger didn't believe in dryers (in addition to human bodies, apparently), so the family's multiple loads of laundry per day all had to be hung individually. I slowly built a jungle of suspended damp cloth around myself as I wondered what the rest of the family thought about Den Metod. The kids were pretty normal, all things considered, and Jan seemed far too simple for craziness on that scale. *You're not a very good cult leader if you can't even recruit your own family*, I thought.

"Natalie?" Inger called down the stairs. "Do you have a moment?"

I jumped. A feeling of guilt welled up in my throat, as if she would be able to see from my laundering style how damaged my opinion of her had just become. Was this it? Was she about to ask me questions about it? What was I going to say?

"Sure," I said as she walked down the stairs. How could this be any worse than the last time she asked me if I had a moment?

"Would you be comfortable preparing Jan's dinner for him this afternoon? I have an appointment in Helsingborg."

Predictably, I had no argument with this. I did, however, feel awash with annoyance at the linguistic format of the request. *It's not dinner*, I thought, mentally noting both the time (11 a.m.) and Inger's seeming refusal to help me learn Swedish by at least using the words I knew in context. *It's middag.*

"Wonderful!" she said, and smiled her enormous, red, crazy-person grin. "Do you know how to prepare fish?"

"Oh yeah," I said. "I make fish at home all the time."

She was delighted, as always. She left "everything I would need" right on the counter for me, and if I could make some potatoes, a dill sauce, and some salad, that would be great too.

Frankly, I was so relieved she was leaving the house, I hardly listened to her instructions. A little physical distance was definitely in order.

So *fisk*, right? I've done this a hundred times. You take it out of the package, defrost it, pop it in the pan–I needed fifteen minutes at most to prepare the whole meal, as Inger said it was defrosting in the sink already. Best if I gave myself a half an hour to boil the potatoes, I decided. Taking full advantage of Inger's absence, I sat in my cellar bedroom for an inappropriately long time, writing in my journal, reorganizing my clothes and doing all sorts of nothing until I figured it was time to get started.

Up to the kitchen I went.

OK. There was the frying pan on the stove. There were the breadcrumbs on the counter. There were the *potatis* and the dill on the table, and I knew the *sallad* was in the fridge. Huh. Where was the *fisk*? Oh yeah! The sink.

When I think back on this moment, it recurs in slow motion with some horror-movie-esque, don't-go-through-that-door music in the background. Because as I got closer to the sink and its contents slowly became clear, I began to realize that I had made a terrible, irrevocable assumption with regard to this *middag* preparation.

Oh yes, there were *fisk* in the sink. There was a shit ton of *fisk* in the sink. There they were, with heads and skin and fins and scales, floating around whole in the sink as if this being dead thing was completely incidental.

Oh. My. Gosh.

And we're not talking lake trout here. These fuckers were what the Swedes call "flatfish." They looked like a regular fish that had gotten run over by a truck. And then attacked by a zombie. Both of their eyes were on top, staring skyward from their flattened, graying carcasses. They weren't just little eyes, either. They bulged out of the tiny, pointed head and were astonishingly non-symmetrical, like each floating corpse was a freak of its own species. Those eyes. They were insane. And they were all looking at me.

"Holy shit," I said out loud with a sudden realization. "I have to cut their heads off."

After a moment of frantic deliberation over how one removes a head from a fish, I found a knife, placed a *fisk* on the cutting board, took a deep breath, and cut its head off.

OK. That worked. Six more to go. But then they still had skin and bones. And though I couldn't see very well down their little severed throat holes, I was willing to bet there were guts inside those disgusting little bodies too. So utilizing every distant childhood camping memory I had, I pried and pulled and gauged. Scales flew everywhere. Long blue sacks of something burst all over the place. After removing everything I was sure not even a Swede would eat, I had a pile of massacred, yet organ-less, headless fish.

Pulling their bones out was about as difficult as it should be for any decently evolved vertebrate. Even after yanking out the spine, there were plenty of skinny little bones to dig out, one by one. After spending way more time than seemed prudent on dissection, I rationalized that perfection was not the theme of today's *middag*, so I might as well just move on to the breading.

The dill sauce I had going was not smelling good. I hadn't even added the dill yet, so the fact that it smelled like anything was probably not a good sign. I rushed over to the stove, with sick *fisk* shit dripping from my hands, to give it a good whisk. Would enough dill cover the taste of scorched milk? And the fucked up *fisk* the sauce was meant for? Sure it would! Good thing the Swedish recipe for salad was iceberg lettuce on a plate. Not only would that be a quick prep, I felt pretty confident that it would be my best dish.

By the time Jan came up to eat, the potatoes were overdone, the dill sauce was lumpy (in addition to stinky), and nothing was even on the table yet.

Jan waited patiently. Once he finally had something resembling food before him, he said it all tasted wonderful, while smiling at me with *potatis* squishing through his teeth. I don't know who he thought he was kidding, since I was eating the same disastrous crap, but it was gracious of him.

Cleaning up the kitchen afterward, I felt oddly proud of myself. Sure, I'd made a pretty mediocre *middag*, but I'd just taught myself how to clean, batter, and fry a terrifying, run-over zombie fish in under an hour. It was a carnal, look-at-me-surviving-in-the-wilderness type of pride—something new to me. And considering I'd done all this immediately after learning my employer was most likely a crazy person, I concluded that it all went sort of OK.

Had I known this was Inger's way of introducing Jan's *middag* preparation into my daily routine, perhaps my warm, fuzzy feelings would have dissipated. But as it was, I didn't even feel my three and half hours of free time a day slip down to two and half. And it was a good thing, as the feeling of genuine levity I was enjoying while cleaning up after myself in the kitchen was my first since arriving. I even started to chuckle about Inger's Metod. Honestly, there really wasn't anything more horrifying to me than the prospect of spending my twenty-third year as a maid on a farm, foreign or otherwise. At this point, I decided that the weirder things got, the better the story would be in the end.

* * *

Inger was cracking up. Sure, she laughed at pretty much everything I said, but as I explained to her my difficulty with the *fisk* the day before, she was really losing it. All of the reddest parts of her face were in full bloom and vibrating.

"Honestly," I went on, genuinely enjoying my own deadpan act. "I had no idea they were going to have heads. I was expecting a defrosting fillet waiting for me. Jan's lucky to be alive right now, actually."

We were at the mall. Yes, we had left the farm. And we were at a mall. And we were having a nice time. Inger needed to pick up some blank CDs (I pointedly asked no questions about what she'd be burning on them) and asked if I wanted to come along.

Did I? Well, I'd been inside the same house for more than a week, and when she asked, I'd been standing tiptoed on a windowsill, washing the top corners of the panes. So yes, I opted for a trip to the mall.

The mall was called Väla, though I never figured out whether this actually meant "mall," or if it was just the name of this particular mall. It looked amazingly like an American mall. Of course, it had Svensk stores and was chock full of actual Svenskar, but it also had McDonald's, Esprit, and something called the "House of Bagels." So it was half-familiar, at least. After a tour and a quick run in and out of the electronics store, Inger and I retrieved a cup of *kaffe* (Made by a professional! At a *kaffe* shop!) and sat in the food court to relax and have a chat.

"Oh dear!" Inger huffed between bouts of laughter. "You should have just left it! Jan could have had leftovers, and I could have shown you when I got home! Ah!! Ha!!"

After she calmed herself down and I assured her I really enjoyed the challenge, we talked easily about the rest of the week. Until she brought it up.

"So Natalie," she began diplomatically, "I am interested to hear your thoughts on Den Metod. We haven't spoken of it since you watched the video, and I'm eager to hear your reaction."

Oh shit. I felt a bit like I was being confronted by a junior high boyfriend I'd already decided to break up with. No good could come from me humoring her, but she was my employer. How could I avoid offending her while clarifying my disinterest in indoctrination?

"Well," I began slowly, desperately trying to think of a response that didn't involve the word "crazypants." "I thought it was really…interesting…"

I could tell by the extreme arch of her eyebrows that I'd already been too encouraging. Better reel it back in.

"But I'm really comfortable with my own relationship with God and my faith," I continued. "Though the underlying sentiment of the philosophy isn't too far from my own, I guess the disagreement between the...logistics of Den Metod and Christianity are just too big for me to really get on board with."

"Well!" Inger looked all too pleased with my answer, "I am so happy to hear that you are so strong in your Christian faith. You may have noticed that Den Metod is based in Christianity, though. I wonder...would you mind sharing with me what the differences are between the two that make it difficult for you to accept Den Metod?"

Was this a debate or an exit interview? Was she really not clear on the difference between Christianity and the concept of sex being an effort to join God's light? And there being no such thing as sin or Hell, and Jesus coming back to dictate a new Bible, and all that crazy brain splitting into pieces bullshit? Was this a real question?

"Well, there's the fact that you don't believe in the resurrection," I started matter-of-factly. "That's a pretty big cornerstone of Christianity."

We discussed the issue gently for about ten minutes. Her therapy, she explained, was the "method" itself. She helped her clients find their first memory of anger, which was the first moment when their brains split, and then they analyzed that moment, and every other moment of anger in their lives to figure out how to embrace love instead of anger from then on. Which, I mean, is fine. What's horrible about that? I was careful to tell my employer and landlady and only friend in Europe, (albeit now my craziest friend in the world), that I found her "philosophy" quite engaging, but kept insisting that I was perfectly happy with the existence of sin and Satan. Totally fine with it. Liked it, in fact. It was a bit like telling a telemarketer that you're perfectly happy with your cable package, thank you, no matter how much cheaper her deal was.

"I do appreciate you speaking so honestly with me, dear," she said. "It seems you are very true to your convictions, which I think is wonderful. Truly, in Den Metod we believe that each belief is true if it is true within the mind of the believer. But dear, should you ever be interested in exploring Den Metod more fully, or attempting to uncover the pivotal moment of your past, do let me know, and I would be more than happy to share."

"Thank you," I said with the most sincerity I could muster. "I really appreciate that."

5
Svensk Lektionen
Swedish Lessons

Saturday, August 24, 2005

Hey Lise,
So Saturdays here are insane. I pretty much have this nightlife to die for. Tonight, I think I'm going to read another chapter from *Frommer's Travel Guide: Sweden, With the Best Castles and Palaces,* and then, if things go really well with that, I might get my journal out. And write about not seeing any of the best or worst castles and palaces.

I'm learning a lesson in slowing down. I had a bit of a panic attack yesterday when I realized that I'm going to be twenty-four in four months, and I'm spending a year on a farm. But I talked myself out of hyperventilating. I mean, it's not like I haven't had my share of partying and being young and stupid. And I'm certainly not ready to abandon that completely when I get home, so I might as well take a break for a year, right?

Learning Swedish is also going slowly. Mainly because the damn class I'm signed up for won't start until they have more students. Why doesn't anyone in all of Sweden want to learn Swedish? In lieu of actual professional instruction, I have flashcards taped to everything in my room. The kids make fun of me. As they should. My desire to learn Swedish is pretty much the pinnacle of entertainment around here...

Wanting to speak Svenska was not just a ploy to get the Swedes to like me. I was genuinely hankering for this portion of my foreign experience. Part of the reason it was so easy for me to decide to pick up and run off to Sweden was that I was so geeked to be immersed in a new language and culture. I figured the learning experience alone would make for an adventure.

Thus, Swedish lessons were a part of the job arrangement I was not willing to overlook. Sure, there was that stuff about weekending on the Continent and vacationing in the South of France in there too, but as those opportunities seemed far less imminent, I decided focusing on the language classes was an OK place to start when it came to contract demands. You really can't go in with guns blazing when it comes to enforcing deals made via Hotmail.

The fact that everyone here spoke perfect English worked out well for me as I got my bearings abroad, but once I was ready to start trying my hand at a bit of Svenska, I was shit out of luck. Svenskar love practicing their *Engelska*, but no one had any interest in speaking their native tongue with me, nor did they have the time or patience to let me try to speak it to them.

With my pocket Swedish-to-English dictionary and constant barraging of the Waaras with questions, however, I was beginning to piece a few things together. It was a surprise to me, for example, that the word "Swedish" does not appear in the Swedish language. In fact, there's no "Sweden" either! I was living in *Sverige*, trying to learn Svenska, a language that rarely, if ever, uses the "w" sound. Veird.

Until my supposed Svenska class filled up, I was more or less on my own. So I taped homemade flashcards to things. I read Svensk grammar books. I tried to force the kids into helping me out. And to Pia's credit, she tried her hardest to teach me to count as we rode our bikes to the train station one day.

"*Tjugo*," she said, peddling away a couple of yards ahead of me. We'd finally made it to "twenty." I was already mentally exhausted. The chilly wind and the bicycling in forty-degree weather weren't helping.

"Choo-go!" I said back.

"*Nej*," Pia said in her soft and lovely voice ("Nigh!"), and then corrected me with a noise that sounded completely otherworldly to me. She was somehow making a "th-" sound, a "ch-" sound, and a "sh-" all at the same time. She had to be making this up. Human mouths don't make that sound. At least mine didn't.

"Chee-ooo-go?" I tried.

"*Nej*!" she said again with a smile, before needlessly repeating the bizarre noise. We'd already had to give up on seven (*sju*, pronounced "scheeww," kind of) and two (*två*, pronounced "tvough," kind of). I had a feeling we were getting to another brick wall. I took the opportunity to briefly close my eyes, let the wind cool my eyelids, and my brain relax. Svenska was beginning to make me feel about letters and sounds the same way I'd been feeling about each one of these Svenskar. They looked so recognizable and straightforward, but were in fact were completely foreign.

As a language, Svenska was completely nonsensical. While it sounded like fun to me, it was difficult to get the hang of, especially when no one was telling me the rules. The language was full of sounds that were not just hard to make—they were difficult to even hear. My ears were managing the learning curve as much as my brain was. And the phonics were just ridiculous. Just when I thought I had something figured out, some crazy new twist came in, and I couldn't keep track of the rules anymore. For example, *kök* (kitchen) was pronounced like "shook," but *krök* (bend) was like "crook." How was I supposed to keep track of that craziness?

Svenska also saw no need for spaces. Long before the Internet boom caused us all to start smashing our words together to look cute and hyperdigital, the Svenskar had a historic affinity for compound words. The English phrase, one-dollar bill, for instance, was *endollarssedel.* A day care manager was a *daghemsföreståndare.* My personal favorite Svensk *ord* was *undersköterskeutbildningen.* Honestly, I wasn't even sure what it meant. It was something to do with education and being an assistant to a caretaker. Who even cared, really? Just look at that amazing, twenty-six-letter *ord.*

Finally, Swedes had a noise—a gasp, really—that meant, "yeah, go on." Or, "OK," or anything they wanted it to mean, I guess. It was a sharp intake of breath that just barely made a sound, and it was interjected in the middle of an opposing speaker's sentences, so as to be maximally confusing when you were trying to say something.

For example, I let's say I'm speaking to Inger, and I say, "Well, the hardest thing about learning Swedish here is that everyone is so excited to speak English—"

"*Jahh-hop.*"

"—what?" I might say, wondering what accidentally offensive thing I might have just said to make her gasp. Bear in mind that the "*-hop*" part at the end sounded very similar to the noise you'd make as you watched someone chop his finger off.

"Oh, please go on, darling, I was just listening!"

OK.

"So anyway, everyone just wants to speak English, because they don't get to use it much, and I'd really like them to give me the chance to—"

"*Jahhhop!*"

"What? Did I say…? Are you OK?"

"Well of course! What do you mean, darling?"

And so on and so forth until you just got used to this apparently half-conscious, panic-inducing interjection flying into the midst of every statement you made.

Despite all its quirks, I was damn sure I was going to learn Svenska before I left Sverige. The challenge actually made it more exciting for me. Being so goal-oriented, in fact, was part of the reason it'd taken me so long to leave Greg. He was great at helping me set goals. The end result of all of our horrid fights was always the same: identifying which of my character flaws caused the issue at hand, and me promising to get better. And then I went right to work on self-improvement. And I don't want to brag, but I really exceled at getting better at things.

Did I hang out with people that made him uncomfortable? That's because I had bad taste in friends. Easy. I'll stop hanging out with them and better screen all future friends. Did my pursuit of grad school insult his status as an occasional community college attendee? That's because I'm arrogant and think I'm better than him. Fine. I can prove my humility. Who needs higher education?

As I waved good-bye to Pia at the train station and turned to peddle back toward Ödmjuk Gård on my own, I recalled the very first time Greg had set such a goal for me. It was right after we had started dating, and I'd brought him home to my small town to meet my family. It was a holiday, so a bunch of my old friends from high school were there, and I did what every small town girl does when she falls madly in love with her first out-of-towner: I took him to a bar full of drunken high-school alumni.

It was so fun. We played pool. We danced. He met all my friends. I drank lots and lots and giggled with plenty of girls and showed off my super cool and fun new man and reveled in how much everybody loved him. And they did. Because he was funny and smart and charming and great. See, that was the thing about Greg. He was dripping with charisma. No matter what room he entered, he was instantly everyone's favorite person there. He could make anyone smile; he made people feel like they had just met their new best friend. I would later learn that there were three distinct sides to Greg: the hilarious, electrically charming side; the brooding, emotional side; and the dark, dark, very dark side. Ninety-five percent of the world only ever saw the first, and I was still part of that happy majority. No wonder I was head over heels for him.

Then, at the end of the night, we got into the car. And I was in trouble. I'd never been in trouble with a boyfriend before, so it took me a few minutes to realize how dire the situation was.

How could I have done that to him, he asked. Why had I taken him somewhere where he was so outnumbered by so many douchebags? Why was I friends with so many douchebags? And why did I think it was OK to just laugh with them and talk to all of them and dance with them? Clearly there were old boyfriends in there. Probably. Don't tell him. He didn't want to know. All he knew was that everyone there knew me better than he did. Did he even know me at all?

How could I have been so insensitive? How could I have acted so selfishly, and, now that I mention it, so sluttily? No one with any common sense could have thought taking him there was an OK thing to do.

Well…I actually had thought it had been an OK thing to do. I thought he would have fun with my friends. All indicators, such as his face and his behavior throughout the night, had led me to believe that he was, in fact, having fun. So in addition to being insensitive, it appeared I was an idiot. I felt awful. And dumb. I wanted my friends to like him; I'd just assumed he would like them.

But I was wrong. And saying I was sorry in the car was not enough. Apologizing for being insensitive once we returned to my dad's house didn't cut it either. We were not finished until hours later, sitting on the floor of my father's bathroom, me in tears, begging for his forgiveness for being "the kind of person" who would associate with such morons, for being "the kind of person" who would have put him in that position.

"It's OK," he comforted me, after I'd finally admitted to my newfound sins. "I know you don't want to be that person anymore. I love you, and you make me so happy. I want to help you be better."

As I put my bike back into the small storage barn near the house, I realized I'd forgotten all about that argument. It seemed crazy now—right?—him offering to help me learn to be a better person when I didn't know there was anything wrong with me in the first place. But, to be fair, prior to that he'd spent months telling me wonderful things about myself, things I'd never known to be true. When Greg told me what an amazing, beautiful, perfect person I was, and how I was the only one, his fated savior, who could finally made his dark and traumatic life worthwhile, I totally and utterly believed him. I mean, I was his fucking fated savior. And, in exchange, he was offering to become mine.

That seemed like a fair trade. So by the time he was filtering through my closet, showing me which of my clothes made it totally obvious that I harbored latent sluttiness, I was grateful. He loved me so much, he was willing to shield me from hard truths, like what a five-foot-two blonde girl with D cups was really saying when she wore a shirt like this. I was just a country girl from Northern Michigan; I didn't know. And what was my favorite shirt worth, next to being the amazing person this man I loved believed I could be? A minor wardrobe change was a small price to pay for getting to be with someone as enigmatic as Greg. It was like being with a celebrity. I understood the costs.

I wished I could think about it without still feeling a little competitive. How had I not followed all of the rules? How had I not reached all of his goals? I was an achiever! I did everything he asked! There was no way he could complain about my performance! Ah well. I may not have been able to reach Greg's aspirations, but now I had something much more concrete in front of me to learn. How difficult could it be to learn a new language after two years of learning how to be a new person?

I was making Åke drill me on my flashcards one Saturday afternoon as we were on our way to some destination Jan kept calling "the dog food factory." At this point, I stopped asking too many questions if Jan was explaining things. I'd just figure out where we were when we got there.

"*Bror*," Åke read from the backseat of the Volvo.

"Brother!" I yelled back. I was way more enthusiastic than necessary all the time around Jan and Åke. Mainly because they were so reserved that shaking them up was a way of entertaining myself, but also because I could tell they quietly loved it.

"*Farbro*—ahem—*farbror*," he went on. Poor Åke. Like any seventeen-year-old *gård* boy with a twenty-something foreign girl living in his basement would be, he was constantly in a state of semi-panic and voice-cracking. I adored him.

"Uncle!" I practically sang, turning around to grin at Åke.

"Åke," Jan broke in, "you do the peoples now. But you should do the doggies and the puppies for we go to get the puppy food."

"Ah…*ja Pappa*…" He mumbled and sat back in his seat. What was he supposed to say to that? Clearly he did not appreciate his father's brilliant suggestions as much as I did. Poor Åke.

But just as he was sinking into a deep pool of adolescent misery, I realized that what Jan had just said made something finally click in my head. Although I'd been there for weeks, it was an ongoing joke that I couldn't pronounce Åke's name correctly. Just couldn't do it. I really wanted it to be "ache" like "your name gives me a head*ache*," but when the name came out of my mouth I knew it was wrong. Lisbeth always seemed to say, "ewwkay," but Inger's pronunciation was more like, "OH-key." No one seemed capable of just explaining to me what sound the letter *å* made. But of all people, Jan had just said it in a way that made sense to me.

"Wait!" I said, looking back and forth between Jan and his embarrassed son. "O-K? Like you're feeling okay? OK? That's how you say it?"

Åke hesitated. "Ah," he started, giving me a bit of a nod, "yeah, it's sort of like that."

And so it was. I wasn't right on, but I was evidently way closer than I'd been with "ache." I could tell by the teenage grin Åke was trying to wrestle off his face that the word rolling off my tongue was close enough. Oh, sweet Åke…

A Svenska victory. They weren't many, but I enjoyed them when they happened.

And oh, we were actually on our way to a dog food factory. Well, sort of. Before long, the old Volvo pulled into the driveway of a nearby farm run by a man named Henrik who had a machine in his barn that made dog food, one bag at a time. Why not? Clearly, a quirky language was indicative of a culture rooted deeply in quirk.

* * *

Whatever help the Waaras were in my quest to learn Svenska, the grocery store beat them tenfold. For this reason, grocery shopping was my most favored of household duties. That, and the fact that going to the grocery store was my most autonomous activity. I drove myself there; I browsed through the aisles at sloth-like speed; I wondered at the amazing foodstuffs, and honestly learned more about Svenska and Sverige from food packaging than I ever could convince a human Svensk to teach me.

So though I often had a difficult time not chucking my dense, grainy breakfast of *kavring* and cheese right at Inger's crackpot face whenever she'd saunter into the kitchen and proclaim, "*God morgon*, Natalie! Today, I wonder if you'd feel comfortable…" for fear of what bizarre new form of hard labor she'd found for me that day, if the sentence ended with an invitation to go grocery shopping, I had a pen and paper out before she was done saying, "Waaaanderful! Good for you!"

My typical shopping list looked like this:

Lisbeth's cheese (*Herrgårdsost*)
Thyme (*timjan*)
Ground beef mixed with other meats (*blandfärs*—other meats?)
Oranges (*apelsin—confusing*)
"Minirit" brand crispbread (*knäckebröd*)
Beef bouillon cubes (*köttbuljong*)
Milk (*mjölk*)
Sugar (*socker*)
Flour (*vetemjöl*)
Ham (*skinka*—that should be easy for me, since I think ham stink-as.)

> Butter (*smör*—also the root of *smörgasbord*! And *smörgas* means sandwich, and *bord* means table! A smorgasbord is literally a sandwich table? Does etymology get any more fun?)

Armed with my list, and literally dangerous behind the wheel of the dilapidated Volvo, I'd venture out to City Gross. Although the store's name loosely translated into something like "town merchant," it was just as enormous and brightly lit as any American grocery chain. Curiously, the monstrosity of a store sat in the middle of acres and acres of empty fields, with no sign of any actual "city" in sight. To get there, I had to drive through three separate, winding villages, each one a cluster of adorably unique coordinating homes, but not one of which contained any type of store. Naturally, I'd get lost nearly every time. But getting lost only gave me an excuse to be gone longer, so I didn't mind at all.

After stalling out a proud average of three times while trying to get the alligator of a car into a parking spot, I'd grab my fistful of cloth shopping bags and head into the store. Sverige, by the way, kicked the US's ass on the bring-your-own-bag-to-the-store trend. I'm sure this was accelerated by having to pay for each plastic or paper bag used instead. Svenskar. They can't decide what they love more—saving the Earth or being cheap. Or making rules. Judging from the fact that I had to stick a ten-*kronor* coin into the grocery cart to "rent it" while I shopped, I'm going to go with being cheap.

One of the most interesting parts of City Gross was the cheese section. Unlike American cheese departments, with their open coolers full of yellow, orange, white, and marbled chunks of cheeses, colorful bags of the shredded kind, and more, the Svensk *ost* shopping experience was considerably less dynamic. Multiply the number of *Amerikansk ost* varieties by ten, and then take away all of their differentiating features of color, shape, and packaging, and you're left with the Svensk *ost* department: rows and rows and rows of white cheese in triangular wedges. How can you tell the difference? You can't. There are labels, naturally, but one would have to be able to read Svenska for that to be helpful. And once you know the names, you also must consider that like milk, each variety of Svensk *ost* was available in particular percentages of milk fat. During the first few weeks, I spent a good hour shuffling through the *ost* coolers, desperately searching for the word *herrgårdsost*. And naturally, the one I brought home was the wrong percentage of fat, always.

Especially enthralling were the foods that had no American counterpart. *Lingonsylt*, for example, was like a jam made out of, well, lingonberries, an entire fruit I had no idea existed. They were first described to me as tasting similar to cloud berries, but that was about as helpful as comparing them to unicorn steak. The closest approximation in the American diet was cranberries, but frankly, cranberries tasted good, and lingonberries didn't. Anyway, this jam-like stuff came in plastic tubes like summer sausage, and Svenskar ate it on anything and everything.

Like what, you ask?

Like meat, *potatis*, and *blodpudding* [BLAD-poo-DING]. Gosh, you might be thinking, *blod* couldn't possibly be what I think it is! But yes, a favorite of the "true Swede's" palate, blood pudding was as common as bologna was in the US. And for the first time ever, bologna ends up being the less disgusting of two choices. As it turned out, "pudding" was a generous term. *Blodpudding* was blood and flour made into a gel/sausage-type substance. You sliced it, you fried it, you put *lingonsylt* on it, and I guess you ate it. I had to fry some for Jan once, and that was it for me. I was done. The single experience of slicing a tube of solidified blood and smelling it sauté was plenty. After that, I just put slices of it on a plate so he could fry his own blood. Which he didn't; Jan liked it raw just as well.

Also in the category of amazingly disgusting Svensk fare were Kalle's spreads. Inside a seemingly innocuous toothpaste-esque tube featuring a smiling cartoon child was Kalle's spread: a cheap, pink, bubbly, caviar paste. Think caviar is gross? Consider how gross cheap-o caviar must be! And then imagine it coming in such exciting flavors as "dill" and "hard-boiled egg." Inexplicably, a popular food item with which to serve hard-boiled-egg-flavored fish eggs is—wait for it—hard-boiled eggs. Inger tried to convince me to try it several times, saying it had so many additives that it was more like a blend of sugar and food coloring than caviar. Yum. Squirt me some of that.

On the more appetizing side, the Swedes do have an amazing aptitude for bread. From their *knäckebröd*, to the soft, chewy disks of *rågkaka*, to the amazingly dense and seedy *kavring* Inger would make, they have really cornered the market on delicious *bröds*. I'd often linger extra long near the bread table at City Gross, wondering if it would be worth Inger's scolding to purchase a new kind of delightful Svensk *bröd* never seen at the Waara house before. After my initial invitation to buy any food I wanted for myself, the policy had quickly changed to any foods I wanted for myself among those already purchased regularly for themselves. Occasionally, after Inger stopped examining my grocery receipts, I'd buy an interesting new roll from the bakery aisle and eat it in the car. Technically stealing? Sure. Worth it? Definitely.

The combination of cultural discovery and personal freedom associated with my grocery store adventures wasn't the only reason I loved them so much. It would be disingenuous of me to leave it at that. The truth was, I was an American consumer, a creature with a decidedly unSvensk mindset. Although I had always considered myself a conscientious consumer in my homeland—a frequenter of thrift shops and avid believer in low-cost fun—hardly a day would go by without purchasing something, somewhere. Buying things is like sport to us, a science, an art, and an exercise we engage in daily. The experience of perusing the brand new, from cars to candy bars, is thrilling. It's just what we do.

Svenskar worked hard to take the fun out of shopping. From their mad *krona*-pinching to the total absence of cart islands in parking lots, the Svensk shopping experience was one that put more burden on the shopper and less on the store. Capitalism wasn't really their thing. Inger even lectured me on the correct way to line up the grocery items on the conveyor belt during checkout.

"It is considered very rude to just toss your groceries down in any which way," she explained. "You must locate the bar code and face it toward the checkout person, one item at a time. Otherwise, they must strain themselves."

Honestly? The checkout people might strain themselves? And as it turned out, I couldn't even chalk this one up to Inger being a complete nut. Apparently, in a nationwide effort to save checkout attendants from the risk of tennis elbow, all Svenskar go through this ritual at the grocery store. I don't recommend skipping it, unless you are hoping to experience the bone-chilling wrath of a Svensk checkout lady done wrong.

As the weeks wore on, my hunger for the thrill and delight of an easy, American shopping experience grew painful. In Kassgården, the gas stations didn't even have convenience stores attached to them. How did people make it to work, I wondered, without the ability to pop into the gas station and grab a Powerbar? Not that it really mattered to me personally; I had so little discretionary money, I considered buying a pop on my occasional grocery trips a luxury.

The shiny exterior of this brand new adventure was slowly being replaced by a rational, if uninspiring, appreciation for the facts at hand. I was living overseas and learning new things about the world. I had lots of peace and quiet. My internal organs must certainly have been pleased by the hiatus from the onslaught of drinking, smoking, and hardly eating that had preceded my departure.

I tried to cheerfully appreciate my limited free time. Between *middag* and the kids' return from school I'd sometimes read, sometimes study Svenska, and I even made myself go on a run now and again. But I found nothing new or exciting about any of these things, and there was only time for one of them each day. Then into the shower to scrub off the morning of horse handling and vacuuming I would go. I tried not to shower in the morning, or after the kids got home. My personal shower was, after all, in the laundry room, which not only was a regular thoroughfare for the family but also had a door that led to the outside. On any given day I'd stand in that cold, strange shower stall, realizing that I hadn't spoken to anyone all day, and laughing at myself for bothering to shower at all, when I would just be going out to shovel horseshit with Lisbeth in a few hours anyway. There was no good time to shower here. And, I was starting to feel, no good reason to either.

6
Den Stillhet
The Quiet

Thursday, August 26, 2005

To-Do List

- Feed horses
- Walk dogs
- Clean linens and take to hostel
- Vacuum
- Defrost freezer
    - Empty freezer
    - Dial to zero
    - Put newspaper on the floor
- Fold and send Inger's invoices–fakturas
- *Middag* for Jan
- Break
- Kids
- Horses

Meticulous didn't really cover it. Excessive vacuuming and dusting were one thing. Ritualistic energy maintenance upon leaving each room was quite another. Now, I'd always considered myself to be environmentally conscious. I recycled. I closed the fridge while I was pouring my OJ. Most of the time. But in this house, energy conservation wasn't an afterthought; any activity unrelated to energy conservation was considered immorally excessive. In a world with nary a room with overhead lighting, this was the required routine upon entering every unlit room:

- Fumble around until you find the cord to the lamp.
- Fumble around until you find the power strip and plug it in.
- Fumble around until you find the wall socket to plug the power strip in.
- Fumble around until you hit the on button to the power strip.
- Fumble around until you find the switch that turns on the lamp.
- Proceed with your mission in this room.

I mean, for effing eff's sake. Wouldn't flipping the stinking power strip on and off have sufficed? But oh no. Each piece of every electrical system in the house had to be completely disconnected and disarmed after each use. The idea that power could somehow be transmitted between the turned off lamp and an unplugged power strip didn't seem like something an entire family of five people could stand in front of you and swear to, but apparently it was. But why would they take my word for it? I was just the lowly house help with nothing better to do than disconnect and reconnect 150 plugs, switches, and wires each day.

Who would want to live like that? My gut was beginning to point toward a possible answer to that question: not Inger. Despite being the one who directed me through the insane home energy policy, she didn't want to do it herself. So she hired me, so I could turn off all of the lamps and unplug the TV and entertain her kids and make lunch for her husband, all things about which she seemed less than enthusiastic. Apparently cleaning, cooking, and horseshit-disposal were cramping her career in peddling pseudo-religion and memory foam.

After accepting that endless cleaning was to be my lot in this Svensk life, I tried to make the best of it. I reminded myself that it was a great way to listen closely to music all day, something I'd always meant to spend more time doing. I'd carry my laptop from room to room, designing new playlists based on what sort of chore I was up to that day. Dusting meant something soothing and reflective. Rambunctious rock and pop were reserved for vacuuming and compost-hauling.

It was the "Window Washing, Introspection, et al." playlist that got to me one morning in the living room. The song that accompanied my cleaning a moment before was suddenly distracting me from the task at hand. It was Thursday. I was dusting. After a week of nothing but awkward Svensk *familjen* time and housework, I was well overdue for a distraction.

I should have given you a reason to stay
Given you a reason to stay…

As if the singer was lamenting my leaving Michigan, I found myself wholeheartedly agreeing with him. I should have had a reason to stay. Did I have one? Did I miss it? Or did he just not give me one? There I was, paused from my dusting, sitting on the dining room table, frozen. The words of the Death Cab for Cutie song assembled themselves into the context of my life and rendered me motionless.

Greg, of course, was the one person who could have changed my mind about coming here. Hadn't he tried?

Maybe he had, a week or so before my plane left. My friends were throwing me a good-bye party. It was fabulous. We drank, we giggled. There were games and balloons. And Greg was there. I wondered whether or not he'd come. Sure, it was only normal for him to go to a party where all of our friends were, and we'd been broken up for months. We'd hung out in the same group since. He'd sort of dated someone else; so had I. But his coming to this party still felt heavy. These were my party friends. Saying goodbye to most of them would be easy. Greg's presence made it feel like I was really leaving something, or, at least, it made my leaving seem real.

I'd already had a lot to drink when he came up behind me and touched my elbow.

"Can you come outside for a sec?"

Down the stairs and into the dark, we were suddenly starkly apart from the glowing party that continued to throb on the balcony above us. Merriment was still plastered to my face as he led me to a dark tree in the neighborhood right-of-way, paused, and then turned to look at me.

His eyes were about to flood. He looked down quickly, shuffling his feet with his arms awkwardly akimbo—an unnatural contrast to his normally commanding presence.

I had to tell myself to stop smiling. Maybe that made me a terrible person, but I was drunk, and I'd been having fun. A heart-to-heart was never what I wanted to do while partying, and that was always when he decided he had something really serious to talk about. And now, today, it was worse. He'd caused me so much pain for so long, and I was in the middle of celebrating with my friends. Why did I owe him the satisfaction of responding to his misery now? I didn't have the patience for it.

"Nat…" He bit his just barely quivering lip and sent his eyes darting for the dark sky above us. It was just as well that he couldn't look at me. I'm sure I was doing an awful job pretending to look sympathetic while desperately hanging on to my buzz. The spare light revealed just how bloodshot his eyes were. He was really upset. And stoned. Reasoning with him would be difficult.

"I'm not…I'm not going to stand here and try to…try to tell you not to go or anything." He was choking on as many of the words as he said them. "I just want you to know that…That I miss you…I mean, already. And I'm sorry, for the way this is."

Even through my insensitive drunken haze, a burning started to spread through the back of my throat. He should be sorry. The last year of my life had been complete havoc, and he had been the center of it all. We lived together, we lived apart, we kept dating, we broke up, we got back together, we broke up again. And I couldn't quite place my finger on why, but from where I was standing, I was sure it was all his fault. That's how I justified my silent cruelty to him now, even if he couldn't see it. I'd loved him; he destroyed me. So now he was sad and sorry. He had better be.

"Greg…" His name was Greg, of course, but it actually felt weird calling him that when we weren't together. No one called him that. Most people knew him as Ory. Neither Greg nor Gregory was rock star enough for him, so to the world he was Ory, or Ory G, or O-Dogg, or The O, or a few other ridiculous variations I liked to pretend didn't exist. To me, he was just Greg.

"…I don't know what to say to you. To that," I stumbled. "I'm sorry too."

I wasn't. And honestly, I really wanted to get back to the party. I had just been upstairs squealing with glee. Now I was borderline emotional. I had to get out of there.

"There's nothing we can do now," I continued, as if I were saying something well thought out and profound rather than whatever was falling off my inebriated tongue. "We just didn't make it. And I've got a one-way ticket to Copenhagen. Nothing you have to say is going to change that."

"How can you…?" His eyes snapped back to my face, just as his voice snapped right back into the caustic tone I was used to.

"What's wrong with y—"

And then it was gone. Uncharacteristically, he retracted the accusation from his voice.

"It doesn't matter," he said. "You're right, and I'm going to go home. Come here."

He hugged me. The bitter tension that had grown between us notwithstanding, nowhere had ever felt more like home to me than Greg's arms. It didn't matter in the least that I'd just been trying to get away from him, or that he'd been nothing but an exhausting and painful force in my life for months. I could have stayed there all night, his broad arms wrapped around me, clutching my little person with so much care. It was there, inside his soft T-shirt embrace, that I had always found a reason to get back together with him. No matter what degrading things his mouth could say or the contempt his eyes could convey, I never doubted his love for me in those arms.

But we were beyond that now. We separated, we awkwardly said goodbye, and I actually skipped my way back up to the party. I was going to continue having a good time, dammit, and I was going on a European adventure. Fuck him and his love hugs.

Now, sitting on Inger's bare wooden dining room table in this cold, orderly farmhouse, I thought about that embrace for the first time since I'd left it. Had it been a reason to stay? Should it have been enough? It certainly felt like it now, but I couldn't have known it then. How was I to know how hard a really good hug was to come by?

If you feel discouraged, there's a lack of color here

The song continued, turning my attention from what I had left to what I now faced here. A lack of color? How about lack of life? Or lack of purpose? Or lack—a lack of anything? I had been dusting virtually dustless shelves, only because the vacuuming was already done, and it wasn't the right day for mopping. I had to be dusting, because the horse-poo shoveling wouldn't happen until Lisbeth arrived home from school, and my hour-and-a-half break wasn't due for forty-five minutes. I never imagined my globetrotting adventure would be so mindlessly regimented.

Worse, I was now beginning to prefer the aching solitude of my cleaning routine to the bitter moments when Inger would flit through the room, correcting every broom sweep and feather dust. "Oh! My dear—ha ha ha!" she would say, "you are doing a fine job, Natalie, but here we use crunched newsprint and vinegar to clean the windows. Vinegar does such a fine job! Please refrain from using such expensive cleaning solutions and paper towels!"

Holy hell, woman. The spray bottle that I found in your kitchen said *glasrengöringsmedel.* GLAS means "glass" and RENGÖRINGSMEDEL means "cleaning agent." I looked it up. You can't tell me that you purchased this glass-cleaning agent for any other purpose than to clean your damn windows. Or that the thirty *kronor* you spent on it a year ago is going to break the family bank. Who the fuck gets a live-in maid from America when you can't afford to use the fucking glass cleaner you already own? And if you somehow couldn't, and it was such a big fucking deal, maybe you should have given me more detailed instructions than "clean the windows on Tuesdays" before fluttering back to your kooky book writing in your office.

She was getting on my nerves.

If it wasn't using paper towels to clean the windows, it was the order in which I vacuumed the rooms, or—the crime of all crimes—being caught with a metal utensil in my hand while cooking in a Teflon pot. I was only using it to stir the liquid, I swear! I wasn't touching the sides! I know your paranoid rules about Teflon! Maybe if you think Teflon is going to kill you, you shouldn't cook any of your food on Teflon!

I assumed the housework would be getting easier as time went on, but thanks to the constant addition of new rules and more tasks, it was proving to be quite the opposite. Napkins and placemats were now laundered every week, which did not just mean washing and hanging them to dry, but also running them through the antique mangle. What's a mangle? It's a wringer. As in, "he ran me through the wringer." In this case, it was a two-hundred-pound, cast-iron-and-hardwood contraption with a hand crank that you ran laundry through to iron it. The fact that the family used cloth napkins three times a day was silly enough; that they needed to be ironed with something that looked like an Inquisition relic was downright insane.

Oh, and my hour of Internet use after everyone went to bed was getting a bit long. Could I cut down on that, Inger wondered? Every minute cost money. And was it really necessary that I shower each day? Swedes tended to shower less often, and it was really better for the water use, dear. Oh, and would I be so kind as to begin showing Inger the grocery receipts when I returned from the store again? She just wanted to keep better track of things better.

Even her attempts to bond with me were becoming unbearable. Gone were the days of her lingering in the kitchen with me after *frukost* to share a *kaffe* and tell me about how much better the world was when you considered the fact that we were already in Heaven, or to tell me about growing up with her traditional Svensk parents. Now, inquiries were annoyingly pointed toward my own personal happiness. Apparently her cult powers sensed my growing dissatisfaction with my life here.

"Naaatalie, darling, how are you this morning?" She grinned wildly at me as she fussed unnecessarily with the French press.

"I'm fine," I replied, pointedly free of any recognizable emotion. In addition to not wanting to talk to Inger about my state of mind, I am generally not a fan of chatting in the morning. With anyone. Mornings are for mumbling and coffee and eating breakfast, not chatting about feelings.

"You've been more quiet during the past week, I've noticed," she went on, either missing or not caring about my disinterest in continuing the conversation. "Is there any reason why? Anything you'd like to talk about?"

Well Inger, I just left my home, my family, friends, the beginning of a writing career, and everything I'd ever known to spend a year being, apparently, a maid on a farm with no human contact outside of your family.

So yeah, I guess I have a few things on my mind.

"Oh, I've just been a bit tired. I might have a bit of a cold. Not a big deal."

My attempt to sidestep the question had the exact opposite effect. Within an instant, her colorful, lanky form had taken up residence on the counter stool next to me, and she was gazing intently at me as I used my favorite new kitchen tool, the *osthyvel*, to prepare my usual *frukost* of *kavring* and cheese. We don't use the spatula-shaped *osthyvels* to slice our cheese much in the US because our cheese comes magically pre-sliced. Even as I took the time to appreciate her countrymen for having the good sense to *hyvel* their own *ost*, I peeked at Inger warily from the corner of my eye with dread. This couldn't be going anywhere good.

"I realize you are happy in your religious faith, dear, but I'd like you to consider this possibility. In Den Metod we learn that illness may become of the body, but it begins in the mind. There is no illness that we do not, in the beginning, convince ourselves to have, even though it all takes place apart from our consciousness. This is why those who are the least satisfied with their lives tend to struggle with illness more than the rest of us. *Ja*?"

Although the outrageousness of this statement caused me to pause in my *frukost* preparations, I was unable to come up with a single response. *Hyvel* and *ost* still in hand, I tilted my head oh-so-slightly toward her craziness. Really? We invent our own illnesses? So all those people who died of disease—and I'm no epidemiologist, but I'm guessing that would be the vast majority of anyone who's ever died—are to blame for their own deaths? Yeah, that makes perfect sense.

"So what I'm asking you now is," she continued, "could there be an unhappiness, or a dissatisfaction with your life which may have caused this cold to come about? Perhaps by addressing this psychological issue, we can also heal your cold."

"Um…"

"Now dear, I know you may not have been expecting to spend so much of your day invested in domestic activities. Ha! I'm sure you have never done so much laundry in your life, now have you?! Ha ha!"

She was completely hysterical; I was completely stunned. All I could do was stand quietly next to her and wait to see where this was going.

"It sounds like you had quite a busy life at home, and this must feel much slower than what you are used to. Could it be, dear, that your cold has been brought on by this change? And could we perhaps investigate that together?"

Now, I realized that this was a perfect opportunity for me. All I had to do was agree with her. Then she would know. At least I would have stated out loud that I'm not cut out to be a maid. Just agree with her. But that was the catch, wasn't it? I wasn't about to agree with anything this batty broad had to say. Just because my current illness was completely fictional, I was about to let that validate her psychological, pretend-Jesus bullshit. I was keeping my fake cold.

"So you believe that all illnesses begin in the subconscious?"

"I do."

"Even cancer?"

"Yes, dear. This is usually the result of many years of dissatisfaction."

"I don't want to seem disrespectful, Inger, but I don't believe little kids who develop leukemia don't have much time to be that dissatisfied with life. Or that too many infants are to blame for being born with AIDS."

"Oh, but the subconscious of mothers can have a profound effect on children in the womb."

Wow. WOW. I bet every parent of a child with a terminal illness would love to hear that.

"Well, that's certainly something to think about." Without giving Inger a chance to divert the conversation back to my own mental/physical/completely-made-up illness, I gave her a polite smile and changed the subject as I reached into the mug cupboard.

"Is the coffee ready yet? It smells delicious."

* * *

In order to avoid these confrontations—both her attempts to befriend me with her cult-talk and her criticism of my every move—I planned my cleaning around where Inger was not. And when she wasn't in the house at all, I slacked off. Like now, sitting on the table, listening to a sad, sad song and staring out the large windows into miles and miles of Svensk farmland.

There was a lack of color here, just as the song was saying. But against my self-indulgent complaints, the singer was offering an alternative perspective to seeing white in all directions.

Please don't worry, lover, it's really bursting at the seams,
Absorbing everything, the spectrums A to Z.

Was that it? Was it just my attitude? If I believed hard enough that I was growing and experiencing and absorbing this Svensk *liv*, quiet as it might be, would I feel better about it?

No. As the song repeated, I found myself parsing fact from fiction. I may have run off on this adventure to escape a life I wasn't happy with back home, but here, I was bored. I was bored with every cell of my body. Perspective meant nothing; this was simply reality. Nothing I knew of, for thousands of miles, could make me feel any less alone.

The song had long since ended. No one was singing about reasons to stay anywhere anymore. That was appropriate, I noted, since no one had given me a reason to stay anywhere either. Jumping off the table, I forced my mind through a series of memories stored away for just these occasions: finding the phone numbers of our mutual male friends mysteriously deleted from my phone; being told his friends would like me more if I was just a little more feminine and less opinionated; telling me that it wasn't possible to be a writer and a truly faithful partner—writers have to let their imaginations wander, experience other people, and other relationships, didn't I know? Anybody could be a writer, but most people didn't have the opportunity to have what we had, he said. Let other people be writers.

Greg's demands and erratic mood swings were nothing to get sentimental about. They were the reason to not stay. I'd chosen correctly. Clearly, I had a habit of letting my emotions run away with my common sense, as I had with Greg, and as I was possibly doing now with all of this self-pity. As soon as I got done with the dusting, I'd go make the most of this experience. I'd go for a run and then squeeze in enough time for one of my self-taught Swedish lessons. And then, I was going to write. I was going to write every day here, and emerge with something really great. A novel, maybe, or a collection of essays. That's right. I wasn't about to let a little light cleaning get in my way. I was having an adventure, and I was going to stinking enjoy it—at least half as much as I planned on telling people I was.

Wednesday, August 28, 2005

Alisa,
The radio here is hilarious. Inger listens to the "slow music" station, which is virtually the same cheesy easy listening station everyone in Tawas listened to ten years ago. I hear Richard Marx, Celine Dion, and Michael Bolton daily. Listening to Richard Marx's "Right Here Waiting for You" when you are actually "oceans apart" from everyone you love is kind of surreal. And the kids listen to this station that plays the "cool music." It's entirely indiscriminate. I heard Jay-Z followed by Elvis. Madonna followed by Toby Keith. You tell me.

Oh, and I forgot to answer your milk questions: rectangular cartons, like giant juice boxes. You can buy milk in plastic jugs too, but they're different than ours, more like a jug of antifreeze. But they're all considerably smaller than gallons or even half gallons. I guess Americans are insane with regard to our milk quantities.

Other stark differences? There really aren't too many. Everything is subtly different. Except that towns don't seem to have stores in them. They're just groupings of houses. The trains take everyone in and out of the big cities where people do their shopping and general commerce things. Isn't that strange though that there are so many "towns" without any sort of industry or apparent reason for existing? How did people decide to build their houses in any particular spot all together like that?

Oh shit, Lise. I can't believe I haven't told you this yet: Hamlet's castle is here. Dude...the actual Elsinore is like twenty minutes away from me. I was on a bike ride with Jan, and he points across the sea and says, "Look, you can see Danish castle."

And I jokingly say, "A Danish castle? Like Hamlet's castle?"

"Yes," he said, "that is the one. Hamlet. Helsingør."

I practically had to change my undies. It's all I've talked about since then. I guess they perform the play there in the winter! I'm going to be here in the winter!!! Ah! I'll have to bring several changes of undies with me! Jan said he'll take me there sometime soon. Score! It will be the first of many trips to Hamlet's home, for me, I'm sure.

If someone with an English degree is good for anything, it's getting inordinately excited about all things Shakespeare. Although I'd begun feeling sorry for myself after Saturday bike rides and one boat trip were turning out to be the entirety of my Swedish adventurousness, I was now excited beyond belief. I was going to see Elsinore, or, as the Dane Hamlet would have called it: Helsingør. Who would have thought that play, written four hundred years ago, was set in a real, live castle that still existed? And right across the freaking channel from where I happened to be living?! This was more delightful to my literary heart than a barrel full of mother-fucking monkeys.

Could in life in Kassgården be even more thrilling? Oh, it could. Although there was no time to plan an Elsinore trip this week, as soon as we returned from the very bike ride during which I learned of its existence, Inger presented me with what seemed to be the beginning of a real, live social life in Sweden.

"Natalie darling, Linda dropped by to see if you would like to go for pizza with her, Hanna and some friends of theirs. Would you like that?"

Would I like that? Would I like friends? Would I like pizza? Would I like to eat anywhere or do anything outside of the confines of this house?

"Yeah, that would be great," I replied in the most nonchalant tone I could muster. "I think I'd enjoy that."

"Waaaaandarfool!" Inger replied. "I'll call Linda back and let her know. I believe they will pick you up shortly."

Woo-hoo! I raced down to my lair to prepare myself. Linda was the dairy manager of the farm. She lived in a house that was all of ten yards away from the Waaras', yet I'd only met her in passing once or twice. Hanna was some other sort of worker on the farm who lived even closer—an apartment that was actually a part of the Waara house on the side opposite Linda's home. When I was told of these people upon getting to Sweden, I thought, *Oh, there are young people around my age who live right here. Genius! I'll never be lonely!* Imagine my surprise when so many weeks had passed with hardly any indication that they existed. I would see random people walking around the farm from a distance during work hours, but where had they been on evenings and weekends? Why hadn't I heard a peep from them before now? Who really cared? They were taking me out for pizza!

Suffice it to say, going out for pizza was way more than simply going out for pizza. I was all gussied up in my nicest pair of jeans and a snazzy top when Linda pulled her little SUV out of her driveway and drove three yards to the Waaras' door.

"You are ready for pizza?" Linda said to me as I climbed into the backseat. Hanna was already in shotgun. I guess the American who lived between them was the only one in need of a valet.

'"Yes!" I said, diving right into the *hi's* and *how-are-you's*. They were fine. Fine, and much more composed about the pizza trip than me.

"We are going to get Bobby," Linda told me, glancing at me in the rearview mirror and pronouncing her friend's name as *Ba-BAY*. "He really likes America. I'm sure he will tell you."

Hanna giggled from the front seat as Linda gave her a concerned glance.

"Oh no," I said. "That sounds scary. Should I be worried?"

"He is nice guy," she said, quickly defending him before jumping right back into to making sure I knew what I was in for. "He just…he is just really thinking of America all times. He is like, thirty-five and is living with his parents. He went to America with his cousin, and it is like, the best for him. Just wait. You see."

Linda's volley of being kind to Bobby and mocking him only made sense after I heard the whole story of their relationship. Linda had a long-distance boyfriend who didn't treat her well and whom she never saw. Bobby was her best friend who was also in love with her and had been for years. If you asked me, Linda's complete disinterest in either situation was because she was more interested in Hanna than either of them. But what did I know?

We pulled into the long driveway of yet another farm, and I realized that Hanna's first dibs on seating put me in an odd position. I hoped to God this Bobby person—or Ba-BAY, I guess—was the funny-spectacle sort, not the creepy-spectacle sort, if he was indeed a spectacle at all. It was already dark by the time Linda yanked up the parking break in his driveway, so I couldn't even get a preview as Bobby walked out to the car from his, or rather, his parents' house.

The backseat door opposite me opened. And in came a cowboy boot. And then in came a pair of ridiculously strained Levis. And then came a wilderness T-shirt with "Colorado" screen-printed in cursive on the crest. And then—and then!—in came a cowboy hat.

This was instantly one of the greatest moments of my life. How I didn't start laughing and crying and peeing immediately, I'll never know. Perhaps it was the shock. Perhaps it was because inside that deliciously trashy American kitsch was the roundest, most clueless, most harmless Svensk face I could imagine. It struck me later that if an American had laughed herself out of bladder control upon meeting him, he would have been devastated. I instantly decided that "Bobby" was a purposely Americanized nickname for something else. Björn, maybe?

"*Hej!*" Bobby/Björn gave me what I now knew as the classic Swedish introduction of a quick *hej*, a limp squeeze of a handshake, a nod, and the quiet stating of his name. "Bobby."

"*Hej*," I said, trying my hardest to create a firm, American handshake out of this mess our hands were now in. "Natalie."

"You are with the Waaras?"

"Yes, I got here about a month ago."

"Where are you from in America?"

"Ah, Michigan," I laughed politely, "You know, I just can't get used to everyone calling it 'America.' I've always referred to it as the US—"

"I spent some time in California, you know." Bobby was clearly very eager to get to his American tale. I could hear Linda and Hanna in the front thinking, *That didn't take long.*

As Bobby went on about where he stayed and what he was doing there, I stared in wonder at his wilderness T-shirt. It had a wolf in the foreground and trees and mountains set behind it. It was turquoise, of course. How did this Svensk in this tiny Svensk village own one of these? I'd thought they were a purely American inside joke. Unfortunately for Bobby, the joke had most definitely not followed the shirt to Sverige. Where else could one buy one of those wonders but a backwoods American convenience store between the Big Gulps and the tackle boxes? And here was the proof that Bobby had been in one of those very convenience stores, poised nobly on his round gut. That wolf was staring at me right in the eye, confirming it.

I could not have been more delighted. Well, I could have been, if there'd been anyone within ten thousand miles who could have understood the hilarity of his wardrobe choice and could have giggled with me. Oh well. It was awesome to simply be witnessing it myself.

"We were planning on staying, really," he was saying of his and his cousin's American adventure, "but the investor of our business fell away, and we came home. The plan was only to return long enough to save money and go back, but now…"

I didn't ask after the current state of his American dream. It seemed like it had to be a pretty sad explanation. And considering how reverently he clearly he felt about his American outfit, and how proud he was to be chatting with an American girl, I wasn't about to open that door. Fortunately, Bobby had no intention of letting me mull over that statement. He was officially the chattiest Svensk I'd met.

"You know, the Swedish culture is most like the American culture of any other country in the world," he said.

"Really?" I asked. *Have you heard of Canada?* my inner voice went on. Or *Great Britain? Or Australia? Or…other places with which the US shares a language and direct historic connection?* But right now, Bobby was my best chance of having a real friend on this half of the globe. I wasn't about to shoot him down.

"How is that?" I asked.

"Oh, well nearly everything," he said, as if this should have been an obvious statement. We were pulling into the pizza place, but this didn't stop him. He continued as we all unloaded and headed inside. As we entered, he was chattering about the Swedish youth and their fascination with American pop culture. Strange, I thought nearly the entire youth world was fascinated with American pop culture. But that was really Bobby's primary argument. Although it took him until halfway through dinner to articulate it, he felt Sweden was the county most like the US, because, in his opinion, they were trying the hardest to be as cool as us. Whether or not a single other Svensk agreed, there was no doubt that Bobby himself fit the theory.

The pizza parlor was a surprise to me. Oddly, I was told most pizza parlors in Sverige were owned by Arabs, not Italians. I couldn't give you the first reason why, but that's just how it was. Most consequently, they weren't owned by Americans; as a result, the "pizza" was quite unlike our bready, cheesy pies made with cheap ingredients. For one thing, the pizza in Sverige was exclusively thin crust. Also, the cheese was a much less prevalent part of Svensk pizza than it was in the American version. It was on there, but it was just one of the toppings. The thin, more mildly flavored sauce could be seen through the intermittent cheese and other tasty accouterments. And it wasn't really sauce, either. It was more like tomato juice with perhaps a mild spice or two in it.

One of the most interesting aspects of Svensk pizza was that it came with a little plastic cup of garlic sauce. And by garlic sauce, I mean something that looked like two tablespoons of ranch dressing but was in fact twenty cloves of garlic pummeled into one tiny serving. It was great, but it was also wicked. Some people would drizzle the sauce over the slice. Others would dip their "crust" in it. The brave would order two extra cups and dip every bite in it. They would then murder every living thing in breathing range for the next three days.

"So you like the pizza?" Linda asked.

"Oh yeah," I said. I was being completely sincere, too. The upside to the minimalist sauce, cheese, and crust was that the mushroom and green pepper took on an incredibly pleasant dominance. "This is actually the first meal I've had outside the Waara house."

"*Ja*," Hanna said, rolling her eyes. "Farmers. They are like that. You should go out more. I work for a dancing club in Helsingborg weekends. You can come, and we'll go out there when I am done."

Pitter-pat! Pitter-pat! Pitter-pat!! Could they hear my embarrassingly loud heart-applause?

"Yeah," I replied. "That would be great! I've really been enjoying hanging out with the kids, but I could really use a night out."

As I was speaking, the Middle Eastern shop owner came out from behind the counter and approached our table, wiping his hands on his smudged apron.

"You are American, no?"

Oh, how to respond? Yes?

"I should have make you pizza with American crust!" He was beaming—and practically yelling. I was relieved.

"No way," I laughed, "This is delicious!"

"Yes? You do think?" His tone was so wide-eyed and pleased, it made me feel embarrassed about my effect on him. Strangely, it seemed that being an American made my opinion something of uncommon value. It made me feel completely awkward—complimented and sort of offended at the same time.

"Yes! Honestly," I continued, "I've never had anything like this before, and I love it. I'm pretty much in love with this garlic sauce."

Overall, pizza night was fun. Linda, Hanna, and I got a lot more chatting time in once Bobby had gotten his "America is Awesome" speech out of the way, and I really liked these new friends. Linda was quiet and kind and pleasantly rough around the edges. Hanna was sassy and clearly too cool for her folksy companions, but still nice enough to me. And why wouldn't she be? I was the American.

On the way home, Hanna told me she'd call me when it was a good night to go with her to the club. We had plans. I was going out.

When I was dropped off at the Waaras' that night, I felt my life in Sweden had finally changed. Yes, I'd had several long, quiet, painfully slow weeks to start things off, but everything was different now. I had friends. Life was about to begin. I fell into the quiet of my stylish-but-minimalist Swedish bed that night just knowing that the adventure I had signed up for was about to unfold.

Good thing I didn't know then that I would never receive an invitation to do anything with any of them ever again. That would have made me notice the quiet.

7
Förehavanden
Activities

Fresh from my peer outing, the next mission to be accomplished in my renewed effort to reclaim my adventure was to visit Elsinore. Fortunately, my enthusiasm for visiting Hamlet's castle had spread through my favorite four-fifths of the family; everyone but Inger came along for the ride one Saturday. Although they'd lived their entire lives a short drive and ferry ride away from most famous castle in English literature, it was a first-time visit for the kids. Jan, ever the fan of castles, notorious or otherwise, had been there plenty of times.

We'd only made it to the ferry, and I was already having a great time. Lisbeth, Pia, and I had been watching the American television series *Alias* on DVD, and we were deeply entrenched in speculation over upcoming plot twists. As the fall sun warmed my forehead, and the sea air kicked and tossed my wavy hair in every direction, I was alternately trying to explain to them why their current theory was way off base and contain my laughter.

"But Sydney was forced to take drugs," Lisbeth was reasoning with me for the third time, "so she must now be addicted. So she shall not be a good spy for a while."

"Right," I said, giggling in a way that totally confused my charges, "but having to take psychedelic drugs once to complete a mission isn't going to make her addicted, or make her a bad spy. I don't think they'll talk about the drugs anymore."

"But why…how could she get not addicted?" Pia chimed in. "She did drugs."

Seriously, what kind of after-school specials have these kids been watching? More importantly, how did I walk the line between letting them in on the ways of the world without suggesting that drugs are awesome?

Wow. Someone really should have done an interview or two before hiring me for this position.

"Well," I continued, "it's just that some drugs are more addictive than others, and if they were going to start a drug-based plotline, they would probably have chosen heroin or something like that."

Two unconvinced teenage girls stared at me from the ferry's railing, scrunching their noses into the sun.

"Or who knows?" I continued, smiling at myself as much as at them. "Maybe she'll get addicted and be a bad spy. I guess we'll have to watch another episode when we get home."

They seemed appeased, and I was glad to be done defending drugs. I asked Lisbeth about the riding camp she'd be taking Grölle to in a few months and she gently chattered away about various riding styles and other things she'd be learning.

I was a little bit listening, but my mind's eye was already peeking into the barely visible windows of the Danish castle that was just coming into view on the approaching shore. Could that be the room where Hamlet was supposed to have crushed Ophelia's heart by commanding her to "get thee to a nunnery?" We were approaching from the sea—certainly we'd soon be upon the platform where the Ghost first appeared? Oh, pitter-pat, pitter-pat! My heart was threatening to burst through my ribcage with glee! Could this ferry move any slower?

Two hours later, I was pretending to read a placard commemorating the Swedish conquest of what I had just learned was Kronborg Castle in 1658 by Carl Gustaf Wrangel, wondering why the these Scandinavians seemed to think their actual history was more significant than the perfectly good one William Shakespeare had invented for them. So what if this was really called Kronborg Castle in the *city* of Helsingør? I wanted to see the place where the immortal Ophelia would have scattered her flowers before her heart-rending death. I wanted to see staged bloodstains on the castle floor from the fatal last scene!

But I found there in Helsingør a gorgeous—breathtaking, even—castle, with nothing but simple, honest history marked upon its floors and walls. It was fine. I learned some historically significant whatnots and was in awe of the architecture and moat and towering walls and all. I even found a brochure in the gift shop announcing the winter performances of *Hamlet* that would take place in the courtyard. So that was something.

Here's the thing about the US though: if the castle made famous by *Hamlet* was in New Jersey, it would be a Bardfest beyond anyone's wildest imagination. The actual history of the castle would play second fiddle to the location's potential as an international tourist trap. It would reek of

Shakespeare. Some genius marketing professionals would have known that's what I wanted to see, and they would have made it happen.

My disappointment wrestled with my shame. Here I thought I was somehow above the caricature of the ignorant, self-centered American, and it turned out I had no interest in this renowned cultural site beyond my own connection to it. But I couldn't help it. I couldn't suppress my searing desire to have my picture taken with a seven-foot-tall Laertes puppet with a silent, waving, underpaid college student inside.

I still mourned the loss of my expectations as we rode the ferry back over Oresund in the chilling twilight.

"You see all you like?" Jan asked. He had clearly been in his glory all day, as one of his goofy smiles was stuck fast to his face. He waited patiently for my response while pulling his sensible windbreaker more tightly around himself. Was I going to tell him was that I was disappointed in both the Danes' most likely pointed decision not to sell out their own history to tourism, and in myself for wishing they had?

"Yeah," I said, with a manufactured smile. "It was nice. It was a nice castle."

I thanked him for taking me there before quickly turning my head to watch the coast of Helsingborg creep closer. Multiple rows of neat, colorful houses ran along the shoreline and through the hills above. I was amazed at how uniform they all were, as if made by the same builder in the same year. Individualists they were not, these Svenskar.

"You like this castle," Jan replied to the side of my face. "You see the Sofiero and Borgeby tomorrow. We go in ride and see tomorrow. Adventure Team!"

Sigh. I was beginning to regret having referred to Jan, Åke, and myself as the "Adventure Team" during one of our earlier bike rides or castle hunts. Both this and my flimsy but positive response to Kronborg Castle were now biting me in the ass. I wasn't sure which sounded worse, spending my Sunday on yet another awkward car ride through the woods to look at a big house from fifty yards away, or wilting away in my room alone. Actually, I thought, I'd better keep the day open. Maybe Hanna would call, and we'd go shopping, or to her club. Better change the subject.

"With Inger leaving this week, it looks like you'll have to put up with my cooking for a while," I said. Inger was about to fly to LA for a cult conference. The whole family seemed quietly elated about it. "I hope you don't starve!"

"No, no." Jan searched for the right words for a moment, looking very, very concerned. "You cooking food very nice. Very good to me. And with you, it is nice to having...quiet."

Funny, he and I always chatted much more when she wasn't around, but I didn't doubt for a second what he meant. Poor Jan. If I found his wife difficult to deal with after a month, I could only imagine how he felt. But he never mentioned any unhappiness beyond the occasional, choppy hint like this one.

"Where we go for castles in Sofiero," he continued, back at the subject from which I'd just fled, "now is the time to see the sheep for the puppies."

"Puppies?"

He nodded excitedly and made a gesture with his hands to suggest something tiny. "Puppies. In the sheep."

"Wait," I said, starting to giggle. "Are they sheep with wool, or puppies like Joe?"

"No dog," he was very serious now, trying to communicate his point. "Sheep…med…med…puppy sheep." Again, he cupped his hands together to demonstrate that he was talking about something small.

"Oh!" His meaning hit me abruptly in the funny bone. I burst out laughing. "A lamb? A baby sheep?"

"*Ja!*" Jan could not be more pleased with himself, and I could not have found the fact that he called all baby animals "puppies" more endearing. I laughed for as long as sense would allow, and Jan joined in with some nervous chuckling. It felt wonderful to be struck by something genuinely funny and for my body to have an excuse to release some joy. A heart-full of stress escaped from my lungs and flew out into the sea air, away back toward not-Elsinore. Thank God for Jan.

I would let him drive me wherever he wanted tomorrow. I'd be a sport for his sake, because honestly, he was a good sport too.

* * *

Before she was due to leave, Inger was hosting "a weekend Metod," a two-day affair that would involve a couple dozen or so emotionally malleable people coming to seek Inger's guidance, and, I could only assume, possibly buy Tempur-Pedic products. They would also need food and clean linens. That's where I came in. And that was OK. The excitement of my recent adventures had recharged my enthusiasm for housework. Between this and the change of pace created by the Metod weekend, I felt fully rejuvenated as I lugged a vacuum up and down the steps of the hostel and tidied each guest room. People were coming! Presumably strange people, but people all the same!

After school on Friday, Lisbeth and I stood in the kitchen preparing some dinner in advance of the guests' arrival. I'd just spent the entire day cleaning both the hostel and the conference room. The grounds were all set; now we'd begin the weekend long endeavor to keep them fed. We were chatting about school, about which Lisbeth had just begun to cautiously open up, when the thin girl paused for a moment and looked meaningfully at me out of the corner of her eye.

"Natalie," she said slowly, as she needlessly stirred the pot of boiling pasta water, "did she show you the video?"

Oh. It was bonding time. I'd made it. I was conscious of the fact, however, that she was asking about something that could very well turn into a wedge between her and Inger, or Inger and me, or Lisbeth and me. I certainly didn't want to do any of those things (I mean sure, Inger's batty, but she is the girl's mother), but I also didn't want to shut down an outlet for her if she wanted to talk. Plus, I'd been dying to bitch about the insanity of that video.

"She did," I said nonchalantly while checking the status of the *grön ostsås*. "Have you seen it?"

"Yes," she said meekly. I was still trying to discern her tone when she continued. "What did you think about it?"

Careful, Natalie.

"Well," I said as diplomatically as I could, "it certainly is interesting. I happen to be a more traditional Christian, so it doesn't line up with my beliefs." Outside, Inger was pulling up the drive with a Volvo-full of guests fresh from the train station. They each emerged, one after the other, as if from the world's nerdiest clown car, looking timidly around, smoothing their garments, realizing with a start that they were on a strange farm in the middle of nowhere.

I know how you feel, I thought at them through the window. Gesturing toward the pile of disembarking people and bags, I turned back to Lisbeth. "But it seems that a lot of people find what your mom does to be very helpful."

Lisbeth nodded and went back to stirring the pasta.

"What do you think of it?" I asked.

She stopped stirring and sighed. Looking around for peeping ears, Lisbeth braced herself to speak. "I think…I think it's a little…weird."

As if she'd just admitted to something very, very naughty, she abruptly turned back to the stove and snapped her attention back to the nothingness she had been accomplishing there before her confession. Inger's voice could be heard from outside the closed windows, directing her flock to the conference center. I moved back to Lisbeth's side and likewise began to quietly fuss with the various pots on the stovetop.

"Yeah," I said. "I think it is too."

Lisbeth looked sideways at me with half of a relieved smile peeking out from behind the bits of strawberry-blonde that had come loose from her ponytail. I gave her a reassuring smile of my own. After only a few seconds, she put down the wooden spoon with which she'd been poking the water, turned on her heel, and left the kitchen.

It was good to know how she really felt, and that Inger hadn't pressed her "process" upon her children. It made me nearly tearful with relief and proud of Lisbeth for her common sense, and for her momentary candor.

Also, knowing the kids weren't on board with this freak show (if obedient Lisbeth was a Metod resister, Åke and Pia surely were too) made me feel freer to shamelessly spy on as much of the weekend event as I could. And I wasn't disappointed.

I had my first glimpse of the magic that evening, as I hauled a large pot of pasta from the house to the kitchen of the conference center. I had been told that this large structure was formerly a milking barn. The expansive building was shaped like a pole barn, though in classic Svensk style, it was hundreds of years old, with stone walls and a wooden roof. The inside had been renovated into a rather nice, periwinkle-toned conference room. There were bay windows with large, pillow-covered sills for sitting (all the pillows had needed a thorough vacuuming, of course); there were two long, broad tables surrounded by chairs (difficult to maneuver a broom around, by the way); and there was still plenty of room for a few chair circles, piles of pillows, and spaces littered with various accessories, such as hula hoops, yoga mats, and Pilates balls (just try and figure out how to dust and tidy those items).

Décor-wise, the place was an appropriate shade of nutbag cheerful. The bluish walls were besieged by bright, handmade artistic endeavors such as quilts and paintings, and there were gauzy scarves everywhere, draped from everything.

All this I already knew well from cleaning, however. The new discovery was what went on inside the sanctuary. I was able to peep in though the windowed door of the attached kitchen as I brought the group's dinner to be warmed. After the pots were securely on the stovetop, I peered through the glass to see what Inger and her culty friends were up to.

There they were, a group of twenty or so moving in an awkward circle around a pile of pillows on the floor. Steel-drum music prodded them along, as did Inger herself, speaking English to the international crowd.

"Leave your insecurities behind!" she proclaimed as she skipped, twirled, and pranced past the circling mass of people, who were clearly supposed to be "dancing" along with her. "Just let yourself be one with the music. There is no body, so there is no shyness of bodily movement!" Some visitors were slowly following her lead, doing a rhythmic shuffle here and a bob of their heads there, as they revolved around the pillow island. Others simply walked, bewildered, avoiding eye contact with anyone.

"Soon we will sit, we will focus, we will search, but now is time to release!" Inger was doing an excellent job of pretending not to be annoyed at the shyer, less enthusiastic circle dancers with her passive-aggressive instruction. "Allow your body to be what it is—a nothingness that cannot be judged!"

One dancer in particular did not need prodding. Inger had mentioned that while her weekends were supposed to be revelatory and only necessary once, some people enjoyed them so much that they came again and again. This "dancer" must have been one of those, moving even more zealously than Inger, bobbing and weaving through and around the stragglers, flailing her arms and spinning and leaping and grinning. What a show off!

"Wowzers," I said under my breath into the empty kitchen. Just as I did, I was startled by the outside door opening. Pia stumbled in with two large baskets full of freshly baked rolls. How I'd pulled those off I'd never know, but they looked and smelled like bread, so that was enough for me. I scurried over to help Pia with the door. She pretended to not notice the loud island music or her mother's bizarre instructions being shouted from behind the other door.

"The bread looks nice," she said warmly, her sweet eyes full of sincerity.

"Thanks," I said. "I hope they taste OK. Are we going to watch more *Alias* tonight?"

The fun, relaxed routine of watching the show together was my favorite part of my time in Sverige thus far. It felt cozy and normal.

"No, I am going to stay with my friend in Helsingborg for the weekend," she replied.

Although I knew her response was meant to be apologetic, I could hear her excitement. She was thrilled to escape Crazyfest 2005.

"Oh, that should be fun," I said. "We'll have to catch up on *Alias* on Sunday night. Let's go get the *sallad.*"

As the outside door shut behind us, I could still hear Inger instructing from within the conference room: "If you feel restricted by your body, your soul is restricted as well!"

Damn. I wish I had a friend in Helsingborg.

* * *

Later, when Inger and her groupies were well into a late-night session, and everyone at the farmhouse was nestled in bed, I took the opportunity to call my dad. Not that I would be telling him, the Skeptic-In-Chief, what was going on in the conference center. It's been disingenuous of me if I implied thus far that this running off to Europe to do who-knows-what for who-knows-whom was a decision unquestioned by anyone. My dad fought the move tooth and nail, or at least with words and sighs. I couldn't blame him; he had absolutely no reason to trust that the friend of the sister of the dude his ex-wife had just married wasn't going to cause his little girl irreparable harm, a hemisphere away from his protection. And he had somehow completely missed the point that the more logical his arguments were, the less water they held for me. He wanted me to get the number of their last American au pair and call her for a reference. How embarrassing would that be? I'd have to ask Inger for her information, implying that I didn't trust her. What if she rescinded the offer? He also thought I should have given the plan more time, asked for more money, and all sorts of super boring things. Suffice it to say, he lost those battles. But from our weekly transatlantic phone calls, I could tell he hadn't given up on the war.

I was not about to let him know I was beginning to agree with him.

"So, learning more than you'd ever hoped to about horses, huh?" He was laughing at me as I relayed yet another horse-poo story.

"Yeah, well they're not as scary or repulsive as I imagined them to be," I replied cheerfully. "They smell like shit, but that's mainly because they, you know, shit everywhere."

"Well, it's certainly something new for you. That can't be all bad. What have you been wearing to the barn?" Dammit. I could see where this was going.

"Um…my suede winter coat. It's been fine so far, but it's getting kind of stinky. I guess I didn't think to bring anything else."

"Well, your money just got here a couple of days ago. Do you have enough left to buy yourself something more barn-appropriate?"

Sigh. Dad was the executor of my lack-of-an-estate while I was away. I still had some ongoing bills to pay, so when Inger had given me cash for my first three months up front, I had immediately stuffed half of it in an envelope and sent it home. I'd left Michigan with a completely empty bank account.

"Not…not really, Dad." Nothing was worse than making this admission. I thought back to the day before when I'd pilfered my precious *kronor* pile to supplement the insufficient sock supply I'd brought with me. And I knew was I'd be needing some new shampoo soon. It wasn't as if I was down to my last *krona*, but this was all my wealth in the world for three months and I was hoping to save most of it for Christmas presents. "Clothes are just really expensive here. I haven't looked at coats, but I'm sure it'd be a pretty big investment."

Wow. I sounded like a Svensk. One thing I'd learned from Inger and Jan's money complaints so far was that when you give 75 percent of your income back to the government, everything is too expensive.

"It's not that big of a deal though," I continued with a blatantly pathetic stab at sincerity. "My coat's getting a little old. I'd rather just get a new one for next year when I get home."

"Natalie. You are not going to go through a winter of caring for horses without the right winter gear. Do you have gloves?"

Ugh. Now I was an annoyed twelve-year-old. "Dad, I can buy myself some gloves when it gets cold enough."

"Well, how about this? What you really need for staying warm and working in a barn is a Carhartt. Why don't I get you one this week, and we'll call it your Christmas present."

What?! Now I was eight years old and finding out that we'd be donating toys instead of receiving them this Christmas.

"Dad! A Carhartt? Honestly? Can you imagine me in a Carhartt? Wouldn't that be a waste for just a few months of work? You know I would never wear it again."

"What do you mean?" he was laughing again. "You don't know what you're talking about. Carhartts are in! Everyone at Jimmy's school wants them. I've got employees saving up to get one."

He was being serious. While my father's and my fashion tastes would clearly never align—mine not being based on what the kids at my stepbrother's rural junior high school were wearing—I was relieved to be disagreeing about something other than the trip itself.

So I let him send me a Carhartt. It came in the mail two weeks later and was about three sizes too big. Maybe he thought his twenty-three-year-old daughter would grow into it. Oh, and in the same box came a sensible pair of black work boots, an early Christmas present from my mom. I was equal parts proud and annoyed by their post-divorce collaboration. Regardless, both gifts were warm, hearty, and made the twice-daily horse tending a far more pleasant experience. So…I guess Dad was right. Never tell him I said that.

8
En Genombrott
A Breakthrough

"Ha ha! You must be feeling very odd that I am going to your home while you are staying here!" Inger was supposed to be giving me last-minute instructions as I drove her to the train station, but instead she was cramming as many irritating statements into the five-minute trip as possible. For the next ten days, she'd be in Los Angeles at her crazy-person conference. I should clarify that Den Metod was not a Swedish phenomenon, nor was Inger some sort of integral, founding member. No, what she was doing at Ödmjuk Gård was more like starting her own local franchise, you know, sort like her Tempur-Pedic venture, or a Burger King, except less healthy. Apparently there were hundreds of these crazy clubs all over the world, which was why she had to fly to LA to convene with all of them. So they could all have sex with Jesus' light in unison or practice not existing together or something. Oh man, how much did I need a break from her?

I gave her a thin, cooperative smile. Was I jealous that it was her ass on the way to the US rather than mine? In a way. However, as a born-and-bred Midwesterner, Southern California was about as foreign to me as Sverige. Take her, LA; you can have her.

"Now, on top of your regular duties you'll be cooking for all three meals." As usual, Inger wasted no time waiting for a response before skipping subjects. "You don't have to wake early to prepare breakfast in the morning, but if you could cook the meat patties the night before and set out the ingredients for Jan's oatmeal, they should be able to do the rest."

Honestly, I thought, *if my family was this helpless, I might try to get an indentured servant too. Or I'd teach my kids to make their own stinking breakfast. And tell my manchild husband where to locate his own oatmeal.*

"Your days certainly will be longer, my dear," she went on from the passenger seat, bumbling through her enormous patchwork purse as keys and boarding passes and various wallets went flying about, "but I know you will do splendidly. We will discuss perhaps giving you a day of vacation when I return."

Wow, how generous. After working from alarm clock to lights out for ten days she'd think about giving me a day of comp time: this in a country where even McDonald's employees get six weeks of paid vacation every summer. I would have been pissed at her if I'd had any intention of actually working that much. Sure, I'd have to take the horses out in the morning, make Jan's *middag*, walk Joe, make the family dinner, and help with the horses at night, those were a given. But I sure wasn't planning on doing any mopping or vacuuming. Oh no, I would be seriously slacking for the next week and a half. I might even leave the computer plugged into the powerstrip unnecessarily for a few hours. I couldn't wait.

Early October was chillier and dryer in Southern Sverige than in Michigan, and Inger's breath was visible as she haphazardly gathered her luggage from the Volvo at the train platform. The minute she gave me a big, red, farewell smile and turned to roll her suitcase along the platform's loud gravel entrance, relief coated my insides like that animated diagram from the Pepto-Bismol commercials. I peeled out of the train station faster than a Volvo station wagon had ever peeled away from anything before. I was going back to my lair to take a nap.

Overall, the beginning of the week was fairly nice. There wasn't quite as much free time as I'd hoped. After all, I actually liked Jan and the kids; I didn't want them to starve. In fact, I secretly wanted them to like having me around as the mom more than Inger. I might have, in spite of myself, actually worked harder. I'd had my mother email me her most delicious and fail-safe recipes. (Note to self: Svenskar aren't crazy about spicy things. Or things with too much taste in general.) I took the dogs for extra long walks because it felt more like fun than work when Inger hadn't put it on a list. On our walks, Joe, the tubby black lab, Agda, the smiling Newfoundland, and I explored new corners of the farmland trails I thought we'd exhausted before. The trees that lined our path—the path that edged acres and acres of farm fields—had already lost their leaves, but recently enough that the ground was now aglow with their fall colors. For the first time since arriving, the countryside looked beautiful, like a place where I might like to be. "So maybe it's not necessarily housekeeping I hate so much," I acknowledged out loud to Agda, who liked to trot closer to me than Joe. "It's just your crazy mom. Good to know."

The best part was dinnertime, or *kvällsmat*, as I kept reminding myself to call it. (Without Inger there I knew it would be at least another two weeks before there was any chance a Svenska class would emerge. Thus, my silent, solitary studies continued.) In the absence of the alpha matriarch, the normally quiet remainder of the family suddenly perked up, and kvällsmat became quite the chatty evening adventure.

"So, what is everyone going to be for Halloween?" I was changing the subject. Lisbeth had been grumbling about an assignment she'd been given at school. It wasn't that she had any argument with the task itself, but the fact that the other girls in her class were not taking it as seriously as they should have been. Of course. Her lovely eyes were steeped in disapproval. I was so enchanted by the lively dinner conversation that I feared it veering toward such a dreary topic.

The Halloween question, however, brought the chatter to a halt. Glances scurried across the table from green eyes to blue, all wide with nerves. Pia looked at Lisbeth. Lisbeth looked at Jan. Åke looked down at his chicken curry casserole, clearly wishing it were *potatis* and *sallad.* I wasn't sure what to make of this response.

"So…you don't know? Or you haven't thought about it?"

"We haven't dressed for Halloween before," Pia quietly admitted for her family. A beat of silence followed this revelation.

"Wait. Halloween isn't just an American holiday," I protested in shock. "Is it?"

"Well," Lisbeth giggled, "yes, I think it is mostly. But some people are starting to celebrate here, a little. Some little kids will dress in disguises. But not many people have candy, so there is not really much places for them to go and ask."

For the record, the US was absolutely not the only country to celebrate Halloween, I would later learn. In fact, it was one of the most global holidays out there—Sverige included. Unaware of this, I deferred to the Waaras' expertise with regard to their own country. I was instantly determined to steal these wide-eyed Svenskar's Halloween virginity.

"Well, we're definitely celebrating it this year," I demanded. "There's no question about it. It's the most fun holiday there is."

The nervous looks continued, but I could sense excitement below their apprehension.

"But…" Lisbeth, as per usual, needed to know all of the details before getting on board with this idea. "There are not houses around our home that will have candy. Where will we go?"

"Go? Candy? Oh my gosh, you are totally missing the point of Halloween!" I was practically shouting with excitement now. "We don't have to go anywhere or eat any candy. The fun is dressing up, decorating, and having a party. Are you guys down with having a party?"

I noted with delight that in any normal household this would be the time when all eyes would dart to Jan for the paternal blessing. There were no such eye darts. Rather, Jan looked to his teenage children with as much hope on his face as each of theirs. Could they have a party? Had they ever thrown a party? Or gone to one? This was all unclear.

Then, out it came. Lisbeth, clearly torn between this awesome-sounding plan and maintaining the status quo in a home where she was second-in-command, vocalized everyone's concern.

"Ah…should we…? Should we have the party before Mom returns?" she meekly suggested. "She might…she might want to…be very involved."

There was a general murmur of understanding around the table. Each delicate Swede stared into his or her plate, imagining their American Halloween party as planned and operated by the family puppet master. I was tickled. Mutiny!

"How about this," I said, clearly having no problem directing this overly-directed family. "Rather than have a Halloween party that's two weeks early, why don't we spend the next few of days planning out the whole thing, and then right before Halloween, we'll introduce it as a sort of surprise for her, and all we have to do is carry out the plan and have a great time."

Everyone loved the idea.

The remainder of the week was marked with a newfound closeness in the Waara-sans-Inger Household. The missing matriarch wasn't mentioned again in any pejorative way, but a bond had formed the minute Lisbeth's uncharacteristically bold statement fell out of her mouth, and the heads around the dinner table ever so slightly nodded in unison. Our Halloween party plan wouldn't be hard to keep secret; part of Inger's week-long seminar required her to cut off all communication with the outside world. No phone calls to family. No emails. No letters. I remembered thinking when she'd told me about this that a) I couldn't have been more excited to be cut off from her; and b) that I was pretty sure all you had to do was Google, "signs you might be in a cult" to learn that purposeful isolation from your family was about as red as flags get.

Regardless, whoever said secrets don't make friends had never planned an illicit Halloween party on a Swedish farm. It was fun to feel as if the kids and I were plotting together. Lisbeth and Pia sat on either side of me on the living room couch—a room that hadn't been used for much "living" prior to this week—looking up fun Halloween recipes on Inger's laptop. The three of us spent hours rifling through boxes in the attic for costume possibilities. Åke even stopped up every once in a while and allowed his sisters to make him showcase a few funny hats and accessories. All three kids wanted to be "something dead." While I'd explained to them that

Halloween costumes weren't necessarily limited to the theme of ghosts and ghouls, they didn't even acknowledge other options. They were doing Halloween, and they were going to do it right. Their enthusiasm was adorable and energizing.

The fun spilled over into us doing other things together. Our routine of watching Alias on DVD became more of an event, with tea, hot cocoa, and even some popcorn added to some sessions. Pia and I went to another exercise class, which was equally as ridiculous as the first one. These were really nice, pleasant kids. Why had Inger gone to the length of bringing an American over to spend time with them for her?

The role of substitute matron also came with increased concern for Pia. I'd noticed before that she wasn't a big eater, but now, as the family cook, I suspected it was more than that. She hardly ate anything, but she would pretend to, cutting a piece of broccoli into seven or eight pieces and slowly chewing each bit. Inger had told me that she'd just recently given up all simple sugars. Why would a skinny fourteen-year-old cut out sugar from her diet? Should I have a talk with her about body image? Should I talk to Inger?

For the time being I decided to not decide. Continual monitoring seemed like the best balance between Pia's well being and getting myself into a sticky, overstepping-my-boundaries situation.

The other small hang-up was Lisbeth. Now, I loved Lisbeth, and while I was quite sure she felt some affection for me too, some notable territorialism surfaced with the absence of Inger. It wasn't that I expected an anarchic, party atmosphere to overtake the quiet farmhouse when she was away, but I didn't expect Lisbeth to be the guardian of the rulebook.

"You know you're not to use a fork with that pan."

The fact that Lisbeth had been secretly monitoring me from behind as I managed four simmering pots on the stove was enough to annoy me, let alone that she decided to startle me with cookery care instructions. How Inger or Lisbeth thought I should test the doneness of the boiling *potatis* without stabbing them with something metal, I wasn't aware. But this week, I thought, I'd be able to stab the damn *potatis* in peace.

"Lisbeth—"

But when I turned to her, she was standing before me with a wooden spoon pointed at my sternum. She was too old to scold. And I lived with her, so I had no desire to start a fight. So I took it. And the *potatis* were going to be eaten however fucking done they were.

Despite the rules, Inger did call a couple of times that week, and during the calls I'd hear Lisbeth whining to her in the same sad, Svensk whine she always used when speaking to her mother. I couldn't help but wonder if she was whining about me this time. Were those Svensk complaints about a homework assignment, or were they Teflon-related gripes? Had she heard me sneak upstairs last night and pour myself a secret glass of wine? Was she tattling on me? Until those Svensk classes started up, there was no way for me to know.

The rest of the week passed easily, but it wasn't as if the family's way of life had suddenly changed. It was nine o'clock on Saturday, so obviously the kids had all voluntarily gone to bed a while ago. Jan had actually gone to Germany for a farm equipment-related event that night, so it seemed especially odd for the house to be so quiet.

For the life of me, I couldn't understand these teenagers. I get the whole we-live-on-a-boring-farm thing, but for goodness sake, isn't doing something out of the ordinary required when your parents are out of town? I was supposed to be in charge, and there I was, itching to be naughty. I would have happily sneaked them a beer if they were interested. Hell, I'd have poured them shots or taught them how to assemble a beer bong. If Swedes didn't place weed on the same plane of evil as heroin, I'd be willing to teach them about all kinds of bongs.

But alas. Although the parents were away, there was no one to play. So I could only be consoled by my nightly routine of creeping into Inger's office, plugging her laptop into the power strip, plugging the power strip into the wall, connecting the phone line to the computer, waiting while the ancient piece of machinery slowly booted up and even more slowly dialed its way into the information superhighway. Holy fucking shit. These people loved making life feel even slower than it actually was.

I tried to wrap my mind around staying in a country full of people I couldn't relate to in even the smallest way for an entire year. My refusal to give up on this adventure was slowly rubbing raw my desire to not waste a year of my twenties in quiet monotony, even if it did have a burst of geniality now and again. Something was going to have to give.

And then there was a knock at the door.

What could this be?

Robbers?

Thieves?

Svensk Jehovah's Witnesses?

From what I knew of Svenskar so far, criminals would certainly be the only humans out on the prowl after the hour of nine. And as I could only assume Svensk bandits would knock first, there was no reason to rule out illegal activity. So that was pretty exciting. I prepped myself for a mild-mannered assault as I approached the door. *Maybe these criminals could be talked into hanging out with me for a while,* I thought. *Maybe they're looking for hypodermics and a tourniquet so they can shoot up some pot in a dark alley somewhere. I am totally going with them.*

I quietly opened the door, careful not to disturb the slumbering kids upstairs.

"*Hej!*" said a thin man with disheveled blond hair. "Is Jan in?"

It was Johan. I sort of knew this guy. Well, I'd had one embarrassing experience with him, making him a large portion of the Svenskar I'd ever met. During my first week in Sverige, just days after I learned to drive a stick shift, Johan was inexplicably at Ödmjuk Gård, and Inger had asked me to drive him home. Not having as clue as to who this somewhat Eurotrash-looking man was, or why he needed my expert driving assistance, but wanting to be impressively agreeable to my new employer, I naturally agreed. To my mortification, I learned on the way over to his house (a two-minute drive that took about ten as I ground my way through the transmission of the poor Volvo) that he was in fact the car guy. He'd been delivering a car to the Waaras that he had repaired. He didn't need me to chauffeur him anywhere; not only was he perfectly capable of being the driver, he also could have walked his ass home.

But why do either of those when he was clearly enjoying himself in the car? He complimented me so dryly on my driving skills that it took me a minute to realize that he was making fun of me. Having a real, honest laugh in my frighteningly unfunny new home made my heart go pitter-pat a bit. *Well, here's a normal person,* I'd thought, fresh off the plane. *There must be more of these around.*

Ha! Oh, how naïve I had been.

Relatable or not, I figured I didn't have much hope of seeing him again anyway. The kids told me he was the "weird man" of the neighborhood. "He has—*gasp*—tattoos all up and down his arms," Lisbeth said, hardly able to stifle her giggles. "And his girlfriend is a priest, and they live together unmarried."

Damn. It wasn't that I was looking for a Svensk fling with the painful remains of Greg still circling my emotional drain and all, but I was disappointed at this news. It didn't seem likely that the priest's live-in boyfriend would strike up a friendship with the American girl down the road.

But here, standing on the doorstep so many weeks later, was a chance to have one more conversation with a normal-seeming person. I'd take it.

He was shocked to find out that both Jan and Inger were out of the country.

"Seems like he would have mentioned that when I said I was going to drop off the car," he said, pursing his thin, Svensk lips as he stepped right past me into the foyer, completely unbidden. Like someone might do if they were hoping to befriend you. I made a mental note not to get too excited, even as my pulse began kicking the shit out of my throat. Friend. Friend. Friend. Friend.

"Where are the kids then?" Johan asked.

"Oh," I said, "yeah…it's pretty late for them. They hurried off to bed about an hour ago."

"When neither of their parents are home?" he asked with flat disbelief. "You'd think they'd be up with a party." He raised his eyebrows and shook his head as he looked around himself, as if taking in both the Waara home and whatever went on inside for the first time.

For joy! He thinks they're being weird too! Could the twilight zone could be getting less twilighty?

Despite the emotional disco in my brain, I was able to maintain a polite, breezy banter with Johan about what I did and where I was from, as well as learning a bit about him. In addition to working on cars, he did a few other things that weren't totally translating for me. There was something about car radios and something else about driving services. Again, I blushed internally that I'd given the "driving services" guy an unskilled ride home. We somehow got on the subject of money when it happened. My entire Svensk experience began to take a whole new form with one sentence.

"And there's another thing," he said, casually gazing toward the darkened wall just over my right shoulder. "I don't like bills. I don't think I'm going to pay them anymore."

Silence.

I almost couldn't breathe. Did that just happen? Did this Svensk just quote the movie *Office Space*? I must have looked like a moron. I just stood there, staring at him. I hadn't seen so much as a fraction of myself reflected in a single soul in this country after five weeks, and this guy in the foyer, on this crazy *gård* in the middle of nowhere, in the dark of night, just quoted one of my favorite movies at me. For one second, I felt at home.

He finally had to break my stupor.

"It's from a movie," he said, "but I do really not like bills."

"I KNOW!" I accidentally shouted. "*Office Space*. I've seen that movie a gazillion times! The two Bobs? The Jump to Conclusions Mat? The-the smashing of the fax, or printer, or whatever in the field with the baseball bat?"

The conversation burst open from there. He fancied himself a bit of an American movie buff. He loved Tarantino, the Farrelly Brothers and—as if I wasn't charmed enough at this point—he told me that *The Big Lebowski* was also one of his favorites, which pretty much sealed the deal on us becoming best friends.

An hour later, with his cell number—excuse me, his mobile number—programmed into the phone Inger had given me (that I had yet to have any reason to use), he finally said his goodbyes and left.

For fucking joy. I might have a friend. Might. Considering how I hadn't so much as heard a peep from my previous potential Svensk friends in more than two weeks, I didn't want to get my hopes up. But they were. Up. My hopes, I mean. Johan, I had to believe, was different. Now that the possibility of a new friend allowed me to admit it, Linda and Hanna had acted a bit like taking me out had been an errand. This guy barged right into the house. And he certainly was better looking than all the rest of them. Not that that mattered, what with his priest lover or whatever.

So when he called over to the Waaras' the following day to ask if I wanted to join him for a ride to the hardware store, I was elated. Of course I wanted to go the Swedish hardware store!! What could I possibly want more?

* * *

What do you wear to the hardware store? The thought struck me as both sadly ridiculous and desperately important. He'd be here in a matter of minutes, so I didn't have much time to mull it over. I'd brought a slew of cute outfits with me, perfect for going out to the bar, to dinner, for a day in the city, but even after being relegated to housecleaning and horseshit clothes since I'd arrived, I realized I couldn't justify wearing any of my finest duds on a trip to the hardware store. Forget what Johan would think; I wouldn't be able to live myself.

So on with a moderately snappy long-sleeved t-shirt, and an extra application of deodorant, and I was ready and waiting. *I bet I'm wearing more deodorant than everyone in this family put together*, I thought cheerfully as I waited by the side gate of the farmhouse that served as a convenient and discrete escape point from my basement dwelling.

Johan's Volvo was way cooler than the Waaras' car. It was a sleek silver hatchback. Well, as sleek as Volvos get anyway. Not until it pulled up did I think, *What reason could he possibly have for calling and inviting me to the hardware store?*

"*Hallo*," he said as I slid into the leather bucket seat next to him.

"*Hej*!" I said, trying not to look as batshit excited as I was to be running an errand.

"*Ah! God eftermiddag. Hur mår du?*" He said this with a completely knowing arch in his thin, blonde eyebrow. Oh dear Lord. He was really cute.

"Ah, yeah. Johan," I said, "I'm bilingual in exactly one word, and that was it." Trying hard to sound casual, I gave him an understated, half-cocked smile. Good one, Natalie!

"Well," he said as he shifted the car into gear and pulled away from the farm, "we're just going to have to change that, aren't we?"

Think of something to say. Think of something…

"So I've been here a month, and this is the first time I've been on a highway," I said a few minutes later, as we merged away from the Swedish back roads to which I'd been confined.

"What? Don't they…take you places? You can't get out of town without getting on the highway." Johan's speech was entirely different than any of the Waaras'. It was equally melodic, but rose and fell throughout his phrasing, rather than just starting at the top of the scale and descending. It was irregular and surprising, like listening to jazz after hearing only waltzes for months.

"Well, apparently I'm supposed to be going all sort of places, like Swedish lessons, 'the city,' wherever that is, visiting their aunt in the South of France. But so far I've been doing mostly vacuuming."

"Excuse me…vacuuming? You're a cleaning woman?"

"And I do laundry too," I added smartly. "And I shovel horseshit every day, so I'd say it's been a pretty well-rounded experience so far."

"You are sar-CAS-tic!" he beamed. "Do you like Jay Leno?"

That was an interesting leap.

"What? You get Jay Leno here?" I was in total disbelief. What Swedish TV channel was he watching? Clearly not any of the twelve that came in at Ödmjuk Gård. He gave me a politely incredulous nod, as if the silly foreigner next to him had asked if Sweden had indoor plumbing. "I guess I like Letterman and Conan O'Brien more, but sure, I guess I like Leno."

"I have a joke for you." His tiny, straight Swedish teeth were poised in a smile chock-full of anticipation.

"OK…"

"What is the similarity between a hurricane and a divorce in Arkansas?"

I had a feeling this joke was being paraphrased.

"Ah. I don't know."

"Either way, somebody is gonna lose a trailer!"

I laughed. It was just an OK joke, but it was hilarious that a Swede was telling it.

"What?" I said when I regained my breath. "How do you even understand that joke?"

"Do I strike you as someone who is stupid?" he asked, still smiling.

"No, you strike me as someone who's never been to Arkansas."

"We have these TV things here, you know."

I was absolutely dumbstruck. Up until three months ago I knew jack shit about Sverige. Apparently, I still didn't know much. And this guy understood jokes referencing sub-cultural nuances from the US.

"I am so happy I get to tell that joke," Johan said, emphasizing his enthusiasm by pounding the steering wheel with his palm.

"Why, have you been saving it up or something?" I asked.

I expected a volley of my ironic tone, but his response was completely sincere. "Yes! I heard it, like, five years ago on Leno, and I've tried to tell it to people, and they just don't get it. I had to wait until I found an American to tell it to."

"What?" This was even funnier than the joke. "You've been saving that joke for five years? That is ridiculous!" I was practically crying. "If no other Swedes get it, why do you think it's so special?"

"I don't know [EYE dunNo]," he said. "I guess it is just because I am so special." His eyebrow was doing that thing again. I had no clue what that was supposed to mean, but it made my stomach do a cartwheel.

"So you decided to invite some American girl you just met to drive to the hardware store with you so you could finally tell your joke."

He grinned. "Sure. That is it," Johan said, looking at me slyly out of the corner of his small, lively eyes. "Why, are you so disappointed that you had to leave the farm?"

"Dude," I said in my most serious voice, "this is the biggest event of my month."

9
En Skymt
A Glimmer

Lise,

...so anyway, we go to the nearby metropolis of Malmö to visit the hardware store. We have fun, laugh, etc. He tells me about his impression of Americans, and I explain my impression of Swedes. Our mutual appreciation for self-deprecation is much a more effective means of transatlantic relations than the UN could ever hope for. How amazing is it to find someone in your Swedish village, population twenty-four, who thinks so similarly to yourself? He starts talking about music, and I realize that my music-dude magnetism has followed me around the globe. And guess what his favorite kind is? Eighties pop.

I know. It's almost creepy.

Later we watch a movie at his house. There is no priest girlfriend, but I can see her remains...some scattered mail, a couple of pictures, and some décor that looks distinctly feminine. She's gone, but evidently, she has not been gone long—after living there for a couple of years. We're just going to pretend not to know that information.

Then we watch a movie. Lots of fun. He turns out to be as laid back and mild-mannered as all the Swedes I've met, but different in that he has this energy that is missing from the others. He's so peppy; it's totally changed my idea of what the typical Swede is like.

And he has the largest Great Dane I have ever seen, who is

the cutest and sweetest ever. His name is Ludde and he comes up to my shoulders.

So, three days after the hardware store, the day after Inger returned (ugh) from her US adventure, he text messages me (the only way to communicate in Sweden, evidently) asking me to come over again...

"Inger," I asked as I started to help clean up after dinner," do you mind if I go over to visit Johan after Lisbeth and I are done with the horses?"

This felt so strange. At twenty-three, I hadn't lived with my parents for years, nor had permission been required for doing whatever I wanted for a long time prior to that. But living with your employer was a breeding ground for unreadable situations. Inger's veritable monopoly over my schedule seemed to necessitate asking permission.

"Of course, darling! I am so glad that you are able to find a friend!"

And now it was beginning to feel weirder. What was I, the socially inept teenager who'd finally found another oddball to hang out with after school?

"Please go. I will help Lisbeth with the horses tonight. You have worked much extra while I was gone anyway. You go have fun."

Although I found her delight in my new friendship predictably annoying, who was I to argue? I made a mental note to become further annoyed at the prospect of this one-hour reprieve from the horses being my comp time for working twelve-hour days for the prior ten days. No time to worry about that now.

Down in my cellar, I grabbed my clumsy, family-issued phone to text Johan:

Is now OK?

A few minutes later:

The sooner the better!

Johan lived in a small, two-bedroom house not far from the Waaras. In fact, when taking the stretch of the country road west from Ödmjuk Gård to the farm where the horses were kept, his home was one of the three houses in the cluster along the way. It felt good to know that the most sane and normal Svensk I'd met so far was a short car ride and/or panicked run away.

Although I'd lived in apartments bigger than Johan's little house, it felt incredibly spacious to me when compared to the claustrophobia I'd been feeling at Ödmjuk Gård. The front door led directly into a modest living and dining room area that attached to a neat little kitchen that appeared to be under construction. Save for a tiny bathroom, that was the entire ground floor. The stairs, I learned later, led to two small bedrooms. I found it adorable. It was no grand estate, but it was just the right size for a single Svensk, his large dog, and three cats.

We didn't watch any movies this time. Johan was determined to prove his love of music to the American, so we spent all night listening to the sleek surround-sound system that was hooked into his computer. To be clear, this was probably six months from the time when Americans really began the migration over to iTunes as their primary mode of music storage, and using their computers with sound systems instead of stereos with CD players. I was impressed.

He made it into a competition of sorts, going through his playlist, finding a track, and saying, "Do you know who this is?" as it began to play. It had been going on for almost an hour. I was doing all right, but he hadn't been giving me tough choices.

"This is the Dandy Warhols!" I practically yelled at him. How did he find that band living in a Swedish farming village?

"Natalie, we have music stations."

"I know," I said. "I've heard them, and they certainly don't play this kind of music. This band isn't even that big in the US."

Clearly proud of himself, he left me mystified as he flipped to the next song. It was some Euro-techno crap I didn't recognize and had no desire to. He flipped again. Again, I freely admitted I didn't recognize what sounded to me like generic hair metal.

"This is Iron Maiden!" he said. "Natalie, this is so American!"

"How about you leave the classifying of American music to the American," I said. Iron Maiden? As a follow-up to the Dandy Warhols? I would just pretend that hadn't happened. "Next, please."

Three seconds into the following song, I just about started to cry with joy.

"The Pet Shop Boys?! I love the Pet Shop Boys!"

"Natalie," he looked equal parts delighted and confused, "are you old enough to love the Pet Shop Boys?"

I laughed. And then I stopped.

"Johan. How old are you?"

Always cool, he replied, "Not too old, but older than you." He was teasing me now.

"You don't even know how old I am. How would you know?"

"This," he said, switching to the next song, "is Bach."

"I know it's Bach," I came back, insulted at his clear bias against Americans' cultural education.

"You *know*?" he said, full of suspicious condescension.

"Yeah, I know. I know my classical music. I've played the piano since I was seven. I can play the trumpet, the tuba, and the French horn, and I was drum major of my high school marching band. I know Bach." Good thing he wasn't familiar enough with American culture to know that this was a blatant admission of my supreme geekiness.

"OK," he said. "You know Bach." He nodded his head. "You are a very surprising girl, Natalie."

He pronounced my name like I'd never heard it before, with a distinct staccato on each syllable, and a different note singing out each one. I resisted the urge to ask him to say it again. That would not have been playing it cool.

"Would you like something to drink?" he said.

"Like something alcoholic?" If his pronunciation of my name got my heart racing, it was now going double-time. My enthusiasm was perhaps not something I should have been proud of, but almost two months had passed since I'd had a drink—a real drink, that is. Not one of the single, four-ounce glasses of wine Inger allowed me to imbibe every couple of weeks or so. The few months preceding my arrival in Sverige were among the least sober in my life. Quitting cold turkey was not serving me well; I was hankering for a buzz. Especially at that moment.

"Yeah, I've some beer or something in there," he replied nodding to the kitchen.

"Holy shit, yes," I said, not caring how much of a boozehound I sounded like. "Please get me a drink."

If there were one thing I could and should have researched about my new home abroad before taking off, it was the alcohol content of their beer. Like many Americans, I just always assumed beer was beer. It had exactly one beer's worth of alcohol in it, and it tasted pretty much like, you know, beer.

Svensk beer, or *öl*, well...it was a bit different.

"Do you know the joke about American beer and the canoe?" Johan asked as he emerged from the kitchen with the tallest can of beer I'd ever seen and two small glasses. I didn't.

"What do American beer and making love in a canoe have in common?" he asked, biting his lip with delight.

"I have no idea."

"Ah ha! Both are fucking close to water. Ha ha!"

I smiled. Whatever. I was so disinterested in the taste of beer that I figured I was immune from distinguishing one from another. But I certainly didn't miss the heightening of the tension in the air that resulted from his sexually suggestive joke. All the more reason to start drinking. He opened one bottle of beer, which I noted as strange, and filled two tiny glasses to the brim and offered up mine. Gosh, I thought, what a puny-ass amount of beer. It wasn't until I'd downed three or four of these little glasses of *öl* before I really understood the joke.

As a result, a few hours later, I was fucking close to trashed. I somehow realized it was nearly 3 a.m., and I had a full day of housecleaning ahead of me.

"Dude," I slurred. "I have got to go. Those crazies are probably totally freaked out. I don't know if these pees-ple can stay out this late without, you know, being a pumpkin."

Predictably, Johan had no idea what that meant, but he laughed. He was somehow sober.

"What? They aren't that crazy, are they? I've been fixing their cars for years, and they seem OK."

"Firss of all," I said, teetering as I tried to get my feet into my shoes, "yes, about those years. You have not tolded me how old you are, which I asked you and you avert-ted my questions. Second! They *are* crazy, dude." I really needed to stop calling him dude. "They unplug everything in their house every night before bed."

"OK."

"They disssconnect the car battery when they park the car."

"Yeah," he said, helping me navigate the doorknob. "I told them they didn't need to do that."

"Inger is a fucking cult leader, man." For the record, "man" is no smoother than "dude."

"What?"

Oh poo. It had been a part of my survival strategy to get to know Johan a little better before I did any shit-talking about the Waaras. He seemed cool, but he did do business with them and had been their neighbor for years. He had every reason to be more loyal to them than to some American girl he'd hung out with twice. And I had to live with these people for another year. Oops.

"I can't…Yeah, I've got a lot to tell you," I said, gratuitously patting him on the arm. In direct contrast to my thoughts, I added, "I'm gonna go now." We'd made it outside, and my hand was on the car door handle. Johan was thankfully helping me climb in. Gosh, he was standing really close to me.

Good thing I only have to drive two miles of farm road to get home, I was thinking, looking down the dark, blurry stripe that was probably the road.

I wasn't sure, but while I stood staring off into the Svensk night, wondering how I'd make it home without killing myself, he might have kissed me on the cheek. Totally unprepared to deal with that, I ignored it, fell into the driver's seat and experienced my first (and only, thankfully) episode in Svensk drunk driving. In retrospect, it seems like he should have stopped me, and I suppose I thought he was going to until he had me tucked into the car and was waving me away. Okey-dokey. American guys usually intervene here, but there I was, starting the car. I only had a mile of houseless, traffic-less country road to travel, I told myself. Even so, I made a slurred mental note that I was going to have to better monitor myself from here on out.

But for the first night in a long time, I did not suffer any insomnia.

* * *

I should have woken up full of giddiness and intrigue the following morning, but I was far too concerned about the state and position of the Waaras' car. As I clearly had been too inebriated to undress myself and get under the covers of my tiny cellar bed, I was loath to imagine how I'd parked the Volvo. I could hear Inger upstairs chattering away on the phone in an aggressive tone I'd yet to hear from her. Had she realized how late I'd come home? Did I drive the station wagon into a tree? Why did Johan let me drive home? Was he drunk too, even though he seemed sober? Had he kissed me?

All of these questions bumbled lazily around my head as I tried to make myself presentable enough to emerge from the basement and peek at the car out a window. But how would I do this? The only window from which a proper view could be had was in the Inger-occupied kitchen.

There was no other option. As I pulled on my hangover uniform of an oversized sweater and glasses, and tied my disgusting mess of hair back in a ponytail, I strategized how I could manage to peep out the window without her noticing, on the off-chance that her thirty-year-old car was wrapped around a tree, and she was yet unaware. Honestly, if I'd crashed the car, there would probably be no need to even look after Inger saw me.

As I crept up the stairs, I could hear her talking, deep in an ultra-serious phone conversation. If her out-of-control American au pair/maid was the subject matter, she made no attempt to switch topics as I entered the kitchen. Unfortunately, she was sitting on the window seat as she chattered away in Svenska, blocking my view of the driveway. Damn. I'd have to crane my neck from the window across the kitchen to evaluate the Volvo's placement.

For an unnatural amount of time, I made like I was searching through the breadbox. I couldn't quite see the car, but I was so close. Inger's voice was getting more frantic! She wasn't looking in this direction yet. I had just a few seconds to use my arms to boost myself high enough above the counter to get a proper view, all the while girding myself for whatever lecture I was about to receive, or the new car I was about to buy them. As her voice became louder and fiercer, I was just about there—I just had to lift myself a bit higher and stretch my neck out a little farther—

Inger was ranting into the phone. I couldn't follow a single word. It sounded like the Swedish Chef having an Iron Chef-style meltdown. As her melodic, looping tirade went on, I strained farther to see out the window while watching her warily from the corner of my eye.

Clang!

Just as the phone slammed down, I finally got a perfect view of the red Volvo, which was parked perfectly in its regular spot, all in one piece.

Oh. What was this nutbag all upset about then?

I was still propped over the counter, my feet six inches above the ground, when Inger directed her attention toward me. She did not acknowledge my odd positioning in the slightest.

"Natalie dear, I do apologize, but it appears I must disrupt your morning with a request. It seems I must go to hospital immediately, and I'd very much appreciate you driving me."

Wow. I was way off.

"Are you OK? What's wrong?"

"Oh—HA HA!—It's nothing, dear. That was just the hospital on the phone, and they are quite certain I have what they are calling an *advanced kidney infection*," she pronounced the diagnosis as if she was reading it out of a book of spells. "It's so silly! See, I've been having a pain in my side since midway through my trip, and I just stopped into the pharmacy yesterday to inquire about it. Well, they insisted I go to the laboratory to allow for some tests. And now the doctors are telling me I must report to the hospital right away! I find it sort of ridiculous, the way these doctors believe..."

Inger wasn't even close to stopping, but I was already in internal hysterics. How priceless was this? First of all, this woman seriously thought I'd be upset about missing my morning of horse-tending and vacuuming to drive her to the hospital. But even more staggering to me was that Inger, who claimed to believe that illness only existed in the mind, had just allowed a kidney infection to get wildly out of control. I loved it. I mean, not that she was actually sick, but I was giddy to hear how she was going to rationalize this.

I didn't have to wait long. We were on the road to the hospital in Ångelholm when she started applying her mystic principles to the situation.

"It must have been the stress of being so far from family that created this mental illness that has translated into an infection," she rationalized.

"So...if the illness was created in your mind," I was being as careful as I could to sound more curious than skeptical. I kept my eyes locked on the road ahead and hands firmly planted on the steering wheel. "Can't you cure it, or make it go away in your mind as well?"

"Well, naturally that should be the case," she responded, clearly welcoming my question, "but it would take much more than a student of Den Metod like me to know fully how to do this. It would certainly be something I would aspire to. But then, if I were skilled enough to perform this, I would most likely not be in the situation in the first place. Ha! How interesting!"

Interesting wasn't exactly the word I was thinking of. *Convenient* seemed far more appropriate to me. Regardless, I had no problem with Inger being in hospital for a day or two. Far be it from me to argue her into trying to stay home and battle her infection with her mind.

In all seriousness, it was a good thing she didn't. Although Inger wouldn't let me come any further than the parking lot—"Just leave me here, darling. I'll call you when I'm ready to be picked up later"—the doctors insisted on hospitalizing her for at least a week. Really? For a kidney infection? Either Svensk doctors were incredibly cautious (and why not, with free healthcare?) or Inger had seriously just nearly killed herself with crazy.

* * *

Although I was ecstatic to have the house back to myself during the day again, I wasn't fully embracing my return to being on-call twenty-four hours a day. I had someplace to be now. My newfound, or rather, re-found freedom made visiting Johan less awkward with no one to ask permission of, but it was still difficult to fit in. I'd purposely neglected to analyze whether or not it was a wise idea to spend all my spare time with him, whether or not I was ready to jump into something like this, or what "something like this" even was. All I was acknowledging to myself was that Johan was exciting, and the Waaras were boring.

Twice during my long day of housework I now had the thrill of passing by Johan's little house on the way to the horses. What was he doing inside? Was he thinking about me? Would we hang out later? What did this all mean? Wise or not, whatever my visits with Johan meant, they filled me with the rush I'd intended my overseas adventure to be full of in the first place.

Not that I was the only one who seemed so keen on what was happening. On one particular afternoon, Johan texted me:

Must come over. Here this excelent song.

Close enough.

Be there after horseshit.

Later that evening, I was barely in the door when he grabbed my hand

and pulled me onto the couch, where we had spent every night so far listening to music and watching movies.

"Are you ready?" he asked, eyes wide and finger poised over his laptop keyboard. I released the tension of a day of cleaning and behaving myself in a sigh, like a bird released from a handhold.

"Go for it." His enthusiasm was amazing. Even over a newly discovered song. OK, I'll admit it. It was probably more than that.

The song was hilarious. I'm not much of an electronic music fan, so it was hard for me judge whether it was good or not musically, but the lyrics of Princess Superstar's "My Machine" were so funny, they practically made me cry. The gist of the song was that the singer wondered what would happen if she had a machine that could turn her into anything she wanted. Somehow she accidently ended up turning herself into a box of cereal, and she sang—nay, rapped—her way through a child's digestive tract. I loved it. I loved Johan's enthusiasm for the song, I loved that he had no idea how awful the lyrics were, and I genuinely loved them for being so terribly, terribly cheesy. Good thing too, because Johan played it on repeat for about five hours.

The beer came out again that night. Now, I would have preferred to return to my normal American habit of drinking myself into oblivion every night, but that wasn't really how it worked in Sverige. As much as Svenskar loved to talk about drinking, it seemed their lack of enthusiasm for spending money disallowed for the type of constant binge-drinking young Americans deemed normal. After that first night, if there was *öl* involved, it was one large can split between our two, moderately-sized glasses. Darn. But whatever, I wasn't being choosey. Johan and I seemed to have a fine time with or without the crazy-strong *öl*.

"I'm really glad this song is good." I said, draining my glass, "because you are sure playing the shit out of it."

"Hey," he smiled, "you find something you like, you just, you know…get really comfortable with it." He pronounced every syllable of "comfortable." I found it adorable—especially aided by the öl. His bleached hair wasn't so spiky today. It was still tousled, but it lay more comfortably on his head. He'd been working all day. His fingers were black and his Eurotrash hairdo was clearly fatigued. Naturally, I found this adorable as well.

"So you are telling me all these things we think about Americans aren't so true?" Johan was back to his list of assumed American qualities, testing me to see which ones he could mark as true or false.

"Johan, there are a lot of us. There isn't a single thing you think about Americans that applies to all of us."

"Well, you are not fat, so there is one." Johan smiled at me.

"And neither are any of the Americans on TV or in movies," I said. "It seems like half of your stereotypes are from the media, and then you still believe the half that are confounded by what you see in the media."

"Ah, Natalie. You are a smart girl." His insistence on calling me a girl wasn't doing much for my confidence about his age. I was, I'll admit, sort of basking in his compliments, however. "So I know you are not a druggie American."

I laughed.

"An American what? Druggie? What are you, thirteen?"

"So it is not true that Americans are all doing marijuana and heroin?"

"Johan, there is a vast difference between pot and heron," I said.

"So you do one of them?" He seemed suddenly serious.

"Well, yeah. I'm completely in favor of smoking weed," I said. "Most people are. It's milder than this *öl*, I'll tell you that much. Heroin, on the other hand, will fucking kill you. So…kind of a big difference. I don't know anyone who does heroin."

Johan was quiet for a moment. I thought he was considering my light-hearted attitude toward pot, but instead he reverted back to the song that was still playing on repeat.

"I'm glad you liked this 'My Machine' after I told you about it so highly," he said cheerfully. "There's nothing worse than having really big hopes for a good song and being disappointed."

"Yes!" I said, turning to face him on the couch far more excitedly than necessary. "Like when you hear the intro to what you think is 'Under Pressure' and it turns out to be Vanilla Ice?"

He stopped fiddling with his computer for the first time all night. He looked so perplexed I thought for a moment that I had insulted some deep-seeded love of "Ice, Ice Baby." Setting his computer down on the coffee table, he turned to face me and was silent for a moment before saying, "Natalie, you have completely changed my view of Americans. You know…so much."

Too flabbergasted to compute. All things considered, it did seem like fairly strong emotional reaction to Bowie-based commentary, but between my buzz and the flattery, that seemed like splitting hairs. I suddenly had the urge to ask him his age again, but was fortunately not that drunk.

"Do you want to go listen to music in my car?"

I had no idea what he meant by that, but yes. Yes, I did.

...So he asks if I want to listen to music in his car. Whatever, I think. This is an odd request, but I'm agreeable.

Lise, he BUILT this car with his hands. The inside looks like a space capsule, and the whole interior is virtually one huge speaker. But it's not meant for volume—it doesn't even get that loud. It's about sound quality; it's this art form I had no idea existed. When you're in the car, it's like you're hearing music for the first time in your life—it's amazing. When you close your eyes, you can see the band in front of you. You can point to where the singer is, where the drums are, where the guitar player is. If they move around the stage you can follow them with your ears. And he did this somehow by the way he built it. He competes with this car in these national shows—and kills everyone because he's the only one who builds his own cars, rather than building systems into an existing car.

Anyway—five hours and who knows how many songs later, he kisses me. We go back in the house and do more of that for a while. A long while. I CRAWL into bed at 6 a.m.

So that's how things are going with me and the incredibly hot Swede who takes me out for ice cream and to browse at IKEA at my convenience. I took a nap at his house Saturday afternoon and woke up to a homemade breakfast. It was 2:30 in the afternoon! "Wake up, beloved," he says, "I made you breakfast."

So what's been going on in the Midwest? Try explaining to a Swede that the American "Midwest" is actually located in the northern, mid-east portion of the country. You can just see the "that's so American" expression on their faces. These are the main stereotypes people have about Americans here—some of which were total surprises to me: 1, we all have guns; 2, we all sue each other constantly; 3, we're all fat; 4, we all smoke pot. I've been trying desperately to explain that these aren't true regardless of the fact that I've shot a gun, been sued, and have smoked plenty of weed. I'm not doing a very good job of dispelling these rumors. Somehow our conversation about suing got around to the symbols on plastic bags that indicate that you shouldn't put a baby's head in one. You know what should make us all feel really embarrassed? Those only exist in the US. Apparently the rest of the world is pretty clear on not putting your baby's head in a bag.

I have all sorts of funny stories to tell you, but I should tell you some over the phone. I have a cell phone here but I don't know if I can call "America" with it. It's so weird that everyone calls it "America." I feel like we're in *West Side Story*. I've got to go. My Swedish lover is coming to pick me up for a night of watching *The Big Lebowski* and drinking white Russians.

med mycket kärlek,

Nat

Home life at Ödmjuk Gård took a strange turn with Inger in the hospital. It was as though her being out of the country was an entirely different state of affairs than her being in a hospital bed in Ångelholm. Maybe it was because she called every day. Several times a day. Maybe it was general unrest from the family being out of sorts for so long. Either way, life was suddenly just as tense and annoying with the Waaras as when Inger was home, but I had more responsibility because she wasn't. Awesome.

It was Wednesday, and I was boiling *potatis.* I'd made it all the way through my stack of my mom's best recipes with no positive feedback. Fuck these Svenskar and their polite dismissal of all my delicious American recipes with their flavors and variety. If these people want plates full of hot, unsalted starch and watery iceberg lettuce, who was I to argue? In the almost twenty-four hours between being in LA and the hospital, Inger had asked me to consider if the tiny package of Philadelphia cream cheese and soft *rågkaka* bread I'd added to the family's massive grocery list weren't just a bit "excessive," so I guess I wasn't allowed to eat anything other than *potatis* and *sallad* now either. Unless I wanted to pay for it myself, she reassured me.

So as Lisbeth approached me in the kitchen with her usual pouty expression, I immediately tensed up. *Seriously*, I thought, *if she asks me what time we're "going for the horses" I'm going to punch her in the throat hole. I'm going to take this* potatis *poker and hold it right up to her eyeball and scream, "What time do we go every night?! After dinner?! Is it a safe bet that we'll probably repeat that same behavior for the fortieth night in a row?!"*

"Ha-looo," she greeted me cheerfully, though her expression was as dull as the meal I was preparing.

"Hey Lisbeth," I said. "What's going on? Did school go OK today?"

"Yes, fine. I've just talked to Mom on the phone."

"Oh, how is she feeling?"

"Well…" I could tell by the hesitation that Lisbeth hadn't asked, nor had Inger even mentioned her health on the phone. Why bother, really? She probably had just spent the last six days thinking happy thoughts and now she's cured. Non-issue.

"She's wondering why I haven't had more piano lessons."

Really? Inger has been sitting around in the hospital thinking of ways in which I'm deficient at my job? How shocking.

"Well," I said with forced cheer, "would you like to do a lesson tonight?"

It had probably been three weeks since the last time Lisbeth and I had sat down at the piano together. In fact, not since the second week, when we'd done three or so lessons in a row had either of us really made the effort to do it regularly. What Inger didn't seem to realize was that Lisbeth didn't give a shit about learning the piano, as evidenced by the fact that she'd never once practiced nor suggested to me that we do a lesson. I was therefore unsurprised at her response.

"Ah…no. But maybe later. We have horses later. But," Lisbeth continued after a pause, "she says you should give me more lessons."

My blood boiled as hard as the *potatis* water.

"Hey, no problem," I said with a smile that absolutely hurt to crack. "You tell me when you want a lesson, and I'm there to give you one."

She lingered for one extra second. I imagined that she was trying to decide if she could flip the responsibility for lesson-scheduling back over to me. She couldn't.

And off she went.

* * *

Hospitals are typically several things—sterile, severe, various shades of taupe—but there's one descriptor that no American hospital had ever struck me as: quiet. As I wandered around the Svensk *sjukhus* pretending to know how to find *Avdelning* C, *Bädd* 4, I began to wonder if I had accidentally wandered into the terminal illness ward—right after everyone there died. The hallways were nearly empty. Only about half the rooms were occupied. Where was everyone?

"Natalie, dear!"

On cue as usual, the voice of my now-healed (bodily, at least) employer saved me from the labyrinthine hallway. She was just inside the nearest doorway, packing up her belongings, which were scattered across what I could only assume was *Bädd* 4.

"Oh, ha ha! You found me!"

Like the Swedish Chef, every time Inger was doing something such as packing a suitcase or mixing ingredients in a bowl, she did so with a joyous haphazardness, causing things (including her hands) to fly in every direction. I wondered if this was an absurd coincidence or an actual Svensk trait somehow perfectly captured by a Muppet. Her careful children sure didn't have it.

"I'm sure it was no easy task to find your way here!" she shouted, shirts and scarves and socks fountaining through the air above her suitcase. Why had she packed decorative scarves for a hospital stay? Who does that?

"Well, it turns out you're practically the only person in the whole hospital, so it wasn't too hard," I said. "How is it that it's so empty here?"

"Well dear," Inger responded, zipping up the miraculously packed bag and striding out of the room and down the hall. "I suppose there are several reasons for that—ha!—but mostly because we are not in an emergency room hospital, so there's less excitement, that is certain. Also—"

We'd made it to the front counter in a quarter of the time it had taken me to get to her room. Inger stopped mid-sentence to chat in Svenska with the receptionist while taking out her wallet. They were clearly talking about checkout. To my surprise, she was handed a receipt and Inger pulled a small stack of colorful bills from her wallet and awaited change. Isn't their healthcare paid for? In a flash, the transaction was done, and we were again on the move.

"Also, dear, we see more bustle at doctors' offices than the hospital. Why, I remember when I was living with Karen in America—" and with that, Inger launched into yet another story about her experience living in Kansas as a teenager. I always found these stories exasperating, not only because I was clearly the last person in all of Sverige who needed to hear an anecdote about what life was like in the US, but also because of the cheerfully disparaging subtext to every story. This one was about when her American sister had to go to the hospital because of a minor injury and had to wait for several hours for treatment.

"And then, you should have seen the hospital bill they received in the end! Oh, my!"

By the time Inger began wrapping up her unnecessarily long story, we had already gotten to the car, visited the *apotek* to pick up her medicine, and had nearly made it back to Ödmjuk Gård.

"And that was in the sixties! I do believe it is much worse now." Normally I would disagree with everything Inger said for the sheer joy of disagreeing. On the topic of the US healthcare system, however, there was no way for me to honestly do so.

"Right, I know," I said, hoping to get back to the question that sparked her story an hour before. "So why did you have to pay as you left the hospital? I thought your healthcare was all paid for."

"Oh, well—ha ha!—there are other things, costs that one is billed for during a stay of that length." Inger's cackling blended with the crunch of gravel below the tires as we slowed into the old, red Volvo's parking spot in front of the farmhouse. "I was charged for my food and stay there, eighty *kronor* per day."

"Eighty *kronor?*"

"Eighty *kronor*. Yes dear, about eleven Euros or dollars." Inger almost seemed embarrassed about this expense as she gathered her bags from the back seat. I was still behind the steering wheel. Even for a country with socialized medicine, eleven bucks a day for room and board was shockingly low.

"It seems they are tightening their budget these days," she continued. "But I don't believe any of that was for the MRI or medicine. That was all part of our system."

Yeah, no, I don't think any of those eleven bucks probably paid for an MRI. I thought of a friend of mine who had recently shattered her collarbone falling down a stairway. After being hospitalized for little more than seventy-two hours, her insurance company received a bill for well over $100,000, and her family owed thousands of dollars in the end. And Inger had just paid eleven dollars a day.

The conversation went on as we unloaded Inger and her belongings into the house. After the apparent shame of having to pay the equivalent of a Starbucks breakfast for a day of hospital care, she was on a narrative warpath to expound upon the glories of the Svensk healthcare system. Did I know that a new parent—mother *or* father, mind you—might take sixteen months off of work at two-thirds pay after the birth of a child? Did I know that it cost no more to treat cancer than the stomach flu? I should be informed that Swedes were far healthier and happier than the rest of the world (read: Americans) because they were encouraged to take sick days and see a doctor the moment they felt sick.

I wondered if I could take a sick day. As I helped Inger unpack, and her lecture began to morph into directions on what to prepare for dinner, I realized that my nearly three weeks of freedom from this woman were officially over—though apparently my new duty of preparing dinner was not. Was I going to get that day off? Maybe I'd been foolish to have felt ready for her to come back, assuming she'd be taking over some of her motherly duties. And how was this whole crazy thing with Johan going to work now?

And I had a right to be concerned; Inger didn't take back a single motherly duty. Although clearly her long absences had put extra strain on her children and her housemaid, it was a perfect opportunity for her to further divest herself of this provincial life. Congratulations, Inger. I was glad this "au pair" thing was working out for someone.

10
En dröm i mej nuet
A Dream to Me Now

The flagship moment of any freshly minted relationship was the emotionally airbrushed all-nighter. You know this night, right? It's that night when you and the new other became verbal and physical explorers, allowing your pasts and your mouths, your interests, jokes, hands, and secrets to float between, on top of, inside, and all around each other, without the slightest acknowledgment of time. These were the magical experiences that by their memory alone could keep the worst of affairs moving doggedly forward. For the best of relationships, I liked to believe, they were but a sampling of what was to come.

Johan and I had weeks of these nights. We were in the happy position of not only having each other's persons and personalities to explore, but also our non-mutual languages and cultures.

"You said good-bye."

Johan made this odd comment after I ended a phone conversation with my mother. I'd begun to transition all of my normal activities over to his house. Why make an awkward, whispered phone call from Inger's office when I could just sit on the couch and have a normal conversation here? Why sit through any more quietly strained meals with the Waaras than I had to?

"Yes," I replied inquisitively to Johan's observation. "It tends to get people off the phone."

"But Americans don't say 'good-bye' before hanging up the phone." His thin, Swedish lips were talking nonsense, but his brown eyes showed no trace of a joke.

Thus began yet another investigation into the world's perception of American behavior based upon movies and TV. It turns out that he was right in his observation that American actors rarely bothered to bid each other farewell at the end of phone calls.

"But what does that matter?" I asked. "Airtime is money. Any moments lost with perfunctory conversation cuts into another scene or advertising time. Of course they don't bother with good-byes."

"Perfun-who?"

"Ah…unnecessary by virtue of being…ah, you know…obvious or, like, customary. Sorry!"

Johan would proudly admit that he was no scholar, but he did love to talk about the English language. So the mention of an unknown word was all it would take to launch another lengthy digression into the meaning or phonetics of a particular word.

It was hours later before we returned to the topic of phone etiquette, but Johan still wasn't buying my capitalist explanation. In Sverige, the government owned the television stations, so the idea that entertainment and capitalism could have such a personal relationship held very little water for him. For example, to convenience the viewer, each hour of TV had only a couple of commercial breaks, each about five minutes long. "How else would you have time to go to the bathroom or make a snack?"

Honestly, until he made this connection between snack time and commercial length, I'd never really understood what capitalism was or how much it permeated everything I knew about normalcy.

"Advertisers don't want you doing either of those things," I said. "Why would they pay for commercials if they knew you'd be pissing in the other room? And the networks are afraid you might change the channel or not come back to the couch at all. Five minutes is a long time."

"Maybe *you* always say good-bye," he said, straightening up on the couch where he had been reclining next to me. The outside light was dimming, allowing the muted IKEA floor lamp next to us to take over the job of setting the scene. The small house, half under renovation, was glowing orange. The rumpled gray couch cover was starting to feel like something I hadn't felt in months—like home. "But maybe [*butte mebbe*, it sounded like to me] you're the only one. There are a lot of Americans, you know," he said, echoing my default reply to many of his bizarre US stereotypes, as a playful sparkle appeared his eye.

"Johan, the entertainment industry is not an accurate representation of American life." I knew he had transitioned into teasing, but once I had a point to make, there was no stopping me. "First of all, one hundred percent of the Americans I've been talking to on the phone on a daily basis for the last twenty-three years are most likely not all in on a massive phone etiquette conspiracy against me, and, what's more, there are plenty of things that Americans do on TV that we never do in real life besides abruptly ending phone calls. Like...do you think we all get in car chases? Do you think we shoot locks off of doors with our guns when we're locked out of somewhere? No. Not true. We never do those things."

His cool and pleasant expression showed his amusement with both my tirade and his success in pulling it out of me. He was now leaning even further into my territory in the center of his tired couch, his hands suddenly full of my blonde hair.

"You're so smart, aren't you?" He spoke slowly, peering at my forehead as if he was trying to see what was inside. "So much of these things to learn from in there. You are..." he paused. Was he trying to think of the right word to make a sincere point here, or was he trying to find the word that would shut my mouth and drop my pants?

"...fascinating." The word—*faw*-SNAY-*ting*, as he said it—had barely rushed from his lips before they were on my neck. What did I care about the true purpose of his choice of words? He barely had a handle on the language, and he'd picked a good one. And that was how each night inevitably ended.

* * *

Thursday, November 3, 2005

Dear Lise,

So would you like to hear more about him? OK. Johan is many things. His main "job" is a car mechanic, which he does out of his house, but to get by, he does odd jobs for nearly everyone in Sweden. He fixes the neighbors' cars and tractors, machines, whatever; he works for his friend Danne's car stereo store, and sometimes works at the local "dog food factory." Mainly in exchange for dog food. Oh, and then there's this: he's also a freelance hearse driver. I don't know the answers to any of the questions you're dying to ask about this, because I really don't want to know them. But apparently, that is a job that exists. And I guess no one has died in the last few weeks.

Basically, Johan does whatever he wants every day. You know how people say they'd like that life where they wake up whenever they want and do what they love and make a living that way? This is what Johan does.

Oh, he's thirty-two. He finally told me. He thought that me

knowing his age would freak me out or something. Freak me out? I'm only going to be here for another eight months, and I'm already working as a maid for a crazy cult leader. How freaked out could I get?

It's just so nice to have someone to really talk to. After speaking to the Waaras in one- or two-sentence conversations for months, it feels so good to just blabber on and on about anything. In the last week, I would bet that we have spent thirty hours talking. I know that sounds like an exaggeration, but I just did the math on my hand with a pen.

I can't believe I haven't even told you what he looks like! He's about six feet tall and ridiculously skinny. He has blond hair that is always sticking up in odd directions and a tiny little blond soul patch. Both of his arms are sleeves of Viking cave-drawing tattoos. Swedes love Vikings—and why wouldn't they? Why don't we brag on the Pilgrims? Who knows? Maybe they didn't pillage enough.

"What are you saying?" he whispered in my ear, as he cradled my neck on one side with his hand and attended to the other side with his lips.

I smiled, eyes closed, and leaned into his nuzzle. I couldn't even imagine what the right answer to the question he was asking me was, but I wasn't about to chance giving the wrong one. I kept my lips quiet—but not sealed.

"Natalie," he said, "what are you saying to me?"

The pressure was on. All I really wanted to do was melt into the couch and let him do to me whatever it was that he was clearly planning to do. Why was he requiring my input? I wasn't intending to say anything, nor was I confident I knew what he was asking of me, anyway. As my sex life prior to this day had never included discourse, I nervously deduced that he was apparently asking me to verbally ask for it. Let me be clear: I'd never "asked for it" in my life. Sex was just something that happened to you, right? I hoped he would clarify this request later. Right now, I was not in the mood to improvise.

But he wasn't letting it go. He slowed the progress of his hands under my shirt, around my ribcage. He loosened his grip.

"You want me to fuck you, don't you?"

Whoa.

Now I was the one loosening up and leaning back.

"Johan," I gasped. I was officially coming up for air. "You don't say that word in that context." As soon as the words came out of my mouth, I could taste their sterility. Even in his second language, so could he.

But he was not daunted. He pulled back from me, but his face was resolutely focused on his line of questioning. He was in pursuit of something, in a way that was as terrifying as it was fascinating.

"It's just, you don't use 'fuck' to describe sex with someone you actually care about," I rationalized. "It's derogatory."

His haughty smirk was undaunted by this clinical explanation.

"Natalie, what possibly could separate one word from another, but what you believe? The meanings are the same. But one sounds a lot...better," he sighed heavily into my ear as his mouth briefly switched from verbal persuasion to a hotter, wetter argument with my neck. "Sexier..."

"I don't know," I managed to say, both in earnest and desperation. "The meanings are different to me. To everyone. Everyone I know."

He pulled me close to him again. "But no one you know is here. And you are to decide what a word means here. Natalie. Do you want me to fuck you?"

Pause. I had to decide now. In or out. Waaras or Johan. Boring life of servitude, or whatever this was about to be.

"Yes."

"What do you want me to do to you?"

Another pause.

So I said it.

* * *

To me, Johan was a sexual revolution. It wasn't as if I was a virgin. With a small troupe of exhaustingly long-term, committed boyfriends behind me, the quantity of sexual partners I'd had at twenty-three seemed adequate to me; not a slutty number, but not a prudish one either. My sexual history was built upon equal parts emotional warmth and fumbling compromise. It's not that I was one of those women who'd never had an orgasm—no, no. At least after I had gotten my bearings in each relationship, I had a success rate of having my own needs met approximately 55 percent of the time. Or 45 at least. That wasn't too bad, right? You really can't ask too much of boys if you want them to stick around, and I hated to be pushy. So only occasionally would I go so far as to answer the inevitable, almost-end-of-sex question, "So...uh...are you good?" with anything other than the affirmative. It would nearly break your heart to have to put them back to work. Ah, sex: just barely worth it.

Warmth and emotion, it turned out, were non-essential ingredients in the recipe for Sex According to Johan. Without going into much nauseating detail, I think he may have been trying to impress me. And I was impressed. My statistics were definitely on the rise.

While these revelations were no small deal for me, I was continuing to try and play it cool with the Waaras. Although it could not have been lost on them that I was now getting back from Johan's anywhere between two and four in the morning on weekdays, and not even bothering to return on weekends, my employers and I behaved like nothing was amiss. This was sort of surprising for me. I'd thought that Europeans, and Svenskar in particular, were known for their openness and matter-of-fact response to sexuality. Our mutual dis-acknowledgement of my new relationship seemed decidedly American.

Even more surprising was learning just how much they'd been discussing it without me. One Monday evening, after finishing with the horses and tossing a few things in a bag, I jumped into Johan's waiting car near the side gate. I'd just bid adieu (without mentioning where I was going, of course) to Jan and Inger who were both in the kitchen and both, I might add, acting perfectly normal.

I joyfully flung my backpack over my shoulder and practically skipped out the side door. Life was finally feeling good.

"Haalow, my love!" Johan greeted me as I slid into the passenger seat.

"*Hej*!" I said back as I leaned over and delivered a hello kiss. Right away I noticed something was off. He was smiling; he seemed in good spirits; but I could sense something slightly brooding in his expression.

"Guess who I received a ring from today?" he said both brightly and testily.

"Ah…well, I don't know that we have many mutual friends," I said. My thoughts ran inexplicably to Greg. Greg? How would my ex-boyfriend even know about this new relationship, let alone track down his name, transatlantic phone number and figure out international calling? It was impossible, though Johan's tone was a perfect mimic of a boyfriend pretending to be undaunted by the appearance of an ex.

"It was your employer!"

Oh fuck.

"Oh fuck," I said. There were endless ways in which this could end in extreme embarrassment. "Inger? Oh my gosh. What did she say? Do I want to know? I don't want to know. She's so nuts…" I buried my head in my hands as the Volvo zipped along the highway.

"Oh, it was Inger," he went on, "but I think it is Jan who is the crazy."

"Jan? Oh no! Is this going to affect your work? Have I gotten you in trouble?" Being the closest mechanic to Ödmjuk Gård, Johan received a good deal of work from the Waaras. As these bonkers people were desperately trying to keep their two twenty plus-year-old cars creeping along until the Rapture, mechanical assistance was needed fairly frequently.

"Oh, well, I dunno," he said, his accent becoming noticeably thicker. "Inger didn't say annythin of that, but she was a leetle concerned about Jan telling her that I had HIV."

My mind went completely blank. I stared at Johan's profile for what felt like several horrible minutes. There was an explanation for this. If I just sat here and didn't panic, it would be explained to me. Right?

Did Johan have HIV? Of course he didn't. Because this wasn't the way that conversation would start, that's for sure. But it had never even occurred to me to ask. Did Johan have any STDs? Did STDs exist in Sweden? Of course they did. But we have a common language about this in the US. The person with the issue is supposed to tell the other person about the issue, and if nobody says anything, nobody has any issues. Right? Why did that not sound right all of a sudden? Was there another way I should have had this conversation with him?

Oh, shit, I thought. *I am an idiot.*

"What?" I said.

"Yeah," Johan nodded, with his widened-eyes set clearly on the road ahead. "You think you're surprised. You shudda be me, the one spreading sexual disease to everywhere."

Apparently, Inger had called Johan under the guise of asking some lame question about headlights. I mean honestly, when you're calling someone to ask them if they are HIV positive and might be passing it on to your housekeeper, why fart around with headlight questions?

Anyway, after this was out of the way, Inger pretended to be getting off the phone when she added, "Oh, and Johan, you are quite healthy, right?"

Johan bull-headedly refused to answer such a bizarrely probing and overly general question. What was she getting at, he wanted to know?

"Well, I've come into the information that perhaps we should be concerned with you having HIV."

"Let me explain this," Johan cut into his story, "I dunno what it is in the US, but here, we aren't all just having HIV whenever here. You are almost definitely a very bad person to be having this. Like drugs, you know? Like you were saying with the pot and the heroin. HIV is like the heroin. It's like, not happening in regular people."

"OK. Um…" I allowed myself to ignore this ignorant and offensive assessment of HIV victims in the light of my slight concern about being one. "So why would they think you have it then? Please tell me they think you get it from tattoos."

"Ah, no. They think I had it because Jan is a moron."

Oh, well, that explains it.

Johan went on to recount a story from more than three years prior, when he was helping on Ödmjuk Gård as a temporary worker during the harvest. During a break, the workers were relaxing at a picnic table when Johan noticed some cows in quarantine boxes and asked Jan what that was all about. Jan explained that they had just been treated with antibiotics, and they had to be separated to prevent the bacteria from mutating and rendering the antibiotics ineffective. Jan had thought this was a pretty complicated issue, and he was quite proud to impart this highly scientific knowledge upon someone. As Johan explained it, Jan was a bit patronizing about it, which offended Johan. To be fair, Johan had once bragged to me that he'd never read an entire book before. So, you know, maybe Jan had a right to be a little bit snotty about it. Still, Johan responded with retaliatory sarcasm.

"Oh yeah," he said to the Svensk farmer who'd never uttered an ironic word in his life. "I know all about that. I have that same problem with my HIV medication."

"That was a joke," present-day Johan said.

"Wow," I said. "Hilarious."

"Well I mean, it wasn't an award-winner or anythin, but come *on*!"

I closed my eyes and leaned my head against the back of the seat. I was mortified, for both Johan and myself. Inger and Jan had clearly been sitting around chatting about my sex life. Even worse, I'd been staying over at Johan's for weeks now! Had their batshit suspicion somehow been true, the tardiness of their concern was practically criminal. Gee, thanks guys.

"I am so sorry," I said. "So, wait—they've thought for three years that you were their HIV-positive neighbor who fixed their cars?"

"I guess," he said, clearly punctuating the end of that conversation. "So, shall we stop at IKEA for some ice cream?"

* * *

"Do you know who *this* is?"

We were back at Johan's after our IKEA trip, back to playing our musical guessing game as if everything was back to normal. I was still reeling inside from the HIV conversation, suddenly confronted with both embarrassment and an eerie sense of reality. This wasn't some fictional overseas love affair. This was a real thing that was happening to my life and my person. How was this just occurring to me?

His eyes darted to me like bullfighter to a bull. I could never tell if he was rooting for me or for him in this game. The song's introduction was familiar, and I knew it the second the lyrics began.

Let us be lovers and we'll marry our fortunes…

"Simon and Garfunkel!"

"And the title?"

"Ah…" Wasn't it enough that I knew the artists from the first line?

"I have no idea," I confessed, biting my lower lip. I would lose major music-smarts credibility for this one.

"Natalie! Ah!" He loved knowing something that I didn't. "You don't know? This is *your song.*"

My song, huh? Now I was even more curious to see what kind of Swedish myth connected this song to me.

"America," he smiled. "It's called, 'America.'"

I giggled. Johan was genuinely shocked at my limited knowledge of this song named for my homeland. To be fair, if Abba had a song called "Sverige," it would probably become their national anthem. Johan would probably have a Viking cave-drawing tattoo of the group singing it on his forearm. But to me, this was just another sixties folk ballad.

The gaming session was over for that song, and we quietly listened to the rest of the song together.

"Kathy," I said as we boarded a Greyhound in Pittsburgh.

The duo hummed through all four ears in the room. I wondered how differently the lyrics, the guitar, and the very ethos of Simon and Garfunkel fell on his ears than on mine.

"Michigan seems like a dream to me now."
It took me four days to hitchhike from Saginaw.
I've gone to look for America.

My heart, the actual organ in my chest, leapt in reaction to the lyrics. I may have heard them dozens of times before, but they had never meant anything. Here, in this little Swedish village, in the presence of this mysterious foreigner who had become my only ally in a hemisphere, it was suddenly the most powerful song I'd ever heard. This was a song about my home.

Michigan did seem like a dream to me now. The mitten-shaped state happened to be where I had spent most of my first two decades of life, but now that I wasn't there, it felt like so much more. I finally felt connected to it, knowing just what it meant to be so far from it. Looking out the window, I noticed for the first time since I'd arrived in Sverige that Michigan was so physically far from me. I could not walk there. I could not hitch a ride there. No one could hitchhike to me.

* * *

I was still in a daze long after two in the morning, when Johan and I finally worked up the motivation to pull ourselves off the couch and into the dark, chilly evening to return me to my lair. I had four more weekday mornings ahead of me, almost an entire workweek before I could actually sleep for an entire night. I made a mental note to again ask Inger about the Svenska classes. At least that would give me something to not loathe about tomorrow.

It was right in the midst of this haze of negativity that we turned into the lumbering, dirt drive of Ödmjuk Gård and into one of the most delightful scenes I'd ever seen.

There were cows everywhere.

There were cows in the driveway. There were cows in Linda's yard. There was a cow standing on the stoop to the farmhouse. Cows, hundreds of them, were mingling from one dark horizon to the other, as if we had just crashed some sort of bovine block party. Johan silently stopped the car. Wide-eyed, I let my gaze wander through each window, not really sure if I was dreaming.

"What…is this? What's going on?" I asked Johan, as if living near a crazy-person farm made one an expert in crazy-person farm life.

"Well, it would appear," he calmly, "we have some escaped cattle."

"What?" I burst out laughing. "Escaped? They're just standing around! They're like fifty yards out of place!"

We were both bent over in the seats of the car, practically in tears with giggles, even as the full weight of four hundred escaped cows hit me. They hadn't wandered very far now, but what if they did? What if they left town? Was I responsible for this situation now that I'd happened upon it?

"What do we do?" I gasped when I caught my breath. "Do we wake Jan up?"

Johan looked at me like I'd suggested we get out and have a manure-ball fight. This night, of all nights, Johan was not doing Jan Are-You-Or-Are-You-Not-HIV-Positive Waara any favors.

"What do we do?" he responded, raising one eyebrow. "We go exploring!"

And with that, he pointed the silver Volvo hatchback toward the pasture, and we took off on a loose-cow stakeout. Not to return them, but to point and laugh. We found some standing on piles of hay behind the barn, some hanging out near the woods, and few on the road into town, looking like they needed directions to the train station.

By the time Johan pulled up to the wooden fence leading to the basement, it was well after three and my stomach hurt from laughing.

"Oh my gosh," I said, holding my sides as I reached for the door handle. "That was awesome. But are you sure I shouldn't wake Jan up and tell him? What if they get away?"

"Natalie," he was smiling too, clearly proud of himself for showing me such a good time, "do you want to go tiptoe into Jan's room right now?"

"Well…no, but I don't want them to lose their cows."

"Natalie," he repeated, "look at the cows." Again, I looked out the dark windows. The headlights shone on a group of four cows ahead of us, slowly chewing on something they'd discovered in the driveway. "Do they look like they are going anywhere?"

"OK, fine!" I said. "You win. But if they lose a bunch of money and have to sell the farm with me still in it, you're to blame if I end up as some weird farmer's sex slave."

"Oh, is that not what you were brought here for anyway?"

"Ha ha, Johan." I pecked him on the cheek. "Maybe I am on my way up to Jan's room anyway."

"Well, have fun!" he called after me as I climbed out the door. "Try not to catch any AIDS or whatever!"

I giggled. He drove away. Despite having horses and mopping to tend to in five hours, and employers I dreaded ever looking in the eye again, life felt pretty good. For a minute.

11
Svensk i "Skam"
Swedish for "Shame"

Perhaps I giggled too loudly and the gods of the karmic universe realized that it was time to intervene.

"What's this?" they must have asked each other, peering over the edges of their clouds or sunbeams or whatever. "Natalie Burg is absolutely not scheduled to be having a good time down there. We must counter this hilarious cow snafu with something absolutely mortifying." Then, one of these gods of the karmic universe must have produced a large remote control, laughed a villainous laugh, and, with his gloved, cartoon finger, pushed a large red button marked VAGINAL AILMENT.

Blissfully unaware, I was still laughing to myself the next morning as I slowly moved through my morning routine. *Should I have woken Jan up? What if there are cows missing?* I wondered as I sat down on the toilet. They'd surely ask me about it later: "Hey Natalie, you didn't happen to notice a few hundred displaced cows wandering around when you came home last night, did you?" Could I lie about it? I mean, the cows were loose, I knew about it, and I did nothing. Hee-hee. I reveled in a fantasy of Inger and Jan running around the chilly farm all morning, swatting at renegade cattle. And then I felt it.

A little burning sensation.

No. This was not happening. Maybe my urine was just uncharacteristically hot this morning. Maybe I was just dehydrated. Maybe…maybe…dammit. I couldn't think of any truly logical explanation. That was because I knew there was none.

Shit.

Now, in the US, I would have ignored the early signs of a urinary tract infection. I'd have tried to over-hydrate myself to see if I could just flush it out without bothering to go to the doctor. Why? Because I'm lazy. And I know exactly how to solve such a problem with a quick trip to the doctor. Why not wallow in wishful thinking for a day or two? Could I do that here? Was there even a doctor to go to? Thanks to Inger's passive-aggressive refusal to properly register my existence, I was an undocumented domestic servant in a nation of socialized medicine.

That's right; I was here illegally, a fact about myself which I had just recently learned. Johan had asked me a few weeks back what sort of visa I had, which would dictate how long I could stay. What kind of visa? How long I could stay? When I told him I'd have to ask the Waaras, he looked at me wide-eyed. If I didn't know the details of my visa, he said, I probably didn't have one. Which was, he assured me, super not-good.

Should I have looked into this myself? Yes. But I think we have established my idiocy well enough at this point. The Waaras had asked me to come here, hadn't they? I was assuming they'd have just sorted all that out. When I asked her about the visa situation, she said there was no need to "declare" me, really. Otherwise they'd have to pay taxes on me. Oh. So that's it.

"If you're really concerned, darling," she'd said, sounding exasperated, "you may perfectly legally visit Sweden for any three-month time, so all you need to do is take the ferry to Denmark every three months and get your passport stamped. If you'd like that, I'm sure we can make arrangements for you."

Golly, how nice of her to offer such a thing, even while sounding so clearly annoyed by it. Surely, it could not be true that anyone could stay in Sweden for as long as he liked by taking a short ferry ride four times a year.

Analyzing loopholes in Swedish immigration policy wasn't going to help with the bacteria in my urethra, however. Was it even possible for me to get an appointment? What would happen if I ignored it forever? Besides bearing the wretched pain of imaginary pins being driven into my lady parts, of course. What did they do in the days before antibiotics? Did people die of bladder infections? Could my funeral really be so embarrassing? Only that would put every teenage girl's greatest fear—the toxic shock funeral—to shame.

"Gee, Nancy, your daughter was so full of life. Too bad it was snuffed it out so soon by bacteria in her peehole."

"I'm so sorry about your loss. So sad and senseless. I mean, really, my cat is at home getting over a UTI right now."

However, that melodrama seemed relatively acceptable next to the horror of asking Inger for help. I couldn't do it. I wouldn't do it. I was determined to figure this out on my own. I needed some cranberry juice, stat.

The first hurdle to solving this problem would be leaving the house. I entered the kitchen, praying that I'd find a grocery list waiting for me. Instead, I found Inger.

"*God morgon*, daaaaahling!" That huge red smile was for once a welcome sign. She was in a good mood. This was a good place to start.

"Good morning, Inger! How are you this morning?"

"Ah!! Waaaandafool!" I gave her my warmest grin as I pulled some seedy bread out of the breadbox. I'd have it without cheese this morning. I knew Inger saw everything I put in my mouth as a hundred-*kronor* piece. My odds of leaving the house would greatly increase if I wasn't looking like an American money vacuum. "And how is your love affair going?"

Seriously? *This* was the question she asked me on the morning that I was medically required to humor her? I instantly felt like a defensive seventeen-year-old girl. Was she trying to be my girlfriend, my mom, or my nosy employer? I couldn't tell.

"Oh…ha ha," I blushed. "I don't know if I'd call it a 'love affair' or anything…I mean, I'm having fun hanging out with him…" I looked up over my breakfast of cold, buttered bread. Was that enough?

No. She was patiently waiting for me to divulge more, with eyes wide, and mouth even wider. When she was excited, Inger looked like someone who had been frozen to death while biting into the world's biggest, most delicious hoagie. I couldn't leave that face hanging.

Sigh.

"Oh, well, I mean, I do really like Johan," I went on. I indulged her by telling the story of him quoting *Office Space* during our first encounter. "It was funny," I stuttered. "I mean, it was funny and kind of amazing to be so far from home and have someone throw a quote at you from a movie you know by heart. Anyway…we have a lot in common."

"Well," she responded, finally closing her mouth with what I was sure was judgment of me spending so much time with someone I was reluctant to call my lover, "I am happy you have that in your life now. I was feeling such pressure that if you were sad or bored here that I was personally failing you somehow. Ha! Ha! No need to worry now!"

It was 8:05 a.m. Cans of worms opened by Inger: two. Urinary tract infections still in need of attention: one.

"Oh, Inger!" I laughed nervously. "Why would you worry about that? I'm a big girl. I'm responsible for my own happiness."

And…curtain. There's nothing like a Tao-ish style retort of self-sufficiency to make Inger feel a conversation had come to a satisfying close. She wished me a good day and floated down to her office. I may not have secured permission to leave the premises, but I'd survived the conversation. That was enough for now. And when I approached her later, maybe her wheels would be sufficiently greased for a favor.

One horse transfer, two walked dog-sicles, and a huge mug of coffee later, I was back in the bathroom recognizing that my slight burning sensation had progressed to a solidly uncomfortable level. I used the excuse of getting the vacuum tubes out of the cupboard below the stairs to pop into her basement office.

"Hey, Inger!" I said cheerfully. I positioned myself politely outside her door at the foot of the stair, my body completely entwined in plastic tubing. I appeared to be on my way up to dutifully vacuum. I told myself that I oozed casualness. "Do you mind if I take the car to the store after lunch?"

She paused, hunched above her keyboard, her two pointer fingers still extended in typing position. Inger had purportedly written an entire book on her computer using only two fingers.

"Well, what is it you need?"

DAMMIT!! How did I not predict this question? Shit-shit-shit-shit-think-think-think-think-shit-shit-shit…

"Ah…I'm just feeling a bit…under the weather…" Oh, I was not doing a good job. "And I was just thinking I'd pick something up to make me feel better."

"Oh dear!" Her fingers were out of keyboard-punching position and she was pushing back from her desk chair. Oh no, oh no, oh no. I'd made a grave mistake! She was standing up! "What is wrong, dear? Perhaps we have something here…" She was already pushing past me and headed toward the bathroom medicine cabinet. What had I done?

"Well…actually…I just have some menstrual cramps, and I have a pretty regular thing I like to take for them." I was chasing her up the stairs with vacuum tubes wrapped around my neck and over my shoulders. She wasn't slowing down. "Really…" I shouted after her, "I think it might be best if I just look around at the store…"

Two hours later I was in the car headed toward City Gross. I'd taken some chalky pills Inger had thrust at me, but stuck to my story of requiring unique and secretive cramping therapy and made off into the gray afternoon with a twinkle of victory in my heart and twinge of pain in my panties. I was going to solve this debacle all on my own.

Or so I thought. To my dismay, I found no such thing as cranberry juice in City Gross. In fact, there were no cranberries at all—not the produce, not the concentrate, not the gel that comes in cans, not even those awesome Ocean Spray hard candies that they had taken off the market years earlier. Who knows? Maybe they had survived here! I looked. But, no.

NO CRANBERRY ANYTHING?! What was wrong with this country? Why would a particular nation be cranberry-free? I'd run myself silly all over the damn store looking for cranberries of any kind in any form and was finally slowing down to a resigned pace in the jams and jellies aisle when I realized why: lingonberries.

These fucking Swedes and their fucking lingonberries and lingonsylt and lingonwhatevers all over their disgusting blood pudding and milk-yogurt! I screamed in my head. I was starting to feel a distinct screaming in my pants. Thanks to the Scandinavian devotion to this subpar cran-wannabe-berry, and which probably had no curative powers over the urinary tract, I was going to have to get actual medical attention for this issue.

I bought some anyway. Unfortunately, Svenskar don't really sell anything in bulk. So I settled on three small glass bottles of *lingonsaft* that would be considered single-serving sized in the US, and chugged them in the parking lot.

Having no faith in that remedy, I weighed my options as I drove home. I could ask Johan for help. No. That would be worse. Asking a crazy person for help with an embarrassing vaginal problem was one thing; asking the one person for whom I hoped to keep up the appearance that I wasn't a disgusting, diseased mess would be a disaster. It had to be Inger.

And it had to be tomorrow. After this lie-initiated failure, I couldn't march into her office and say, "Well, they didn't have my special cramp medicine, so I'm going to need to see a doctor about my burning pee." I would spend the next eighteen hours drinking buckets of water and readdress the situation the next day.

* * *

The pain woke me up before my alarm the following morning. I'd made an unusual exception to going over to Johan's the night before, citing extra work and exhaustion. I made it through breakfast, but didn't even try to start my chores before marching into Inger's office.

"Um…Inger? What do I do if I need to go to the doctor?"

"Well, what is it that you need?" The déjà vu of her reply made my blood pressure rise. If she was going to go rustle around in her medicine cabinet for a chalky pill to give me in lieu of a doctor's appointment, I was going to start packing my suitcase and have my issue solved in Michigan. "Are your menstrual cramps giving you problems still?"

"No," I said matter-of-factly, "they're fine. This is something else. I believe I have a urinary tract infection, and I need to get antibiotics."

OK. I said it.

"Oh! Oh, well is that all? I'll see what I can do!" she exclaimed as cheerfully as ever. And for a few minutes, I let myself sink into a feeling of relief. God bless this woman. She was a nutbag for sure, but she was going to help me, and all I had to do was ask. Why had I been so nervous in the first place?

She started chattering to me about Pia's recent visit to the doctor, and her lab work as she rustled through papers for the doctor's phone number. It turned out that her easy-as-pie solution was to call a doctor and tell him that Pia needed to revisit the lab and have her urine tested for a UTI. But instead of Pia going, it would be me! Then we'd take the falsified lab information to get a fraudulent prescription for me.

Terrific, I thought, *medical fraud. Why not add that to the whole cult thing and the illegal foreign worker thing?*

The next two hours were spent with Inger on the phone trying to lie her way into a cheap fix for my UTI and me waddling around the house gratefully trying to do chores that didn't irritate the now nearly constant throbbing. Finally, she called me back down to her office.

"Unfortunately," she began, "getting you medicine under Pia's name is not going to work. They need her to appear at the lab, and they would then clearly see you are not her."

"OK, so I need to make an appointment myself."

"Yes!" Inger agreed. But she wasn't about to help with that. She wouldn't even give me the number of the doctor to whom she'd just spoken. Perhaps that would have made her act too transparent. "It occurred to me when I was making my calls, dear, that this is something you should probably take care of with Johan."

"What? Why?" This wasn't going anywhere good.

"Well, darling, it would seem that the nature of this sort of thing is that you need to discuss it with him so he can get checked and treated. Otherwise you're just going to pass it back and forth."

Huh? What? I couldn't even reply. One might expect such a rudimentary understanding of a simple UTI from say, an eighth grader. Or a Franciscan Monk. But here was an educated, worldly, professional(ish) mother of three in the twenty-first century suggesting to me that the negative reaction my immune system was having to some Svensk bacteria was an STD.

"Well..." I racked my brain, trying to grasp at the straw that might prevent me from having to tell Johan about my burning urethra. "How will that go in terms of payment for the doctor? I mean, how will that work when I'm not a part of your Swedish medicine program?"

"I don't know, darling. That is what Johan will have to help you find out."

Oh. I get it. This bitch was all about helping me out of my nasty-pants jam when she thought it would be free. But she wasn't even about to make me an appointment with a doctor lest I think that she was going to foot the bill. Or if there was going to be some record of my existence tied to her. Once again, the lines from Inger's original job invitation email started ricocheting around my brain like angry popcorn. "We'll take care of all your living expenses," and "you'll be a member of our family," were clearly open for interpretation. I should have known that if toothpaste and shampoo didn't count as living expenses, medical care wouldn't either.

Who actively recruits someone from overseas to come work for her with the plan of concealing her from society the whole time? Or without enough money for the slightest contingency? Did she really expect that a year would go by and there wasn't any chance I'd need to see a doctor?

As I drove myself over to Johan's, my mind felt numb. I'd just spent twenty-four hours in pain to delay exposing my embarrassing medical issue to Inger, and had been flat out rejected. What if the same thing happened with Johan? Honestly, he would have every right to say he had no idea how to help and send me home. At least he had far more a right to do so than my employer and guardian did.

But he didn't. The remainder of the day was long and emotionally exhausting, but I explained the whole thing to Johan and he helped me get a doctor's appointment. He wasn't overly tender about the situation, nor did he seem enthusiastic about helping, but he did, and I couldn't have been more grateful. Although it took a couple of phone calls and exasperated English to Swedish translations ("not a fungus, Johan—*nej svamp*—a bacteria! No, I don't know what that is in Swedish…"), he found the right doctor and made me an appointment that same afternoon. By evening, we'd made it to the office for a quick visit, to the *apotek* for some antibiotics, and we were back on the couch with me on the mend. No one had questioned my citizenship. Apparently, in Sweden they consider healthcare something humans are entitled to, regardless of legal status. Doctors do, at least, if not employers. And though getting the help I needed from Inger and Johan was mortifying and awful, the doctor couldn't have been nicer, and the whole thing cost me about twenty dollars: impossibly cheap by American standards. But it was good to put a price on the value of my wellbeing in Inger's eyes.

"I assume I will have you here in recovery for tomorrow, my dear?" Now that he'd gotten his skinny ass reacquainted with the couch, Johan warmed right back up to me. The next day was Thursday. I hadn't even considered taking the day off.

"You know," I said, "normally I'd be going to work, no questions asked. But fuck that. If Inger wanted to have a loyal employee, she should have been a loyal employer. I'm staying here tonight."

Johan then launched into a whole explanation of why it was ridiculous to take less than three days off in a row for illness according to Swedish workplace regulations. I wasn't paying very close attention, but apparently you get monetarily rewarded for taking three days off, as opposed to one based on what percentage of your pay you get each day.

"It makes you think twice about taking one sick day, but you gotta take three..."

I lost the rest of the sentence as I slipped into sleep on the deflated, gray couch pillow. I'd let Inger figure out on her own that I wasn't coming in tomorrow. Maybe I'd keep her guessing about Friday too.

* * *

The weekend was quiet. I did go back to work Monday, more out of boredom than to demonstrate my superior American work ethic. You know how when you spend an entire Saturday at home, and then you don't even realize until Sunday that you never left the house, and it's kind of embarrassing? How you might call your best friend and giggle, "Oh my gosh! I just realized I never left the house once yesterday! How crazy is that?"

As it turns out, not leaving the house for an entire day was par for the course for Swedes; two or three in a row was a great achievement. At twenty-three, I didn't understand the concept of doing nothing all evening—let alone all weekend. The world from which I'd just extracted myself was one of visiting friends, going to the bar, eating out, and seeing movies several times a week. My friends and I didn't consider ourselves to be excessive partiers; we were all college graduates who worked hard and spent our free time having fun, rotating from one gathering place to another, going shopping, partying, giggling excessively, and generally making the most of every day.

Bored we were not. And now, after the brief interlude of the beginning of Johan's and my new relationship, I was back to being bored. I was shocked to learn that my exciting new boyfriend spent the majority of his weekdays lying on the couch, typing away on his laptop with a cat curled up under his arm. Didn't he have work to do? Weren't there cars to repair? Shouldn't someone somewhere be dying and in need of an indie hearse driver? Sigh.

So skipping work on Thursday and Friday was dull. And then the weekend was dull. Midway through Sunday, I was about to burst.

"Johan, don't you want to do something? I cannot watch another second of downhill skiing with Swedish commentary. This is the worst."

"Well, honnnney, you are in Sweden," he replied. "You might expect people to speak Swedish on television."

"That isn't really my point."

Johan still had not once looked up from his computer, where his eyes had been for the last two hours straight, making his insistence on determining our TV choices even more annoying. He didn't reply. He was too busy typing what I could only assume was some smart-ass, bullheaded, poorly-typed argument about amperes on an online car stereo forum.

"Let's not watch TV at all," I whined, albeit in the flirtiest way I knew how to whine. "Let's go somewhere. Let's go out to lunch. See a movie. Let's go to the mall. Don't you need something from the car parts store? Or the car stereo store? Or the grocery store? Or the sock store?"

I was probably on my fifteenth store suggestion when Johan finally looked up.

"You want to go to the grocery store?"

"I'll do that. You need groceries?"

"No. And there's no cash to waste on any of those things. Besides!" No one could pronounce a preposition more enthusiastically than Johan. "We are doing something! We are relaxing!"

And he went back to his computer. I wandered into his kitchen and organized his Tupperware cupboard. An hour later, with nothing left to do, I was back on the couch. We "relaxed" for the rest of the day.

* * *

Monday morning, therefore, felt particularly odd. I dreaded it, as always, but this time my mood was a depressing blend of misery and relief. At least I was doing something. Something that didn't involve winter sports commentary. For fuck's sake, I had no idea anyone actually watched biathlons outside of the Olympics. As far as I was concerned, combining cross-country skiing and shooting at a target and calling it a sport was like mixing Draino and antifreeze and calling it a party drink. All things considered, I would have preferred the Draino cocktail to watching another damn biathlon.

This line of grumbling ambled around in my brain as I greedily heaped a third and fourth scoop of coffee grounds into the French press after lunch. I'd heard it said that the only thing that made a substance a drug was how you used it. Thanks to Sverige's strong, dark *kaffe,* my general malaise, and the lack of accessibility to my usual rotation of wine, marijuana, and clove cigarettes, I very purposely chose to use *kaffe* as a drug. Maybe I had been hitting the party wagon a little too hard at home, I considered, as I poured boiling water into the thick glass vial and watched the *kaffe* grounds spin and dip with the rising water level. But there was nothing to be done about that now. Now I actually needed some chemical dependency. I needed to let my heart race or slow down at will. I needed to feed my brain something artificially stimulating. In this household, I needed to abuse a drug—any drug. And *kaffe* was all I had.

That secret abuse was the only thing I had completely to myself. Between Inger's insanity, Jan's quiet sadness, and Lisbeth's alternating neediness and snottiness, I could kind of see how Pia might have developed an eating disorder. I'm a pretty big fan of eating, so instead of starving myself, I drank nearly toxic quantities of coffee. It made me feel good.

In the morning, I'd share the pot of French press that Inger prepared, but in the afternoon, after the stealthy lunch I'd squeeze in after Jan had finished his own *middag*, I'd make an entire pot, twice as strong, all for myself. There were large porcelain cups in the cupboard—from IKEA, of course—that reminded me of an old-fashioned milkshake glass. I'd pour about a quarter cup of milk into one of these, and then fill it to the brim with the dark *kaffe*. This glass, I'd chug. Then, as the hot caffeine jittered into my veins, I'd assemble a refill to take with me to the next task of the day.

Laundry was next. There were loads of whites and colors waiting to be hung on the line in the basement. There were at least two more of each waiting to be put in the dual washing machines. Not that I cared. I was glad of the large amount of damp clothes to be pinned to the line. I was safe down here. Because my shower was also in the laundry room, no one, save Inger, would come barging in looking for me down here. I wanted to be alone with my *kaffe* and my music.

My laptop sat on a wooden workbench, singing at me as I pulled each flattened, cold piece of wet laundry from the machine and suspended it from one of the many plastic-covered wires strung from one end of the room to the other. As a computer, it was unusable for anything besides this. A few seconds after turning on, the screen would begin to flicker, and within minutes, it would turn to pure white. But it was long enough to find the right playlist and hit play. The machine was just good enough for this task, like the caffeine overdose was just good enough to make me feel slightly intoxicated. It was good to feel something, I thought, my heart galloping from the caffeine. I cringed, realizing that this sentiment had crossed my mind on Saturday night too.

Johan and I had already decided to go to bed. Rather, as usual we'd fallen asleep on the couch with the TV on, but I woke up around one in the morning and insisted we go upstairs. I'd learned that if I didn't take this initiative, we would sleep on the couch every night. Johan complained that it would be cold up there, but I was not about to sleep on the same couch where I'd also spent the last thirty-six hours. We stumbled upstairs and slipped into his chilly queen-sized IKEA *säng*. Minutes later, I was wide-awake. I'd done nothing all day. I was restless, panicked even. I couldn't recall another day in my whole life when I literally had not done a single thing. I had to do something today. I reached over to Johan and wordlessly convinced him to have sex with me. He obeyed.

"There," I thought ten minutes later as I allowed myself to drift off. "That was something. I didn't do absolutely nothing today."

Why did that make me feel dirty, I wondered as I stood beneath the growing, drooping canopy of wet clothes. I couldn't put my finger on it, but I knew it felt off, to have asked for sex out of boredom, and to have allowed it to appease me. But it wasn't a big deal, right? We'd had sex plenty of other times. Nothing was any different that time other than the motive. Unsure of how to explain this odd feeling of—guilt, was it? Shame? I ignored it and instead focused on the voice serenading my chore.

You seem so out of context in this gaudy apartment complex…

I sang along to yet another Death Cab for Cutie song as I shook out a pair of heavy, wrinkled jeans.

A stranger with the door key, explaining that I'm just visiting.
I am finally seeing, I was the one worth leaving.

I always thought of Greg when I heard this song. I would obsessively imagine where he'd be, and what he'd be doing when he'd hear that line and think, "Oh my God, *I* was the one worth leaving." Then he'd know. Even now, four thousand miles and three months away from home, I felt overwhelmed with desperation for him to consider this premise. At some point he'd realize he'd treated me poorly, right? I might have physically left, but he couldn't blame me if he realized that he was worth leaving, right?

But today, I heard it differently. I felt differently. I knew the reason I felt so conflicted about my last sexual encounter with Johan was because of Greg. He would be disgusted if he knew that had happened. There were so many rules with him, including rules about sex. He liked to make a point of not following anyone else's rules in life, but he lived strictly in accordance with his own standards—and expected me to as well. These rules were based on some system I'd never entirely figured out, but I knew it when I transgressed. For example, seeming to be interested in sex, even with him, always got me in trouble. I learned to wait for him to decide when it was time for us to be intimate. So yeah, Saturday night was definitely a rule-breaker.

And suddenly, I was laughing to myself. Laughing at myself, actually, out loud, while leaning against one of the washing machines, with half a load of damp clothes waiting to be hung. How ridiculous was I? Not only was I worried about what Greg might have thought about the fact that I'd had sex with someone else, I felt guilty that I had enjoyed it. Greg and my sex life had been awful, hadn't it? When the person you're sleeping with believes you harbor dormant sluttiness, there's no way to win. If you initiate sex, you are proving yourself to be the very slut you are training yourself so hard to not be. If you only await an invitation, you are the cold, conservative, intellectual prude that all your fancy schooling would imply.

With Greg and me, there were too many complex emotions, too much psychology involved, which was pretty much the opposite of what had just happened with Johan. The fact that I'd be leaving in less than a year made this relationship completely different than any other. It was based on having fun and immediate gratification. Wasn't it? I shuddered to think what Greg would say about that.

Then I stopped laughing.

Oh my gosh. I know what he'd say. He'd say he was right about me.

What if I had been the one worth leaving?

Greg had always said that it wasn't anything I'd ever said or done that made him not trust me, but instead, it was what I was capable of. This had always infuriated me. There had always been a bit of me, however, wondering if he was right. Was I capable of infidelity? Or other, generally immoral behavior? Although nothing I'd ever done before had fit that bill, I felt entirely different about the idea today. I knew in my gut that this was what he had meant. And apparently, he had been right.

Shit.

Inger, as per usual, came bursting down the stairs at that very moment to disrupt my wide-eyed thoughts.

"Ah! Natalie! Here you are!"

Her presence jolted me into action. There's nothing worse than your boss popping in on you when you appear to be slacking off, but were in fact taking a momentary breather from being genuinely busy. Especially when I was usually so strategic about my slacking off.

I pushed my way through the thicket of garments to respond.

"Yup, just down here getting through some of this laundry."

"I see, dear. That's wonderful! But I wonder if there was a reason you aren't lunching with Jan anymore?"

It took all my might to not reply with the exact same question directed at her. He was her husband, after all. I hesitated, not only because I was stifling this response, but also because I didn't really have a good answer. I liked Jan. If I had to have lunch with someone in this crazy house, I'd just as soon it was him. But I was in protest of every bit of my life in Ödmjuk Gård. Wracking my brain to come up with things to chat with Jan about each day over lunch, and then losing half of the conversation to our language barrier had really lost its charm.

"Oh, I just wasn't hungry yet, and that's just how the timing worked out with the laundry getting done."

Inger couldn't have cared less what my lame excuse was. "Yes well, I'd really like to suggest you take the time to lunch with Jan."

Oh, would you?

"He does really enjoy your company, dear. I understand you weren't lunching with him much during my absence either, and he does like to spend time with you. He very much enjoys your company."

"Well…ah…yeah, I'll try to make a point of that…"

"Waaaaaaandofoool!" she said, clearly considering the matter closed. "And it has been some time since you and he went on one of your adventures together, so please do consider doing more of that. It is just so nice when you spend time together."

I was so stunned at this request I could hardly imagine what an appropriate response might. Should I have said, "I'm not an escort service, bitch"? Or "Entertaining middle-aged farmers was not in my job description"? Or "What the fuck is wrong with you? You have lunch and adventures with your husband if you care so much about him being lonely"?

It was too late anyway. Inger was nodding and exclaiming, "Splendid!" while retreating up the stairs even as my non-committal response was bumbling out of my mouth.

What just happened? I slammed the rest of my *kaffe*, trying to pretend like my completely awful job hadn't just gotten worse. Knowing I'd now have to choose between losing my peaceful, solo lunchtimes and being blatantly disobedient should have stressed me out of my mind. But in the midst of this hot, delicious caffeine rush I really didn't care. I could hardly wait until Johan heard about this.

12
Besöker Vi, Göra Saker
Going places, doing things

"Yeah, she said he 'really likes my company,' and would appreciate it if I spent more time with him. Can you believe that shit?"

I was feeling better than I had in more than a week. Johan and I were on our way to IKEA—and not to buy one-kroner ice creams, like every other time. We were going to buy more parts for his kitchen. Somehow, after a weekend of insisting there was no reason to go anywhere or money to spend on anything, Johan had decided to end his months-long hiatus of working on his half-finished kitchen cupboards. I was delighted. It was sunny, and we were going somewhere to do something. And I had this juicy piece of Inger-crazy to bitch about.

"I don't...I don't really understand," Johan furrowed his brow at me. "He sent Inger to ask you to spend time with him? Is he a little boy? Can he not ask you to lunch himself?"

"That's the thing," I said. "I didn't get the feeling that he had anything to do with it. Like Inger realized I'd been skipping out on lunch, and she took it upon herself to pimp me out to her husband."

"Pimp you? Honneey, don't you think that's a little...you know, much to say? She was just asking about lunch."

"Well yeah, it's just lunch, and those stupid bike rides we used to take on the weekends. But she's in the freaking house during lunchtime, and on the weekends. She's only asking me to keep him company because she clearly doesn't want to, and any time any woman asks another woman—especially an employee—to do something with her husband that she doesn't want to do, that's just...it's just ick, that's what it is. I'm not going to be

Jan's *middag* wife. Not opening that door."

"Hey! How do you know anything about what she does or doesn't want to do with her husband?" Johan seemed surprisingly defensive about the Waaras' marriage all of a sudden.

"Because she told me," I shot back. "Back when I first started working for her and we were best friends and talking all the time, she said that she was some young, wild hippie, and Jan was just supposed to be some farmhand fling, but they got pregnant, so here they are seventeen years later. Of course, she said it was all meant to be, and the happiest accident ever or whatever. But obviously that is bullshit."

"Natalie," Johan replied to my perfectly logical and succinct argument, "that is how marriage happens here."

"By accidental pregnancy?"

"Yeah, well, they aren't all accidental, but we aren't always proposing and having big weddings and then having kids," he said, as if that was the most antiquated sequence of events imaginable. "We are always living together first, and there is no reason to be married until there is a baby. Usually, your friends are having a garden party at their house, and you arrive and they are instead getting married. The Waaras are not so weird all the time."

"Johan, they sleep in separate rooms."

"Ah…*jaaap*, that one is pretty weird."

Johan could argue that I was blowing things out of proportion if he wanted, but being recruited to entertain someone's husband at any level made me nauseated. I just wouldn't do it. Not to mention that this extra "chore" would virtually eliminate my lunch hour. Although I was working my hardest to not work my hardest during the other nine hours of my workday, I really took exception to her adding a tenth.

"So what did you say?" Johan asked.

What else could I have said to the crazy person on whom my livelihood depends? But I knew I'd go on missing lunch. Actually, now I could skip out on him without the guilt. Before I felt bad for Jan when I'd sneak out on him, but not now. The concubine-ish overtones of Inger's request had officially gotten me off the hook as far as I was concerned. I wasn't about to help her shoulder the guilt of being married to someone she clearly wanted nothing to do with.

With my hackles already raised, it was easy to become annoyed with Johan, whose hackles were clearly unmoved by this story. Although I'd been very consciously appreciative of the many ways in which Johan was different than Greg, his lack of any sort of protective instinct was a little insulting. If Greg had heard that story, that would be it. No more working for the Waaras. I mean sure, he went overboard from time to time, but generally, it felt good to know someone was protective of me. When I'd gotten a job in the men's department of Marshall Fields and was tired of being hit on all the time, he bought me a beautiful ring to wear on my left hand. Not an engagement ring, mind you (and yes, it was momentarily confusing when he presented it to me), but something to connect me to him and fend off the creeps. And it worked! Most of the time.

Greg was the kind of boyfriend who always walked on the street-side of the sidewalk, did all of the driving, and was constantly wary of how others treated me, male or female. It was, undoubtedly, the result of growing up with a younger sister and single mom. He was just a sensitive guy. It was easy to forget, in the midst of the torrent of post-breakup horror stories, why I had fallen in love with Greg in the first place. Sure, he was controlling; yes, he was emotionally explosive. But that all came from this place of being so sensitive that he always felt the need to protect me—and to protect our relationship—from threats, real or imagined.

As we drove along toward IKEA, I looked out the window and stifled a smile, remembering one Christmas Eve when Greg, his mom, and I sat at the bar in her basement, drinking rum and Cokes – rubber Cokes, as she called them – as Greg told us the horrifying story of what had happened when our roommate Dave had come home earlier that week and encountered Greg's cat's new haircut.

"He just stood there, and looked right at her, and then he just started laughing," he said intensely, leaning forward as if he was sharing the most scandalous of gossip. "Can you believe that? He just laughed in her face, for like five minutes. Right in front of her. How was that supposed to make her feel?"

He was genuinely upset. It was adorable. His mother smiled and took a slow drag from her cigarette before turning to me.

"I'm sure there are some big advantages to having a sensitive boyfriend," she said, as if her son was in the other room. She paused for another quick puff. "But I'm pretty sure that isn't one of them."

The two of us erupted into laughter. Eventually, Greg smiled along with us, though still protesting in favor of the poor cat's feelings. How his mom got away with making cracks like that, I never learned. Had it been me, it would have started a fight. But his mom was always able to add a little levity to Greg's deep and serious side that I'd found reassuring. If she could do it, I could learn to do the same.

Just as I was stifling a giggle at the cat-haircut memory, I was relieved to see we'd arrived at our destination, an appropriate distraction from my trip down memory lane. We were at IKEA, pronounced by Svenskar as "ee-KEY-ah."

"Doesn't it drive you nuts that the rest of the world calls it '*eye*-KEY-ah?'" I asked Johan. I was constantly appalled at how easily Svenskar dealt with Americans pronouncing everything wrong. I mean, it was their store—their retailing claim to fame worldwide. Shouldn't someone have mentioned to the US branches that they were saying the stinking name wrong?

"Nah," he said, shaking his head as we entered the store. "Why should we care? It's the same store. We don't care that you call us 'Sweden' when we're really 'Sverige.'"

"Yeah, but you should! Put your foot down. It's your identity we're getting wrong. Wait—where are we going?"

This may have been my first time past the ice cream counter in a Svensk IKEA, but I was familiar with the fiercely regulated layout of the store. When you do an IKEA, you do it in the way IKEA intends you to do it. There are arrows on the ground. You follow them. Oh, Svenskar and their rules.

But not this Svensk. Johan had come in through the exit doors and was darting through an empty checkout line in reverse, dragging me along with him. I looked around in a near panic. Was this allowed? Would we be arrested? I felt like a chewed up piece of *blodpudding* being forced the wrong way through a digestive track. How was this going to end?

"Here!"

The clearance center. Johan explained that the only real way to shop IKEA was to start at the end, with the clearance department. "Otherwise, you get everything you need and then you look through and find half of your purchases are here and cheaper. Then you gotta walk back through and take shit back."

Seriously, it was kind of genius.

Forty-five minutes later, I was nearly asleep on a display model couch when he finished scouring the clearance items. He'd found two hinges and a knob that matched his cabinet pattern.

"Great!" I said, hopping up. "Now we're off to get the rest of the pieces?"

"The rest? Nah, this is all I need."

Did he have cabinet doors somewhere in his house that I'd never seen? Was he indeed only looking for a knob and two hinges? Somehow these questions were really difficult for Johan to answer concisely. It took me the entire ride back and most of the night to piece together that this was how Johan was re-doing his kitchen. Once every few months he'd go to the clearance room and see what pieces from his cabinet set were available for nearly nothing and only buy those. If a piece never made it to clearance, he didn't buy it. Which was why, two years after beginning this project, he had a kitchen that was still torn to pieces and only one cabinet with a door on it.

I did clarify that he was buying his shit from IKEA, right? Where a cabinet door costs like seven dollars?

According to Johan, this was how all Svenskar shopped at IKEA. In fact, he asserted that this was the only correct way to shop there. The whole point of the store, he said, was that you could walk in and buy a coffee mug for one *krona* and then walk out. Knowing how cheap the Waaras were, and having witnessed that every last home accessory they owned was from IKEA, I had no choice but to believe him. Incredible.

At the risk of supporting the already entrenched image of the American gluttony in his eyes, I didn't even mention to Johan why this was so shocking to me: this was the opposite of the American IKEA shopping technique. The entire reason Americans loved the place was because we could spend the same amount of money we would elsewhere and get more stuff. We loved more stuff. Was there a bookshelf at Home Depot for $250? We'd go to IKEA, where they sell for $150, and buy two. The magic of this store to us was that we could totally drown ourselves in pre-punctured plywood without any regard for whether or not we had a need for it.

Regardless of any interesting transatlantic cultural dichotomies exposed by IKEA, the trip was an odd one. I'd been pleased to be going anywhere, but the entire experience would have been more satisfying if Johan had actually gotten down to business upon arriving home. Instead, he tossed the new pieces onto the roughed-in kitchen counter where they have remained, to my knowledge, for all eternity. But who could blame him? We'd left the house for more than an hour: he clearly needed to rest up.

* * *

Instead of having an early Halloween party before Inger's return from LA, we were now preparing for our late Halloween party due to her illness. It was nearly mid-November, but at least we were still doing it. After the past few disjointed weeks at the Waara house, it was fun to be engaged in a project with the kids.

It was a Saturday morning when the four of us spread our recipes and decorations out in the kitchen. As we'd plotted nearly a month ago now, all the planning was done, and we told Inger all she had to do was sit back and enjoy. I suppose that was fairly naïve of us.

"Don't you think it would be best to put the cotton on the ceiling if it's supposed to be cobwebs?"

Åke and I were standing on chairs on opposite ends of the archway between the kitchen and the dining room, mounting the sheets of packing cotton we'd been so lucky to find in the attic.

"Like…flat against the ceiling?" I asked, cobwebs laced between each finger and tumbling to the ground. I had to give Inger credit for enthusiasm, as despite the ridiculousness of her suggestion, her über-smile was out and shining as she gazed upward at our work.

"Yes, you see, darling," she pointed toward the fifteen-foot ceiling with one hand as the other sat akimbo on the hip of her long linen skirt. "If you were to put something sticky all along the ceiling there you could cover the whole area, rather than waste so much drooping off of the walls like this. She gestured toward the cobwebs I'd just carefully stretched from the center of the archway to a framed photo on the wall. What did she think we were trying to do, insulate the house? How often to spiders spin webs flat against a ceiling?

"Well," I said, looking to Åke for help, as if there were any chance this timid boy cared one way or another how to best hang cotton spider webs. "I think we'd have a really hard time getting up there."

"Oh, we could get you a ladder." She was already walking toward the door. "Here, just wait one…"

"You know, Inger," I cut in, "it's a good suggestion, but it's really not worth the trouble. This is exactly how cobwebs are typically hung at Halloween parties. You know," I gestured toward the mass of cotton Åke had just strung across the archway corner, "like a spider spun it like that. The stuff hanging down gives it the look of being haunted."

"Haunted?"

"Yes! Haunted! That's what we're going for, right guys? The haunted kitchen!"

My enthusiasm was met with meek nods from the three ghouls-to-be in the kitchen who were, I knew, in total agreement with me. Lisbeth and Pia didn't even look up from the recipe they were working on.

And so it went. We managed to create a semi-haunted looking kitchen and dining room, as well as some typically faux-gruesome Halloween snacks. Inger questioned the rationale of each appetizer.

"But will raisins taste appropriate in smushed potatoes?" she asked of the mashed potato ghosts' raisin eyes.

"Oh my! I'd think we'd be quite surprised to find such brightly colored worms in actual dirt! And then to want to eat them!" she said while watching Pia put the final touches on the Oreo "mud cake." Yes, Inger, we should have bought the flesh-colored gummy worms. And then not eaten them. I saw her eyeing the Philadelphia cream cheese on the counter called for by the mud cake recipe. I could feel her tense up, just barely restraining herself from bringing up the "needless expense" for the second time.

On that one count, she did manage to control herself. She even played along for the costuming, digging through her belongings, and coming up with a Russian outfit of some sort. I'm not really sure what made it Russian, other than the fuzzy hat, but apparently she'd bought it in Russia, so I guess she got some points there.

The rest of the family's costumes were hilarious manifestations of their quasi-understanding of Halloween. Åke was some sort of Charlie Chaplin fellow with a suit and a mustache. There was nothing silly or odd about his suit, so I guess he really was dressed up as a guy with a mustache. Not bad though, for a shy guy like him. Lisbeth and Pia were both various versions of "dead girl." I gave them low points for creativity, but the pre-party dress-up and makeup session was genuinely fun girl-time for us.

I had found an old floral print dress in the attic and, appropriate to Helsingborg's most exciting feature, dressed as the dead Ophelia. I even found fake flower petals and attached them to my dress. No one understood the reference, but they seemed to enjoy my wild hair and eye makeup.

Amazingly enough, the most original costume prize went to Jan. He dressed up as a Chinese gangster, complete with suit and tie, slanted-eye makeup and Fu Manchu mustache. Where he came up with such a creative (if startlingly racist) costume, I'll never know. But he was pretty proud of himself, that's for sure.

And Johan came as a dead hippie. Oh, did I not mention that Johan came? Yes, I thought it equally weird. It shouldn't have been, really, since he'd known the Waaras for much longer than I had. But he had no idea that his neighbors knew him as the odd, tattooed, priest-fucking, car-grease weirdo guy from down the road. You'd think the HIV thing would have clued him in a little.

It was actually Lisbeth's doing that he was there at all. A few days prior, we'd been on our way to the horses. Lisbeth's big, lovely eyes were just peeking out between her powder blue hat and mismatched brown and orange scarf. They rolled dreamily along as we passed Johan's little house, watching as we crept toward it, then drove by, and then as it fell to the rear of the chilly Volvo. Although I wasn't convinced that her fear and/or disdain of Johan had changed at all since we'd started dating, she was clearly fascinated by our relationship. It seemed that seeing Johan made me far more exotic than my being American ever had.

"Will Johan come for the party?" she asked in her tentative, dainty style.

I laughed. She didn't.

"Seriously?" As I said this word, I glanced over at her, and my mittened hands moved the steering wheel ever so slightly in the same direction. Just a bit. We didn't even go onto the shoulder. This didn't, however, prevent Lisbeth from flinging both arms to the dashboard and bracing herself for impending face trauma.

She looked at me with panic in her eyes. "Take care!"

"Lisbeth, I've been driving since you've been shitting without assistance. Lighten the fuck up."

This was neither true, nor was it what I actually said. I had no doubt that such condescension toward Lisbeth would only get me further into the passive-aggressive twilight zone with her mother. Furthermore, given her innate gift for anal retentiveness, Lisbeth had most likely been fully potty trained at birth.

"I've got it," I really said as I turned slowly onto the dirt road leading to the horses. "Don't worry. And what's this about bringing Johan to the party? Do you think he'd really want to come?"

"Ah…" Lisbeth giggled. I was relieved to have her distracted from that horrid-driving report for Inger I was sure she'd otherwise be concocting in her mind. "Yeah, he is your boyfriend, right?"

Now there was a thought. "Um, I guess so," I said. "I guess he's my boyfriend. Is that like, a normal, Swedish thing to do? Bring your new boyfriend over for a Halloween party with your family?"

"Yes! You should!" She was delighted with herself.

"Would your parents think that was weird?" Not that I should have cared if the world's weirdest people were to consider me weirder than they must have already thought I was, but in that moment I felt a flash of shame. The truth was, if this were my real family, I wouldn't bring Johan home to meet them. He'd never read an entire book. He was a little crass, even for my taste, and I was getting the feeling that he was a tad lazy. But what did I care what the Waaras thought?

"No. Why would they?"

I wasn't about to expound upon the question, but to please Lisbeth (a lofty goal, if there ever was one), I asked Johan to come. And he said yes, sort of to my delight. And surprise. And horror.

But it wasn't at all bad. Johan the dead hippie came over, and even Linda joined us from next door, though she didn't have a costume. Johan was more of a Jeff-Bridges-as-The-Dude hippie than a Jimi-Hendrix hippie, which was a little non-traditional, but how was he to know the difference? We had fun. True, the Halloween music only lasted about twenty minutes ("Ha ha! Lovely music, dear, but could we quiet it for dinner?"), but that allowed for awkward chatting and intermittent silence to became the equally spooky soundtrack. Not to mention that although the assortment of Halloween food was great, and even contained potato-product aplenty, the habit-loving Waaras kept sneaking to the fridge mid-*kvällsmat* to grab some *sallad* or leftover meat patties. Like they couldn't go one stinking meal without a plate full of iceberg lettuce or ground *blandfars*. Whatever. Everyone looked silly. Jan and Johan each had a beer (a light *öl*, with hardly any alcohol), and Inger and I drank a glass of wine. Rather, I had one glass, and several quick extra shots of wine as I kept making excuses to go back into the pantry, wine glass in hand.

After the dinner wound down and the hot cider pot was nearly empty, I took Johan down to my lair.

"You *live* down here?" he laughed, bouncing slightly on the tiny, squeaky bed.

"Well, 'live' is sort of a strong word choice, but yes, this is where I sleep and keep my crap. Do you want to see the laundry room where I shower?" I offered. "It's even more dungeon-y."

"No, I do not," he replied with a grin. "Not unless you are in it."

And with that, he got up, closed my bedroom door, and we made out like teenagers in my room. After rolling around for a while, or the closest approximation to rolling around that my tiny bed would allow, Johan pulled back and gazed sweetly into my face as he tucked my hair behind my ear.

"I am going soon with Danne and some friends to a sound event in Stockholm. It would be a few days, and you might have to take time from work, but," it seemed strange how hesitant he was to finish his sentence, as if he were proposing something truly dramatic, "would you...would you like to come to with me? I would so much like you to come."

Me? On a trip to Stockholm? Not since being invited to the hardware store had I been so excited about anything.

13
Stockholm

Monday, November 21, 2005

If I could package and reproduce this Monday morning, I'd take a case of the Mondays every day.

For some odd reason, the Waaras decided it would be easier for me to take care of the horses if I stayed at Johan's last night. Inger actually called me at his house on Sunday afternoon and asked me to try spending the night to see how that worked out with my schedule.

What was I to say? I followed her instructions.

Sunday night was delightful. We listened to music as he played around online, and I wrote. Eventually we got tired and climbed into his chilly bed, warmed each other up and talked until we fell asleep.

I asked him how he felt about being in a relationship with an expiration date. At first he pretended that he didn't know what I meant, like acknowledging the fact that I am only here temporarily was the thing that would make it true. He said we never know what life could be like in a year, and he wasn't going to think about it. The one thing I do know about my life a year from now is that I won't be in Sweden, but I found his response endearing. The fact that he found my inevitable departure too troubling to think about was a satisfying nugget to extract from the conversation.

This morning we woke up naturally with no alarms, no

> checking the clock. Can you imagine? A life without alarm clocks? He simply doesn't use them. He doesn't need to. We chatted for a bit, and then I wandered into the cold to take care of the horses. Johan was waiting for me when I arrived back at his house. He had to drop me off at work, so I was powerless to stop him from steering his Volvo away from Ödmjuk Gård and toward Helsingborg. We went to breakfast in a little café. We had baguettes, which apparently is Svensk for a sandwich for breakfast. He had ham salad; I had a delightfully magenta sandwich filling—a genius blend of seafood parts and beets. We shared a pen and solved the sudoku in the newspaper together. It may have been the best Monday morning in recorded history. No pressure, no hurry, just starting out the day together.
>
> Then I returned to the Waaras, and Johan went to work on a car. Really, he was doing actual work that day. I know because he was all dirty and greasy when he picked me up this evening. Later, he told me about his life goal: to buy from his friend Henrik (the dog-food factory fellow) a piece of land that has been set aside for him. Then, he's going to build his own house there, doing all the work himself. I could see on his face how much the dream means to him. He was really excited. The guy puts in a day of actual work, and look how inspired he gets!
>
> So it turns out the occasionally employed relaxation king who's never read an entire book has some long-term goals. Good to know.

That would be how, without ever making a conscious decision to do so, I began living with Johan. Inger decided for us. I was unsure if I'd just been kicked out of the Waaras' home, or if Inger had been assuming that's where I would prefer to be and was saving me the awkwardness of asking. When she asked me how the morning went, and I said it was great, she suggested I just keep doing it. Being compulsively easy-going where I was concerned, it was unsurprising to me that Johan agreed.

"Natalie, I am happy when you are here, and when you are not here, I'm wishing you were here."

"So you're OK with me being here. All the time. Even though you barely know me and have no idea if I'll turn out to be a crazy person. That's what you're saying?"

We were watching TV on the couch, naturally, as I attempted to force

Johan into verifying that mine was a wanted presence in his home. His last intense, long-term relationship had just occupied this same space, and it hadn't ended all that long ago. How long ago was a little unclear to me, but if he couldn't bring himself to say he didn't want me here, I'd just have to assume that whatever time and space he needed had been satisfied. Really, I'd have to. I was sort of following Inger's instructions at this point.

He smiled, put his arm around my shoulder, and shifted our mutual attention back to the television with his body language. "I think the Waaras are the only crazies we need to worry about," he said. "Now *that* looks interesting!"

He was gesturing toward the reality show on the large flat screen. It was one we'd been watching regularly (what show hadn't we been watching regularly?) and it was also one that totally floored me every time I saw it. In the style of *Supernanny* and *The Dog Whisperer*, it was yet another program in which an expert would enter a dysfunctional home and use her wisdom to heal its occupants. But rather than naughty dogs or wayward children, these families had varying degrees of sexual dysfunction. The sex expert lady would interview the couple, talk about their copulation schedule, analyze their intercourse environment, and, of course, examine their sex toys. Oh, and there were hidden video feeds to review too.

So yes, interesting was one word to describe that. The sex show was on commercial when Johan's phone rang. He picked the cordless handset up from the coffee table, looked at the caller ID, and without any facial expression handed it to me.

"Say I'm not here."

I looked at the phone in his hand before me. This didn't seem like something I was likely to do.

"Johan, no. No, I'm not a-"

But before I could finish my sentence he'd hit the talk button, tossed it on my lap, and got up from the couch. What was this? Naturally, I did the last thing I should have done: I picked up the phone and spoke.

"Hello?"

"Ah...hello," the confused female voice on the other line said. Clearly, it was not just my gender that was taking her aback, but my language. "May I speak with Janne, please?"

It was Annika, his ex-girlfriend, and I knew it. "Janne" [YAN-nay] was a nickname for Johan, like "Johnny" for John, which I did not know until that very second, though it was as clear from the context as her identity. I couldn't believe this was happening.

"Oh, I'm sorry," I said obediently, not knowing what else to do. "He's not here right now."

There was a beat of silence while Annika considered this lie. "Are you sure? I could have sworn I just heard you speaking to him before saying,

'Hello.'" Annika spoke beautiful English, far better than Inger, even. So she was smart, and ballsy for even challenging my lie. So far, I liked her.

"No, he's really not here," I said, hating myself a little. "I dropped the phone, and you must have heard the TV. I don't think he'll be long though, if you'd like me to take a message."

I was making a point to be very polite. It was clear to me that no one on this phone call was to blame for this supremely awkward situation. I wished there was a way for me to make her understand the same.

"Sure. You can take a message," she said. "Please tell Janne his girlfriend called and she needs to speak with him as soon as possible."

Now it was my turn to absorb a small shock with silence. His girlfriend?

"I'll let him know."

"Thank you," she said. "Just so you're aware, you seem very nice, but I don't for a minute believe that he's not there right now."

"Um…I'm really sorry about that," I said, briefly considering validating her suspicion. "But he should be back shortly, so I'll tell him you called."

Johan had disappeared into the kitchen, from where he had yet to emerge. It wasn't that big of a kitchen, and there was nowhere to sit in there. He was clearly just hoping to wait out my initial reaction, which was a wise move considering I was fuming. I was angry not only at the fact that Johan had put me in this position, but that I really had no recourse for expressing myself. What was I going to do—scream and yell and demand better treatment? To which he could say, "Well, if you would rather be sitting in the dungeon of the Crazies' house, feel free to go back there. I didn't invite you here. I never even told you whether or not I still have a girlfriend somewhere."

I couldn't put my foot down, because I had no stable footing here. And the truth was that I would still rather be here with an asshole than back there with nothing.

Eventually, he came back into to the room. I told him about the conversation, we had a discussion about what she meant by "girlfriend," which he swore was a language error, and let it drop. I was just fine believing it was simple translation issue, regardless of her seemingly flawless English. Honestly, I'd been there nearly every day for the last three weeks. And now I sort of lived there. I knew he wasn't hiding anything. End of story. Sort of.

Thursday, November 24, 2005

Dear Lise,

I'm beginning to get the feeling that our dream for this to be the classic overseas romance with no worries and no strings attached is getting increasingly far-fetched. Given the sort-of moving in together and now this crazy, but not actually crazy-seeming ex-girlfriend reappearing, I think this relationship could probably use some reflection. But I'll try to limit it to just a little bit of reflection in the hopes of keeping our dream alive. Fair? OK.

The fact is that we can't become too attached, can we? I'm certainly not going to become a permanent resident here, and I don't see Johan going anywhere. Not that this debate even matters though; I am clearly Johan's rebound girl, and he is clearly an I'm-living-abroad-for-a-while fling. So whatever the deal with this woman is, it isn't really my concern. Right?

But here's the thing: she called him a few days ago to tell him that she had had a miscarriage, and that it had been his. They'd been together for two and a half years, and now that they have broken up, she claims to have been pregnant? And didn't tell him? If it's true, why tell him now? And why wouldn't she have told him about the pregnancy before it was gone? If it's a lie, what is she aiming to do? Hurt him? Win him back with sympathy? I guess this at least narrows down the question of how long ago they broke up to "really not super long ago."

After this fiasco had marinated for about twenty-four hours, she called him again. She wanted to talk about me. She's disappointed in him. Because he's already in a new relationship? Because of my age? Because I'm American? It's not every day that you deal with the sudden appearance of an emotionally charged, recently miscarried ex-girlfriend of your new boyfriend. Who is some sort of clergy, apparently. What is the appropriate response? Where is the line between being supportive and being nosy or defensive?

Perhaps the most annoying thing is that I'm compelled to really not care. So what if he really loves her and eventually goes back to her? I'll be long gone, right?

As much as this reaction seems sort of icky to me, it's also freeing. For the first time in my life, I find myself completely free of the typical emotional weightiness of a relationship, while enjoying all the fruits of one. I'm with Johan because every day I wake up, and he is who I want to be with. Granted, my options are quite limited here, but I choose him. I have no delusions of him being "the one." He just is, and I just am. I don't know if I've ever been in a more honest relationship in my life.

* * *

I was completely worthless at my duties at the Waaras at this point. I'd begun to realize that I wasn't the only one confused about my role in their home. No one besides Inger seemed to know what my mission was. This made it increasingly easy to make my own rules and priorities. And horses were definitely not a priority to me.

I used to try and help Lisbeth with the horses, but she was so freaking uptight about how they were brushed, how the hay was laid out, how their poo was placed into the wheelbarrow, and so on, I eventually gave up. By this point, in fact, I wasn't even standing around in the barn, awkwardly quizzing Lisbeth about her depressing social life. I decided my task was truly to drive her the two miles to the horse barn, help her scoop the poo, and then let her do whatever else she wanted, all by herself. It sounds really jerky of me, and it was. But she didn't like me to take initiative and do anything myself, and she was as weary of coming up with menial horse tasks for me to do as I was of asking for them. And I was burned out on every aspect of my job, so I didn't care. I'd take my journal into the barn's little kitchenette and pretend like Lisbeth wasn't slaving away just outside the door without me. Serves her right for insisting she own two enormous, expensive animals that she never rode. Ugh. I wasn't even allowed to own my own cream cheese.

It was in the midst of this now highly dysfunctional horse duty when I received the following text from Johan:

Going to be at Dannes for awile. Call when back, sweety!!! :-)

Oh, was he?

Earlier that afternoon he'd mentioned that he had to go over to Annika's at some point to pick up her car because he'd been putting off fixing it for a few weeks. His explanation of the alleged car issue was so incoherent that I was left with the impression that there was something urgently wrong with her glove box. So that seemed a little bit like bullshit to me. And now it was after nine, and he was at Danne's, huh?

I returned to the Waaras' and waited. I fidgeted. I packed an overnight bag, a bag that I'd been continually packing, bringing to Johan's, and then returning empty to the Waaras' the next day. I still did laundry at the farmhouse, and I didn't have a closet or anything at Johan's, so it wasn't like I was moving things over there en masse. I was glad of that, as I had no key to his house, nor a car to get there. At least I was still in possession of my belongings. If he was going to "be there awile" at 9 p.m., why would I even assume I was going to make it over there to sleep? And if I was truly suspicious that he was at Annika's rather than at Danne's, was I really going to sit around hoping for him to show up and take me back to his place when he was done? No. But that might still be better than staying here with awkward questions about why I was swaying from the new plan.

An hour later I received a text that reported that he could be there "quite late." Maybe it would be best to see me tomorrow.

My reaction clearly should have been *OK. See you tomorrow.* We'd already seen each other once that day. And we hung out every day. And we'd only been seeing each for a couple months, *and* he had never actually asked me to live with him. But no, as I lay on my cold, industrial, basement bed with the display of my cell phone suspended in the air above my face, my reaction was, precisely, this:

HANGING OUT WITH DANNE, HUH? THOUGHT YOU HAD TO GO DRIVE AROUND WITH ANNIKA. FUNNY HOW YOU HAD TO DO THAT AND THEN SUDDENLY BECAME BUSY ALL NIGHT. YOU'RE FUCKING HER, AREN'T YOU? IT'S THE ONLY EXPLANATION FOR WHY YOU'RE SPENDING ONE NIGHT WITH ANYONE BUT ME, REALLY. AND IF HER CAR HAS NEVER HAD A FREAKING GLOVE BOX WHY IS IT THAT TODAY IS THE DAY YOU'RE INSTALLING ONE FOR HER, NOT WHEN YOU WERE ACTUALLY LIVING TOGETHER, AND WHY DO SWEDES HAVE SO MANY FUCKING N'S IN THEIR NAMES?

Perhaps this internal rant should have been mitigated by the fact that he continued to text me throughout the evening, checking in, and saying he missed me. Instead, every time my phone beeped, I became even angrier. As one who had never felt jealous before, it was really taking me by surprise. Especially due to the whole I'm-having-a-fling-abroad thing, and the he's-clearly-on-the-rebound thing. He'd been honest with me about the fact that he had to get Annika's car, so why would he lie now? No, it made no sense. I also considered whether or not I was actually jealous or just angry that I couldn't really justify living with Johan if he was sleeping with his ex. Could I?

* * *

It took all of twelve hours for me to get over my angst. Johan sent me a text when he saw me drive by to tend to the horses the next morning asking me to stop by on my way back. He missed me. Danne's was "sort of dull," and "nothing like time with my American girl." After a few of these sentiments in his doorway, I knew (read: decided) everything was fine.

Besides, we were only days away from our Stockholm adventure. What's more, we actually had plans for this weekend as well.

It wasn't as if we never did anything on the weekends. Johan occasionally took me to the baguette place for breakfast; there were sometimes IKEA trips; and we'd stop into his friend Danne's car stereo shop now and again, just to visit—rather for Johan and Danne to talk for hours in Svenska while I studied Svensk magazines and exchanged glances with Ludde, who always came along. Ludde and I did a lot of bonding on those trips, having a relatively equal role.

Bur first real excursion together was to be this weekend. We were going to a Christmas bazaar. Sure, it was still solidly November. But without Thanksgiving to act as an arbitrary border between Christmas and the rest of the calendar, Svenskar have no reason to restrain themselves. As soon as it gets chilly, it's all-*jul* all the time. *Jul* means Christmas. Isn't that adorable?

Inger told me all about these *basars*, the Svensk, *jul*-filled markets, and with no pilgrims or Indians to hold me back either this year, I was champing at the bit to experience a true Svensk *jul* atmosphere. It took a bit of convincing to get Johan to take me.

"Are you sure you would want to go?" he asked when I made the request. "They're just so…what is the word? Corny?"

"Johan! Christmas is corny! It's the time of the year when the cornier everything is the better. By telling me that your Christmas bazaars are corny you are further convincing me to go."

"Mebbe…mebbe 'corny' wasn't the right word."

"You're just trying to get out of it!" I cried. "Dude. What is your beef with Christmas bazaars? They sound awesome."

"They are, I guess…" Johan became, for the first time since I'd known him, strangely introspective. I would have none of that.

"So…they *are* awesome, you guess? So you should probably take me to one? Come on, it was Thanksgiving in the US this week and I missed it. I'm down a holiday." If my persistence didn't have him, I was sure biting my lower lip, creeping over to his side of the couch and sliding my hands under his shirt and around his small, warm torso would seal the deal. It did.

For the sentimental lover of traditional Christmas trappings and bustling commerce, the Svensk *julbasar* was a must-see, must-hear, must-taste, must-smell experience. The one we visited took place in the middle of nowhere (a popular Svensk location, apparently), in a little cul-de-sac of barns on an expansive working *gård*. Booths were set up wall-to-wall inside the barns, each with a unique theme. There was the *mat* barn with hams, beet salads, bread, cheeses, and the quaint if-you-didn't-ask-what-it-was

Svensk *lutfisk*. In the *dricka* barn, Johan taught me how to drink my first cup of *glögg*, a mulled wine served warm with crushed almonds and raisins. The key was to sip the warm, spicy brew, slowly stirring it with a tiny spoon, so that by the time you reached the end of your small cup of strong cheer, the almonds and raisins were sufficiently wine-soaked. Using the spoon to fish out almonds and raisins, the last drink of *glögg* was actually a hot, sweet, crunchy bite.

The gift barn was really a sight. It was packed with vendors selling handmade goods, from scarves to candles to fine art, to things carved out of reindeer parts—all of which completely delighted my pants off. Johan was clearly less enthused with this portion of the *julbasar* experience, but I didn't care. I took my time wandering from table to table, touching hand-knit mittens, rubbing shoulders with dozens of heavy-coated shoppers, and smiling warmly at the vendors whose wares I found particularly charming. This was the greatest number of people I'd seen at one time in Sverige. Just being a part of a genuine crowd was invigorating.

Everything was too expensive for me to buy, but I bought something anyway. It was a six-inch-tall metal sculpture of a leafless tree with a tea-light holder at its base. There was no way I could ship it. Bringing it back on the plane in nine months was not going to be practical. But it looked just like a tattoo Alisa had on her shoulder, so I absolutely had to buy it for her. The fact that it cost just under 50 percent of my Christmas gift budget was beside the point. Look at this place! How could I leave empty-handed?

Back outside the warm, sweet-smelling gift barn, ridiculous purchase in hand, Johan and I weaved through outdoor vendor booths, each steaming with hot, homemade delights like candy and donut-type treats. It was as charming as a Dickens-fucking-village.

I wanted to never leave. I soaked in every bit of wonderfulness from each booth. I touched everything, talked to every vendor, smelled every item, and fantasized about buying it all. Well, not the *lutfisk*. I preferred my fish to be unrotten, non-gelatinous, and not soaked in ice water and lye. The Swedes and their crazypants traditions! After a century of refrigeration technology, isn't it high time to let the poisonous fish recipe die?

Hours later we were back on the couch, as Saturday began slipping into evening. I was lost in my daydream of *lutfisk* jokes and delicious *glögg* remembrances when the man lying next to me woke me with a surprising confession.

"I'm feeling very…heppy that you made me go today," Johan said. He was picking his words cautiously, sans the humorous tone in which he usually spoke. He rotated his head around so that his eyes looked directly into mine. "Thank you for insisting. I'd forgotten how…nice they can be. It reminds me how long it's been since I've been to the *basar*…"

"When was the last time you'd been to one?" I asked.

The last time he'd been to a *julbasar*, he'd been there with his father and one of his two sisters. What he'd forgotten until today was that his mother had been there too.

"I've never heard you say anything about her," I said. "Where is she?"

"I'm not...I don't really know," he said. "That doesn't seem very peecy, does it?"

Peecy? PC? As in politically correct? I mean, I guess it's not exactly politically correct for a grown man to not know where his mother was, but it would still be a pretty generous use of the term. Whatever. Not important.

"Yeah, I suppose not," I said. "Why...why don't you know? When's the last time you heard from her?"

The long and short of it was that Johan and his mom didn't talk much. She reached out to him occasionally, maybe once a year, but ever since she and his dad split up five-ish years ago, he'd been pushing her away. He gave no further explanation for this, nor would I ever find out more. But he was thankful for the memory, and I was thankful for the *julbasar*, so this American girl didn't feel like she'd missed her Thanksgiving one bit.

* * *

Although I couldn't have cared less about the car stereo sound competition that he and Danne were so obsessively preparing for, I would have gone to a Miraculous Process convention with Inger at this point if it promised me travel and social engagement. Besides, we were staying in a hotel! We'd be eating at restaurants! All of my eight-year-old aspirations were suddenly once again relevant. Maybe I'd get to use a vending machine at some point! What if there was a pool? Anything was possible!

I did about as much pre-trip research on Stockholm as I did on Sverige before coming over, so I had absolutely no idea what the city had to offer. Who needed tourist info when you were traveling with residents though? Maybe we'd even do something cultural. Who knew?

I took the liberty of believing Stockholm included, at the very least, people—people who might be doing things like walking around, exchanging dialogue and engaging in some sort of observable behavior. It was a bold assumption, but I was banking on it.

Johan and I arrived at Danne's shop to begin our cross-country adventure late on a Thursday evening. Johan had dropped Ludde off at Annika's house earlier that day, so we were footloose and ready to roll for a weekend of excitement. Danne would drive separately in his car, as it was a competition submission. Johan's car wasn't competing in this show, but we would be carpooling up north with their friend Jakob, whose car was in the competition, along with his girlfriend, Louise. A girl. My age. Given my failure to sustain meaningful friendships with Hanna or Linda, I wasn't going to get too excited. Except that I knew we were going to be the bestest best friends ever. And we'd go to bars and coffee shops and have shopping escapades together all weekend. And with her, whoever she was, my Svensk adventure would truly begin.

Louise was blonde and round-faced and totally fucking pissed that we were still at Danne's shop at eleven o'clock that night. I liked her. In the three hours we'd spent awkwardly standing around the garage ("There's no need to unlock the store and sit down, Honnnnaaay—we're just about to leave..."), I learned that Louise worked in publishing (a meaninglessly general assertion, but one that sparked my interest), I'd shared with her that I was a writer (an equally unclear assertion coming from an illegal American housekeeper, I'm sure), and we established that neither of us had the slightest interest in car stereos. We were both on board only for the getaway.

"Honestly, I'd rather Jakob do just all bad," she said of her boyfriend's competition entry within easy earshot of him, flipping her long, shiny hair over her shoulder. "Maybe then he gives up on Friday, and we can spend some vacation day doing something fun."

Louise was sort of a bitch, which made me feel deeply tickled about getting to spend time with her. Every Svensk I'd met so far, whether good, evil, friendly, or otherwise, was just so damn passive. Not Louise. She was so cutting, in fact, that I ordinarily would have felt bad for her tall, soft, polite boyfriend. But not now. Jakob was surrounded by a nation of polite, passive Svenskar. He was on his own on this one.

Just before midnight, we finally climbed into Jakob's car and took off. My heart raced as we drove into the night. We were on a six-hour road trip. I might have been a stranger to so many things here in Sverige, but I knew road trips. I knew family road trips, friend road trips, school road trips, and weird high-school-Christian-choir road trips (yes, you read that correctly). I loved to be on the move, and after three months of going nowhere, I was moving.

I was asleep in an hour. What? It was dark. And no one was talking. When we stopped for gas (petrol, rather), Johan and Louise teased me. How could I be sleeping through this exciting late-night adventure?

"How could I not be sleeping?" I laughed. "It's 3 a.m., and no one was talking. It's not like I was getting a guided tour of Sweden's finest landmarks or anything."

Apparently Swedes don't take a lot of road trips. "Such a waste of petrol," Johan had said. The distance from their most southern city to their national capital was just six hours by car, and most would rarely, if ever, make the trip. Americans drive from state to state on whims, for weekend trips. To a Svensk, the trek from Helsingborg to Stockholm was an annual one at best. Sigh. I was going to have to show these Swedes how road trips were done. Now that I was awake.

Jakob was gassing up, and I was relieved to find out that this was the first Svensk petrol station I'd encountered that not only included a convenience store, but that was also open past 10 p.m. Was it possible that we had officially departed the middle of nowhere?

"Anyone else going in?" I asked as I started to climb out of the car.

"What do you need?" Johan asked, "Are you really needing to spend money now?"

I was stopped in my tracks. We were traveling. We were at a gas station. If we didn't get out to at least buy some gummy worms—if not ginger ale and pretzels—what were we doing? But Johan was right about the money. I didn't really have any to spend. Johan was my meal ticket this weekend, and I wasn't even sure if he knew that. Plus, all that sitting around on his couch for the last month had really not done great things for my waistline. I guess I didn't really need to get something. But now I was halfway out the door.

"I have to pee," I said. "Anyone need anything from inside? Snacks? Water?"

"Ahhh…I'll go in." Johan sounded exasperated, as if my bathroom break necessitated a chaperone. Once we were inside the brightly lit petrol station, I regained my feeling of normality and authority over the scenario. This not only looked and smelled and felt like a late-night visit to a gas station during a road trip—it was one. The convenience store was like any American one, well stocked with snacks and drinks and normal travel necessities. So of course, I found myself standing in an aisle, staring at the snacks.

Screw these guys. I was getting a snack. Maybe I'd even get those shrimp-flavored potato…was that "sticks"? Shrimpy potato sticks? And was that egg-flavored fried potato chips next to them? Awesome. I got gummy worms. Johan talked me out of buying a Coke too, as he was buying the world's largest bottle of water. You know, so it could last us the rest of the trip up and the trip back down on Monday. No really, that's what he told me.

Back in the car everyone accepted exactly one gummy worm from me as we restarted our journey northward. Louise and I chatted for about twenty minutes or so before the car fell silent again. Although it only took me another few minutes to nod off against the window, I'd already blazed my way through most of the candy. *Who eats just one gummy worm?* I wondered as I drifted off. *On a road trip no less?*

Mon, November 28, 2005

Hey Lise!
The weekend was fun. Well, it was both great fun and greatly boring. It was fun in that it was awesome to get away for three whole days and see a ton of people and be at a big event that was ripe for Swede-watching, a sport that has quickly become a new love of mine. For example, I can't explain how many skinny, blonde, twelve-year-old boys I've seen wearing FUBU this weekend. Yeah, I have a feeling that pale, effeminate Swedish adolescents aren't representatives of either "us" intended by the acronym. And how about the fact that there are all of these Swedes wearing trucker hats like they're Ashton Kutcher? I mean, I'll give them that it's trendy, but I'm beginning to get the feeling that car stereo competitions are sort of the Swedish equivalent of—dare I say it—NASCAR racing here. Do they not realize that the trucker hat trend is supposed to be ironic? Of course not, that would require context.

The weekend was boring in that the car stereo competition was the entire weekend. While we were technically in Stockholm, we never left the conference center. Since it was a few miles from the city center, it was a far cry from a touristy or cultural trip. If someone were to ask me if I've even been to Stockholm, I'd be totally lying if I said yes. We ate in the cafeteria there, we slept in the hotel there, and in between, my new friend Louise and I literally sat in lawn chairs by her boyfriend's car and talked. For three days.

All expectations for a Stockholm adventure aside, however, it was exciting to meet some new people. Louise is really cool, and for the first time in months I felt like I was really just hanging out with a girlfriend. It was also incredibly helpful to hear another perspective on Sweden. She lives in the city of Malmö, which is bigger than Helsingborg and more metropolitan. She goes out with friends, just finished school a couple of years ago and now works in the publishing industry. And guess what? She thinks it would be really easy to find a magazine that would want to publish essays on an American's cultural experience in Sweden! She said that the publication she works for wouldn't be the right one, but she would totally find me the right venue and help me get published here. How exciting is that?

It was exciting. I tried not to act too outlandishly geeked about it, but meeting Louise felt like the biggest breakthrough of my entire Svensk experience. It was amazing that she thought she could help me get published while I was there, but it was also just nice to chat with a girl. Louise and I talked about everything from *kaffe* to college to tampons. Apparently, *kaffe* wasn't just my favorite thing about Sverige, but most young Svensk adults' as well.

"You don't *fika*?" She was incredulous.

"Ah…I don't know if I *fika*," I said. "What is *fika*?"

From the way she talked about it, I was sure I'd missed a prime cultural experience here that was about to change my life. Everyone *fikas* in Sverige, she says. At least all the young, hip people do. I wanted in on this.

It took me about ten minutes to piece together that a *fika* was a coffee break. And the act of taking one, apparently.

"But we're not just drinking coffee. We're being social," she explained. "It's a part of our every day. It's how you know people and get to know people. But it's hard to explain too."

Yeah, no, I think I got it. Drinking coffee with friends wasn't exactly something I did or didn't *do*, as much as it was something I'd never classified as a *thing*. My new friend momentarily stopped watching the crowd and focused inward with a furrowed brow to find the right words to describe the ritual. Really, it was this reaction more than anything else that clarified what an integral part of Svensk culture *fika* was. It would be how I would look if I were trying to describe the significance of pre-football tailgating. I got it; it was a thing.

While it wasn't clear where or with whom I could *fika* back in the village, it was at least reassuring to know what I was missing—to be able to recognize the right thing to be a part of if it came my way.

"So Americans don't *fika*?" She looked at me very, very seriously as she said this.

"Um, well I guess we do *fika*," I said carefully. "We just call it getting coffee. And a lot of times the coffee is beer."

We talked all day. Louise was fascinated by the American education system. It blew her away, for example, that I had a job while I was in college.

"That is like…" Louise rolled her eyes and shook her blonde head at the notion. "You would have to be a very poor person to be working during university."

"Wow," I said. "In the US if you're very poor, you're probably working full time and going to college part time. Everyone I know worked during school. If you didn't work at least part time, your parents would have to be totally rich."

She asked some of the questions I'd heard before—like whether all Americans were lawsuit-happy, and if we all smoked pot all the time—and then some new ones, like why our tampons had applicators. Obviously, I did not know the answer to all of them. Not that this prevented me from taking a stab at each one anyway. I really thought I was going to have a good answer for the applicator question, until I started listening to myself try to explain it. We don't have good aim? We're too prudish to put our fingers certain places? Could we just be *that* lazy?

"I don't know, actually," I laughed. "You got me there."

Our hours of sitting and chit-chatting were way more exciting than looking at muffler displays and talking with Svensk tire salesmen, which were the only alternatives. While the bulk of the building was full of cars with varying types of stereos in their trunks and doors and wherever, a huge section of it was a bunch of typical industry vendors. Whenever I was tired of sitting, Johan and I would take a gander through the car crap sales area. It was sort of awesome for my ego, as he was clearly showing me off as his young American girlfriend. I scored lots of giveaway industry junk and cheesy English phrases from various salesmen of car parts.

"Well HEL-LO, beautiful AMERican!" they would say, shoving a fistful of car battery-themed lanyards under one arm to offer me a limp Svensk handshake with the other. I would always act very impressed with their English skills, as showing them off seemed to be the root of their enthusiasm.

"*Jaaap*!" Johan would nod. "This is Natalie. She comes here from Detroit."

At this point in my stay, I'd stopped clarifying that I was not actually from Detroit. Although Michigan meant very little to Svenskar, Detroit was a concept about which they were very excited to demonstrate their knowledge—especially these car guys. The fact that my visits to Detroit had been limited to a handful of Tiger baseball games and a fourth-grade viewing of *Joseph and the Amazing Technicolor Dreamcoat* made me want to look over my shoulder every time this happened. Surely someone was going to call me out on this. I was raised in a quiet, rural, northern Michigan town almost homogeneous enough to pass for Sverige. But no one in Sverige wanted to hear that. They wanted me to be from The D. So I was.

"From Detroit, *ja*?" they would say. "You must be very tough girl! A very brave!"

Yes. I was A Very Brave, I would agree, nodding and smiling.

And then Johan would launch into a conversation in Svenska.

"*Ju, så jaghor attdessa nyabilbatterierverkligen ärvärt det omdu kan få demtill ett bra pris...*"

Johan and the vendor in question would then and have lots of laughter and brouhaha, leaving me with an inner monologue that went something like this:

OK...they're laughing. I should smile. But it would be crazy for me to think Svensk chatter about car batteries is funny, so if I smile they'll just think I'm an idiot. But looking like an idiot is better than looking like a frowning bitch, right? But what if that guy is saying something really crass about me? And I'm smiling? Do I look away?

And that was how I spent about four hours of each day at the conference, just hanging on Johan's arm, intermittently half-smiling into space and half-smiling at people speaking Svenska. It was this exercise, however, that made me realize just how much of the language I understood. Apparently learning to understand spoken language was far easier than learning to speak it yourself. This should be obvious to anyone who has interacted with a two-year-old human or a dog, but it caught me by surprise. My delight at realizing I understood nearly everything Johan said and about half of what those with non-Skåne accents were talking about was very soon squashed by the fact that all of the conversation was exclusively about car parts. No matter how intently I'd begin listening to their chatter, a combination of a few missed words and the mind-numbing subject matter soon left me back inside my own bored, bored head. It felt exactly like when I was five and my mom would stop in the grocery store or after church to talk to another adult about adult things. For. EVER. It was so boooooring. It was so unjuuuuuust. Someone pay attention to meeee! Doesn't anyone care about meeeee?

But you know, I reminded myself, I am a much cooler girlfriend than that. I love going places and socializing, and just because car stereo sound was the subject at hand didn't mean this wasn't my opportunity to make these excellent qualities known. So there I was, trying to maintain the aura of being an awesome girlfriend who isn't a bitch about car shows, like Louise. I was really just lucky to be taken along. I was determined to look grateful, no matter how close I felt my brain matter was to collapsing in on itself.

But just because it wasn't the getaway weekend about which I'd been dreaming, it wasn't all for naught. Johan and I did have fun. While canvassing the event, between Svensk car vendors, we held hands, giggled, and whispered snide comments about people walking by. Four or five times each day, Johan would receive a text from Annika giving him updates on Ludde. He'd share them all with me, pictures or text, and I was comforted by that, feeling that sharing this information was less disconcerting than concealing it would have been. It was annoying, but I refused to make my annoyance known. How could she even think of five things to say about Ludde in one day? He was one of the most mild-mannered creatures I'd ever seen, not one to exhibit surprising or reportable behavior. Clearly, this was altogether excessive. Whatever. She didn't ruin my time with Johan, despite the fact that she was clearly trying to do just that.

Whenever our group, which consisted of about ten other car friends of Johan's, would lump together and start discussing a plan, I would start to panic inside. I loved making plans. I had ideas for plans. I wanted to be in on the plans! But they were speaking Svenska!

"Johan, what are they saying?"

"Ah…they just…" he was half-answering, half-listening to the conversation. "They just discussing if we go out to the city for food or we eat here."

"Here," was the cafeteria. We'd eaten "here" for two days.

"Let's eat in the city! Johan! Tell them we want to eat in the city!"

I was back to being five and pulling on my mom's sleeve again.

"*Nej*, they just decided we're eating here," he said as the group started to move toward the cafeteria. "No one wants to spend cash. We go to the city for drinking later."

We did not go to the city for drinking later.

Later, we were back in our hotel room instead, which was nice and tidy and overlooked the actual, if far-distant, city of Stockholm. I was looking out the window at the skyline, wondering what there actually was to do to in the city. There must be bars and restaurants—or at least some things to walk around and look at. And it was only eight o'clock!

During my gazing, Johan had transferred himself from the shower into the bed. I turned around to see what appeared to be his sleeping form under the covers. No way he'd fallen asleep in under a minute. I took a flying leap and jumped onto the mattress.

"Natalie! You wake me up!" Johan was giving me a hard time, but he was smiling.

"Johan, come on, get up! Let's get dressed and go into the city!"

"How do we get into the city? Jakob's car is sort of busy on display and inside a building."

"Well…" While I hadn't considered that, I wasn't going to accept that Johan had known all along that we were actually going to a building for the weekend, not the city as he'd promised. "How were we going to go earlier?"

"Ah, we'd had to take a shuttle to the city," he groaned. "And then we might need a taxi…It would be so expensive."

"I'll pay for it."

"Natalie. You don't have any money."

"I have a credit card."

"Beauty, I am tired. I was driving all night," he cooed. "Just come to sleep."

I came to sleep. But I wasn't happy about it. We were leaving the next day. Johan had in fact driven *part* of the night, but that was actually two nights ago. I was beginning to feel like Svensk circadian rhythms must be wildly different to those of Americans. Like, ours had some actual rhythm to them. His was switched off and would not be revving up again that night.

So it wasn't the sort of weekend I expected. Johan and I didn't explore the tourist haunts of Stockholm (whatever they might have been) or dine by candlelight in exotic eateries or sip dark *öl* in northern Svensk taverns with the city folk. Talking about car stereos and looking at car stereos was, evidently, as adventurous as this adventure would be.

Getting to know Louise, however, really made my weekend.

"So why don't people just to go school forever?"

We were in the car on the way back south. Louise could not get over the education-costing-money thing. I could not get over it being so stinking free.

"Well, some sort of do," Louise said, looking alternately at her nails and the back of Jakob's head in the drivers' seat in front of her. "But mostly people just want to get done and get job, you know? Make money and get on with it."

Jakob, it turned out, was one of those Svensk rarities who did still go to school, but worked as well.

"He's on like, year seven or something ridiculous like that," Louise said of her boyfriend who was not three feet from her mouth.

It seemed he liked his job as an engineer, but was getting more training in another field. And there was all of the car stereo tinkering too.

"He's so boring all the time, with all of his things," his pouty girlfriend told me. "He's never around for weekends or nights out with friends because there is always class or this junk." She gestured at the car. Louise and Jakob had been together for more than three years. I assumed this banter must be a part of their dynamic. He must find her snarky comments and cold attitude adorable, or this wouldn't be going on. So I giggled at nearly everything she said.

Meeting Louise felt like a physical weight lifted from my chest. I wasn't compelled to be nice to her because she was my employer, or because she was allowing me to live with her. I didn't have to vie for her attention from TV and an internet forum by waiving sex under her nose. She wasn't taking me out for pizza once to please her employer only to never bother acknowledging me again. Louise clearly didn't give a shit about pleasing anyone. For once in nearly four months, I didn't have to either.

In fact, she seemed genuinely excited about meeting me. I hadn't been sure how serious she was when she first mentioned helping me find a publication for my writing, but she kept bringing it up again and again. Every time we'd hit on a new topic about American or Svensk culture, she'd say, "Oh, that would be perfect for a magazine. Everyone is going to love what you say about this one."

I was also feeling closer to my goal of getting a glimpse of "normal" Svenskar. It was becoming increasingly clear that the Waaras did not fit into this category, which was enormously validating.

"Anyway, you are more fun than *him*," Louise continued, again referencing Jakob. "You can come to Malmö and we'll *fika.* We'll talk about your writing for the magazine, we'll do other fun things too. You could use it. You need to come every weekend, I think."

Holy fucking shit. There is a God.

14
Fokuseras
Focus

There's nothing like being out of town and getting a fresh perspective to embolden one's sense of reality, is there? When returning to the Waara household on Monday morning, I determined it was time to open a Pandora's box that I'd long been ignoring. Would I confront Inger about her maniacal effort to gradually unload all of her familial obligations on to me? Would I insist that she legitimize my status in her country? Would I tell her that Svensk lessons were a part of our agreement and she needed to get my ass in a class ASAP? No. None of these things. So I and my reality-sense were only partially emboldened, I suppose.

I had decided that I was at a breaking point in my concern about Pia's food issues. I'd watched her more and more closely over the past several weeks, and her preoccupation with eating very little while taking pains to appear to be eating normally seemed to be increasing. Her desire to go to the gym had been steadily doing the same, and on the many nights when tending to the horses with Lisbeth interfered with me taking her to workout, she'd take the dogs out for endless walks that she clearly did not enjoy, sometimes in total darkness. For exercise. And she was just so skinny. The girl was way too skinny.

My internal battle at this point was between talking directly to Pia or discussing the issue with Inger. Because my role in their home was still so awkward and undefined, I decided that morning I'd have to take it up with Inger. If I was going to do the right thing here, I should probably do it in the right way, right? I wasn't going to try and overstep my bounds.

With my confidence regained from meeting Louise and her promise of writing work, I felt sure that this careful measure was exactly what Pia needed from me. She needed me to be one sane person in her world. Feeling preemptively heroic, I arrived at Ödmjuk Gård to find Inger in the kitchen. I greeted her and strode toward the fridge to grab some morning frukost. I was aware that me eating meals from their kitchen even though I lived at (or had been relegated to) Johan's was a point of tension, but what was I going to do? I was hungry, and Johan couldn't afford to feed me.

Fortunately, Inger was cheerful this morning.

"*God mooooooorgan*, Natalie!" she grinned "What a delight to see you! How was your holiday in the city? Do sit and tell me now."

Good 'ol Inger. Regardless of her ill and passive-aggressive treatment of me as an employee, she sure was warm and inviting when it came to small talk. I sort of liked the friendly side of her crazy.

"Oh, it was nice, Inger," I said, grabbing the *herrgårdost* from the refrigerator. "It was mostly just looking at cars, but it was nice to get away."

"Do sit," she repeated, patting the bench seat next to her by the bay window. "I want to hear about your adventure and what you took away."

Ugh. *I just did, lady,* I thought.

It seemed, however, like the perfect opportunity to have a nice, open conversation to lead into her youngest daughter's possible eating disorder. So I sat.

"I am sure it was terribly romantic to be with your lover in the city!" she exclaimed.

Holy shit, she really needed to stop calling Johan that. Particularly when the image of him I equated most with the weekend getaway was him faceplanted into the hotel bed as I thumbed through Svensk tourist materials and stared out the window. I was getting rather good at reading Svenska.

"Ha! Well, Johan was really occupied with the car show," I said. "You know, that was really the point of him going. I was just tagging along. But I met a really nice girl named Louise who lives in Malmö. Her boyfriend was in the competition, and so they were both with us the whole time."

Inger's mouth was frozen wide with this juicy detail. I could have reached over and put my fist in her mouth. Don't think I wasn't tempted to.

"It was so nice to spend the whole weekend with a girl my age," I continued. "We really got along well."

"Oh! Natalie! I am so very happy to hear this. And you shall become good friends and you will so enjoy her company in the future, I am sure. Now, I have something to ask you."

Inger was a transition ninja. It was anyone's guess when she'd close a conversation right up and start a new one before you knew what happened. One minute we were sitting together, having a nice meaningless chat, and now she wanted to ask me something. Excellent.

"I wonder if you'll humor me a moment and allow me to walk you through one of the exercises from Den Metod. It is but a brief series of questions, and I dare say I think you'll find these questions will lead to deep answers you may have been looking for for quite some time."

I let this inquiry sink in for a moment. I can't say I wasn't curious. It felt a bit like being tempted by a palm reader or reading a fortune cookie—except with even less confidence about the validity of the outcome. But okay, I'll bite.

"OK," I said cheerfully. "Sure, let's try it."

"Wooooonderful!" Inger was pumped. She dove right in.

"Now, Natalie, let us begin with agreeing to the premise that though you are here physically and we are so very glad to have you, and you are veeeery welcome here, that you might be not fully here with us in your mind. That there may be something from your home that keeps part of your mind attached there."

Hmm. This was curious. What should I reveal to her? I thought of all the bits of my life from home I could toss at her, to let her bat around like a kitten with a minnow. Should I tell her about Greg? No, that was too personal. My family? My missed career opportunities—whatever they might be? Should I tell her I missed being twenty-three and having friends and co-workers and going to the bar and being loud and having fun? I decided I could go down a road that would allow her only a measured amount of meat to sink her teeth into.

"Yeah, I guess that's true," I said.

"Natalie, I would like you to answer without thinking," Inger said, giving me plenty of time to anticipate her question and prepare an answer. "What is it from your home that you are feeling attached to at this time?"

"Oh, my family," I said. "Without a doubt, I miss them every day."

"Mmm…I see," Inger said, nodding thoughtfully. She paused for a moment and then continued. "And what feelings do you feel when you say you 'miss' them?"

"Well," I said, "I guess I feel guilty. I am sad about them not being in my life every day, but I guess not being there makes me feel guilty more than sad. The last few years have been pretty rough for my family. I feel that I left to go off and have an adventure, and they're still there sorting everything out."

There we go. That was truish.

"I understand that must be very difficult," Inger said. "And how does your presence there benefit your family?"

"I'm…well, I'm the only kid in the state really," I said. "My sister lives in Texas, and she has for four years now—ever since right after my parents divorced—so I'm the only one there to really…I don't know, be there, I guess."

"Tell me now, dear—and please don't take offense, but answer directly—why do you believe your physical presence to be so important to your mother and father?"

Well, I mean, not every parent rents a foreigner to care for their children when they're bored of them, I thought. *Some of them just like to be around their kids.*

"It's not that *I'm* that important," I said out loud. "But there aren't that many of us. I'm 25 percent of my immediate family, so…we all sort of matter a lot."

"But your sister left."

"Mmm. Yeah. That's true," I said sadly.

My voice and eyes said we'd hit on a deep family sore spot, but inside I was giggling uncontrollably. My sister, who by all accounts inherited all of the kind, thoughtful, well-meaning genes in our family, was an excellent placeholder for whatever deep-hidden truth Inger was so eager to uncover in me. Sure Inger, my unhappiness in Sverige isn't so much about being at the mercy of a slave-driving cult leader, but because my sister moved to Texas four years ago. Do go on.

And she did, for some time. Finally, she asked a question I knew was coming. She had told me back when first explaining the tenets of this pseudo-religious psychology thing that the real breakthroughs always happen when she surprises her clients with the request to quickly recall their earliest memory. When they do this, they invariably produce the first moment when the root trauma of their existence took hold, and they can then work through a lifetime of issues by resolving that moment. The idea was that before that first moment, we don't even exist. We're like God—who, if you recall, doesn't know that He or we exist at all. So our first memory marks the initial trauma that wakes us up to our existence. It all goes downhill from there, apparently. Because existing is bad, and you probably need an unbalanced Svensk housewife to fix it for you.

So I was ready for it.

"Natalie dear," Inger pursed her large, brick-red lips with surprising success. "Think quickly now to the first moment of your life that you remember. Quickly—what is your first memory?"

"OK," I said in a serious tone. I took a second to sigh and widen my eyes as if overwhelmed with such an intense task. "My first memory is when I was at Disney World with my family. Well, I know my whole family was there, but I only remember my mom. I'm in a stroller, and my mom spins me around and tells me to look up at Donald Duck in a really excited voice. I look up, and there's—you know, the huge Donald Duck character, staring at me, and waving."

I paused for a moment for dramatic effect.

"I was so scared! I knew I wasn't supposed to be scared because my mom was excited, but I was just totally freaked out about this huge duck monster wearing a hat and waving at me. I don't know if I thought he was going to eat me or what, but I was super scared. So I cried."

I looked up at Inger with a smile. Analyze that.

Inger nodded for a minute while staring blankly at me, making some "hmmm" and "ahhh" noises under her breath as she did so. Clearly, she was trying to come up with some way of connecting my guilt of leaving Michigan, my sibling angst, and my fear of Donald Duck. She had nothing. I felt pretty proud of myself. I also really wanted to change the subject before she came up with something.

"It is striking," she finally said. "Sometimes we must explore deeper, after the mind has had time to rest, to truly interpret what all of these things mean."

"OK," I said. "Yeah, I can understand that. By the way, there's something I've been meaning to ask you about."

"Oh yes, dear? What is that?" Inger was suddenly just as eager to change the subject.

"I wonder if you have had any concerns about Pia's special diet."

"Oh! Ha HA!" As usual, Inger was quick to laugh at the least funny statement in the conversation. "I know, dear! It does seem a bit odd, doesn't it? *Jaaapp*? I felt the same way when she first proposed cutting out all sugars, but I must say, I'm quite happy with the result."

"The result?"

"Why yes," she continued. "Had you been here just a few months earlier—and we would have so welcomed you then, the summer was sooooo busy!—you would have noticed the difference. Pia came to me and said she'd been feeling 'puffy,' particularly in her face, and she wished to try this diet that she thought would be healthier for her. Indeed! Her face is visibly less puffy now! I am so pleased!"

"So…was she overweight before?"

"Oh goodness, no," Inger was in hysterics now. "She is such a tiny girl, now isn't she? But her face was just truly quite puffy, and I have a client who comes to my Metod weekends who had some excellent recipes for Pia's diet, and she came to the house and taught us to make some of them, and we're just so pleased! Now, I don't doubt I couldn't benefit from being as faithful to her diet as she is. I look in the mirror now, and I can hardly believe what I see!

"Oh! Ha HA! NAAAAtalie! When you are an old lady like me you may feel the same way. I have this stomach—" she leaned toward me and forcefully groped her lower belly as she spoke, " that I cannot seem to make smaller no matter what I try! And I was such a tiny girl as well when I was young..."

Inger continued her rant about her extremely fit youth and how proud she was of her daughter's unhealthy eating patterns for quite a bit longer before laughing me off to make her husband's bed.

Inger and I were equally unsuccessful in our ulterior motives that morning, I decided as I looked for a safe place to put Jan's dirty underwear, stuffed inside his pillowcase as always. I shook them out, put the pillow into a fresh case, and used the old linens as glove to stick the rumpled undies back in place. This was my job.

I was feeling defeated. The Pia-conversation had gone exactly the opposite of how I hoped it would. Inger seemed to be not only a supporter, but also possibly the instigator of the problem. How can your mother, who doesn't believe her body exists, still manage to pass on her body image issues to her kid? Going to Pia about it now would be far more complicated. Maybe I should just leave it alone, I considered. Can you just leave such a thing alone?

***

My concern for Pia could hardly suppress my excitement for my new focus in life: being published in Sverige. True, everything else I'd gotten excited about thus far had turned out to be a bust, but what Louise was offering me was different. Writing was familiar territory. It was something I knew I was good at, and I knew made me happy—two variables that had been entirely missing in every Svensk endeavor I'd thus far undertaken. This could conceivably be a whole new reason to be in this country. I dared to wonder whether, if it went well, I could even quit the Waaras completely. I couldn't wait to get started. I just needed access to a computer.

With my little laptop not in working order, I was a bit lost. A typical member of my generation, this left me completely unable to compose any serious material. Was I supposed to write it by hand? With a pen and paper? That was fine for journaling and all, but for writing a refined piece of editorial journalism, a keyboard was an absolute necessity. How could I write with an appropriate narrative voice if my longhand couldn't keep up with my thoughts? How would I know if I'd overused the passive voice were the little paperclip man not there to alert me?

But Johan had a computer, so he could be my savior. However, since he spent every waking minute belittling the under-informed on his car stereo forum, I'd already been pushing his patience with my one email check per evening. I couldn't write clever articles about an American's perspective on America for Svenskar under such constraints. I needed time to hem and haw and stare at the screen and alternately type nonsense and delete the nonsense. I needed my fingers to quicken and slow with the pace of my thoughts. The only time I'd been allowed or had time to use the Waaras' computer was after everyone had gone to bed, and I was no longer there after they'd gone to bed. Dilemma!

There was only one answer: go rogue on the Waaras' computer during work. Even the slightest potential of getting a writing gig in Sverige was obviously far more important than the Waaras' hallway being vacuumed and mopped for a third time in a week. I therefore felt completely justified in allotting myself an hour a day to work on my writing, working off notes I'd begrudgingly written by hand the night before.

The stealthy new habit did require Inger's absence, however. Fortunately she'd taken to having many errands and "special sessions" with "clients" nearly every day. As soon as her large red head was carried away by the larger, redder Volvo, I'd prepare a big pot of French press *kaffe*, fill my large IKEA cup to the brim, and steal over to the family computer. Unlike the one in Inger's office, this desktop was on the top floor, right in front of a large window. It allowed me to keep tabs on the entire front yard and driveway. As the damn thing took seven minutes to turn on and off, this was an absolute necessity. Once I had everything up and running, it was just me and writing, my greatest love.

These were my best hours in Sverige. It was a little shocking and more than a bit disconcerting to realize that nothing I'd found on this side of the planet was as delightful as exactly what I'd been doing before I'd left. Sure, I'd just been freelance writing for the city newspaper, writing entertainment reviews after putting in a full day at a regular job, but after three months of vacuuming, I couldn't seem to remember why I'd left such a great gig. Apparently, I thought I needed to broaden my horizons and find something new and challenging to write about.

Well, I thought, as I stared at the blinking cursor on the old desktop monitor that first day, *if I want being a maid on a farm for a crazy family and their cult-leader mom to count as broadening my horizons, I'd better make this happen.*

My heart racing from equal parts caffeine, clandestine behavior, and excitement, I opened my notebook on the desk, positioned my fingers gingerly on the keys, took a breath, and went to work.

Hey Louise!
How's your Tuesday going? I'm done with a first draft of the shoe etiquette piece. It works as an intro to the whole idea of the column too, so let me know if you think it works. I definitely need some Swedish feedback. Johan will only say "It's good," and he's probably just saying that to be nice. Be honest! I'm so excited to

get started on the next ones!
nat

Here's the draft:

Shoe Etiquette and Nylon Ropes: Why American behavior shouldn't be based on Tom Cruise

When I moved to Sweden three months ago, I asked my employer why she and her family looked in the US for an English-speaking au pair when Great Britain is so close by. Her answer shocked me:

"The kids wouldn't have it. It's much cooler to have an American around."

Really? These kids had never met me, and they supposed me to be cooler than everyone in Great Britain? I wasn't sure whether to be impressed with myself or crumble under the pressure. Mental note: write home. Tell everyone how cool I am.

Now, I've been to high school; I understand being seen as cool because of the clothes you wear, the music you listen to, or the friends have. But for simply being from the US? For all these Swedish kids knew, I could be a Texas cowgirl, an East Coast career woman, or a Californian valley girl. Would they have thought me equally cool were I any of these things? How could I be cool simply by having the dumb luck of being born somewhere between New York City and San Francisco?

While I'd never complain about being cool in the eyes of teenagers (don't worry, I'm quite sure I've debunked their suspicions by now), I have found that their assumption about my coolness was only one of many ideas people have about Americans.

As it turns out, life as an American abroad can take on many forms; sometimes I'm treated like a celebrity, at others as an annoyance, and even occasionally like an interesting specimen to question and study. The only thing that is true across the board is that everyone seems to have the impression that to some extent, they already know me. I'm American, after all, so there must be a few things that are absolutely true about me. Here are a few of the generalizations I've heard thus far:

"You must be one of the few fit Americans. Most of you are fat."

"Have you sued anyone? American sue each other all the time."

"What's wrong with you? You and all your American friends love Bush."

"How is it that Bush is president when all Americans hate Bush?"

"Americans all smoke marijuana, don't they? How often do you do drugs?"

"How does it work to be walking around in America when everyone has guns? Isn't it scary?"

I can't even begin to explain how varied these statements are in terms of truth and complete nonsense. Let's just say that it would be a stretch to say that I personally am a fat, litigation-crazy, Bush-loving, Bush-hating, pot-smoking gun owner. I'm really only two of these things. Which two? Well, let's get to know each other a bit better first, shall we?

For the sake of simplicity, let's begin with an easy one: shoe etiquette. I was recently asked by a Swede why Americans don't take their shoes off when they enter houses.

"Well," I responded, "we actually do take them off when requested. Some houses are shoe-houses, and some houses are no-shoe houses. You just have to ask when you get there."

This caused an intense moment of confusion. My Swedish friend decided there was no way we didn't have a national shoe etiquette policy, and I therefore was wrong. No, he said, Americans just don't take them off ever, which is apparently incredibly rude here.

Besides, he told me, he watches plenty of American TV and movies and no one ever takes their shoes off when entering a house. As far as he was concerned, this proved it.

Let me clarify: in the twenty-three years I have spent living in the US, I've been in a quite a few houses in quite a few states. It's a big country with lots of different types of people and climates. Some people want you to take your shoes off. Some people don't care. End of story.

But let's back up to the fact that my friend's entire defense of his opinion of American shoe-wearing behavior was based on what he had seen on TV and in movies. I suddenly think I see where some of the confusion about all sorts of American behavior comes from.

I have a secret to share: Americans don't barge into every house without taking their shoes off, and they don't do much dangling from nylon ropes in tightly-protected vaults to steal large diamonds either. Tom Cruise does that in nearly every movie he's in, but that says nothing about typical American behavior. I don't even know where one buys nylon rope, let alone those weird chest straps he's always wearing.

If there's a reason behind the lack of shoe removal in the American media, I can pretty much guarantee that the matter all comes down to dollars and cents. Just as entertainment producers know that Tom Cruise dangling from a nylon rope will attract viewers, they also know that watching Tom Cruise pause at a doorway to untie his sneakers isn't all that thrilling.

The moral of the story? We're a nation of incredible variety, and you'd be hard-pressed to find a single behavior that "we all" do. One thing we don't spend much time on is the shoe rule. Call us slobs, but in my experience, even those who care enough to ask people to remove their shoes don't care all that much. The greater moral? Don't take anything you see on TV and movies as a reflection of typical American behavior, whether it's perfunctory household etiquette or high-adrenaline diamond heists.

But as far as assuming I'm super cool because I'm American goes, you can feel free to continue with that generalization. I like that one.

And *send.* It had been all of two days since Louise and I had parted when I eagerly sent this first essay to her inbox. I decided to hold off on sending any more until I'd gotten her feedback on this one. After all, this could be nothing like what she expected. Perhaps she'd find the tone insulting to Svenskar, or there were other major adjustments to be made.

Although I was still waiting to hear back from her by Friday morning, I couldn't have felt better. I may have been taking inappropriately long writing breaks every day, but I was also working twice as hard as I had been before; that was to say, I was back to working at a regular pace. I had my writing to think about all day as I scrubbed and dusted. I had a whole new future. There was no stopping my hopes from climbing as high as they could.

By the end of the week, I had one more essay finished and about three more I was itching to write over the weekend. I had plenty of time to write after work that night, as Johan was in Helsingborg at a *julbord* with Danne and his wife, Bergit. Apparently I wasn't invited. Or, as Johan said, "It is not the sort of *julbord* you would want to be at." Not having been to a *julbord* at all, I assumed any *julbord* would be a *julbord* I would want to attend. There would be other *julbords*, he assured me, and I would go to those. But I really wasn't listening, nor did I care what his excuse was for not taking me along. I had writing to do.

Oh—what is a *julbord*, you ask? My, my. Where do I begin?

A *julbord* is a Christmas dinner. It's a buffet. It's a Christmas buffet over which Svenskar go apeshit. Well, as much as Swedes go apeshit over anything. Much like *fika*, the word *julbord* seemed to work for the meal itself, the party around it, and the act of attending the event. You could have them at home with small groups, or in restaurants with dozens of people, or in huge banquet rooms with hundreds of people. Most Svenskar went to multiple *julbords* per year, and pretty much every Christmas party was a *julbord*. It was, essentially, Christmas itself.

But the thing that made *julbords* weird was their uniformity. It didn't matter what the size or venue of the *julbord* was, it was always the same food, prepared in the same way. Now, I know Americans have similar menus for Thanksgiving, so I can't be too critical there. But outside of turkey, stuffing, and cranberry sauce, each family has their own take on the meal, including secret turkey basting recipes, or unique stuffing philosophies.

Not so with *julbords*. The *julbord* meal was the world's most predictable buffet. Here was what's on every stinking one:

Köttbullar (Swedish meatballs. Not too bizarre.)

Kåldolmar (Cabbage rolls. Think stuffed grape leaves except, you know, with cabbage.)

Potatis Korv (Christmas sausage. As with all sausage, I was completely uninterested, but did roll my internal eyes every time I heard the name, noting that Svenskar would naturally put potatoes in their sausage.)

Kokt Rödkål (Red cabbage. The recipe is so fancy it's described in full by the dish's name: cooked red cabbage. Mmm…)

Fiskbullar (Fishballs. Yup.)

Doppigrytan (Literally, "dip in the pot." Dip what into a pot of what? Bread into hot ham juice. Also an idiom for sex. Because apparently

nothing turns on a Svensk male more than thinking about dipping his bread into some fine lady's hot ham juice.)
Matjes Sill (Some sort of herring)
Sill i dillsås (Herring in dill sauce)
Sill i vitlöksås (Herring in garlic sauce)
Kippered sill (These fuckers are wild about herring.)
Lax Kallrökt (Smoked salmon, in case your seafood itch has yet to be sufficiently scratched.)
Jansson's frestelse (Jansson's Temptation! This is essentially scalloped potatoes with a secret ingredient. Can you guess the secret? It's anchovies!)
Julskinka (Swedish ham. That hot ham juice has to come from somewhere, right?)
Sillsallad (Herring salad. Are you surprised at this point?)
Fyllda Ågghalvor (Deviled eggs. Now there's some good 'ol Christmas food!)

It was one weird, overloaded, awkward celebratory meal in which every item appeared to be a side dish. But I'm getting ahead of myself. I was still a week away from learning all this by attending my first *julbord.* On the night in question, Johan had disappeared to one such mysterious event and/or meal, leaving me to my task. Knowing the Waaras were taking me to a *julbord* the following week with some farm association people, I was quite happy to be writing in peace on Johan's laptop without him or his skepticism.

He was skeptical of Louise. He didn't seem to think she was in any position to just look around and find a place for me to be published. I also had detected that he wasn't a huge fan of Louise as a person, based on the number of times he'd said things like "Louise is a total bitch." But that was fair; Louise was a total bitch to Jakob, who was Johan's friend. And I was clearly way more excited about this writing project than I'd been about him or his stupid car stereos for weeks, so I could easily understand his negativity. Still, I wasn't about to trust that someone who had never read a book knew anything about the Svensk publishing industry. The population of this country was about the same as that of New Jersey. I was pretty sure that their publishing sector couldn't be all that huge.

And so I sat down in Johan's quiet, dimly lit house with Ludde at my feet, and I began to write. I wrote, happily and manically. Hours later, I overcame my concern about sending Louise additional essays before hearing back from her and sent her two more. Realizing that it was past nine and I hadn't eaten, I decided to scrounge around the kitchen for some food.

Its state of mid-renovation made Johan's kitchen feel constantly disastrous. We really only ever went in to retrieve food, which was always eaten on the couch. Not spending time in the kitchen well served Johan's quiet disdain for supplying me with food. I understood that having another mouth to feed hadn't exactly been carefully calculated into his budget, so I tried to minimize the burden all I could. There was no standing with the refrigerator door ajar, hunting for just the right snack to satisfy a specific craving. There was ascertaining what food was available for consumption, and the acquisition of said food.

Tonight I took the time to browse. There honestly wasn't a whole lot to look at—just a couple of different cheeses, and some tomatoes sitting on the top shelf of the fridge. I'd already resolved to make myself some pasta when my eyes drifted to the door in the far corner of the tiny kitchen. It led to the basement. I'd never been in Johan's basement. He'd never allowed me. To be fair, his secrecy was out of embarrassment; he said the basement was so disgusting, so filthy, that he was ashamed for me to see it.

"I'll clean it someday, and you will see," he'd say, sprawled out on the gray, rumpled couch. "It's not so awful when it's tidy, but you got the laundry and the cats' boxes there too...you just don't want to bother. It's not good."

Sure he'll clean it. Like he'll get around to finishing his cupboards one of these years. Curiosity got the best of me now. How bad could it be? I walked over to the door and pulled it open. The stairs were right before me, but where they led, I couldn't tell. It was intensely dark, but as I stepped down onto the landing that preceded the steps, I could see there was crap littered all up and down them. Boxes, laundry, tools, what have you, the stairs seemed to be swallowed up by the junk as much as they were by the darkness. How he made it up and down to do his laundry, I could not even imagine. Not seeing a light, nor encouraged by the influx of trash or distinct smell of dirty litter boxes below, my curiosity was officially satiated. Wanting to get back to the pasta, I turned back toward the doorway when a small whiteboard on the basement-side of the door revealed a handwritten note:

I love Janne!

The bubbly exclamation was surrounded by hearts and enthusiastic scribbles. Well, I hadn't written that. Unlike me, the person who did had clearly loved Janne. Or still did. Seeing Annika's handwriting proclaiming her love broke my heart a little. She had not been in the same kind of relationship with "Janne" that I currently was. It wasn't just about how deep her feelings for him were; I couldn't understand the cultural nuances that had tied them together, like knowing the nickname for Johan, or writing love notes in a mutual second language. It was also a stark reminder that I truly had no idea how or why or even when their relationship ended. Who knows how long ago she'd written it? Did the timeline, or her current feelings, really matter? Johan was the one who hadn't erased it.

When I sat down on the couch, Ludde immediately jumped up from his bed and set his enormous droopy face on my knee. I loved Ludde. He was the one Svensk who let me speak his native tongue to him. Unfortunately, my dog-command vocabulary was limited to "*gå och ligga*," so I lost my giant friend back to his bed for the sake of speaking and being understood. Everything I did here was for the wrong reason.

Any amount of grimness I'd felt from having bumped into Annika's note instantly disappeared when I sat back down at the computer with my bowl of pasta. I had an email waiting from Louise:

> HI!
> I like it! its really good! I want to read more! hehe. And i want to know wich of the two things u are.. hehe.. are u a gunowner or what? Iknow ure not fat so.. haha. Pot smoker? *smile*
>
> Perfekt! I really really hope that the magazine will think this is as good idea as we think!!!!!!!!!!!!!
>
> :-)
>
> Can u send a photo ofyourself and a short story about you? I think I need to send that withthe e-mail to the magazine.
>
> I was thinking.. or rather: I was talking to my co-worker here about the idea *smile* and the magazine I suggested is a magazine with the target group younger women and I said, I don´t know what´s best, this magazine or maby a smaller newspaper. And she asked why not Aftonbladet (the biggest swedish newspaper). Well I said. Yes why not.
>
> What do you think.
>
> A magazine (smaller target group comes out once a month) or a newspaper (the biggest in sweden? comes out everdy day maby your artikle would be online at www.aftonbladet.se)? Is it aming to high?
>
> Louise

What did I think about her trying to get me published in Sweden's biggest newspaper? Ah…I'd take it! I immediately went about reediting my three additional essays and sent them off. I'd chosen the topics of Americans suing each other all the time, Americans being fat, and Americans all carrying weapons everywhere. I couldn't have found myself more charming, informative, and dazzlingly clever. I couldn't wait for the entire Swedish populace to find me so as well. But I had a lot of work to do. Louise had attached a long list of interesting topics she thought Swedes would love for an American to address:

- What aboul that Bush (All love or hate Bush)
- Drogs/Marijuana in the US. Dos everyone do it?
- Are Americans stuiped about the politics.
- Education system, high scool, college and so on. Who pays for it and so on. Facts about the educational system. How many goes to scool.
- Political system, what the f*ck went on (during the election) inFlorida? Facts about the political system.
- Social sercurity (a big/important issue in sweden), poverty and homeless people. Swedish prejudice: U don´t get ANY help in the US whatso ever. If ure fucked ure fucked.
- Partying, bars pubs, discos, kareoke and so on. Who goes where (allages).
- Vaccation - do u have vaccation time? When, were and how. (Swedeshave 4 - 5 weeks off work in the summers and 1 - 2 weeks at x-mas. Thisis holy to swedes).
- I would be scared shitless to get muged, raped, carjacked, ormurdered if I went to the US. Crime. Can I walk down a street in a bigcity without getting killed?
- Native americans way of life. Where are the native americans and dothey ride horses like way back when..?
- Fashion, where u buy your clothes (We have HM, what do u have?)
- What is the strangest thing about the US in your opinion?
- Does americans care about the rest of the world or just themselfs?

So much to analyze and write about! These topics could keep me going for years. Or, given my current pace, at least three weeks. I went right to work. A few hours later, I'd finished a first draft of a smart little piece on fashion and was just dozing merrily off on the couch when my phone beeped with a text.

Ah…Johan must be on his way back to me just in time to climb into bed and keep me warm. Yea.

N., we are need ride. You can come get us Honey? You're beutyfal!

What? I sat up and looked out the window—it was practically a snowstorm outside. I not only had no idea where he was in Helsingborg, but I also had no car. Really. Johan, knowing he'd be gone before I was done with work had had me take a little old car that belonged to one of his clients over the Waaras' and back. He was supposed to be fixing it. I had no idea what was wrong with it, but he assured me it would make the five-minute round trip just fine. But an adventure to who knows where in a blizzard? At—what time was it?—2:30 in the morning? No. He had to be kidding.

You're kidding, right? I wrote back. *I can't drive a broken car to Helsingborg. I don't even know where you are.*

I confidently put the phone on the coffee table and closed my eyes. I might as well fall asleep. I wasn't about to go anywhere.

But five minutes later, my phone beeped again.

Honey you are have to come. We are sooooooooooooooo drank... We all want to see you and be safely. Danne an Bergit need you to ride too.

This was ridiculous. Two minutes later another text came in with completely hopeless directions that I could never follow. I broke the cardinal sin of cellular phones for cheap Svenskar: I placed a phone call.

"Johan, you're crazy. How do I know the car will even make it to Helsingborg?"

"Ahhhh! Iss not bad, Natalie. It will be make it fine. We are way stuck though if you don't come. We have no where to stay and no way to get home."

I let the line go silent.

"Natalie?"

"Yes."

"You want me to come home, yeah? You miss me?"

Sigh.

"Yeah, I miss you, Johan. Where are you?"

An hour later I was driving white-knuckled through winter slush on the Svensk freeway with Johan riding shotgun and Danne and Bergit roaring with laughter in the backseat with some dude I'd never seen before who either spoke zero English or was too drunk to try.

Unfortunately, the other three of them had no problem communicating with me.

"Natlie," Bergit was laughing, "are you really so young, because you are driving like you are so very old!"

"Really," Johan said, pretending to be way more sober than he was and seemingly embarrassed by my driving. "The limit is ninety, and it's really fine to actually drive at ninety."

They'd been doing this for twenty minutes straight. The speed at which I was driving was alternately annoying and entertaining them to no end. Danne and Bergit also seemed to have completely different ideas of how to get to their house. *That asshole in the backseat had better be planning on going home with them*, I thought. I sure wasn't making another stop after Danne's, and I was in no mood to be polite to houseguests. My ears and cheeks were burning. Johan, apparently, was still waiting for an answer.

"Natalie. You're driving eighty-five."

"Yes, Johan," I said quietly and sharply. "I realize that. I also realize that eighty-five is not that much fucking slower than ninety. And you should realize that it's after three in the morning, the roads are terrible, it's snowing, and I'm in this country illegally, driving a car that doesn't belong to me. Or you."

Well, that worked for about five minutes. That was how long it took for Danne and Bergit to again disagree on how to get to their house, and the entire car to forget that I'd prefer not to be made fun of for how I was driving after picking up their drunk asses in the middle of the fucking night.

But as pissed as I was that moment, I knew I had a whole weekend of writing ahead of me. I couldn't have been more delighted. I began to outline my next essay in my head—which would obviously not be about Native Americans' horse-riding behavior—and finally was able to block out their harassment. Smiling to myself and making plans to wake up before Johan could get his hands on his computer, I slowly pushed the accelerator down, inching the needle toward ninety-five.

15
Klart som Korvspad
Something becomes obvious
Literally: As clear as the leftover water from boiling sausages.

The following Thursday came, and I hadn't heard from Louise since sending off my latest batch of articles that weekend, but I wasn't too worried. She was probably entirely overwhelmed by the volume I'd generated already, and had her hands full enough trying to make all the right contacts and whatnot to make it happen. And she had her actual job. I'm sure she was busy with that too. Besides, I would be going to my first *julbord* with the Waaras the next night, and my brain was already spinning with anticipation of the potential essay that could emerge from what would surely be a content-ripe experience.

Meanwhile, I was busy making Johan join in my revelry. I forced him outdoors to go on chilly walks with Ludde and me, made him dinner (complete with ingredients pilfered from the Waara kitchen), I kept him company in the garage as he worked on his crazy sound car, asking all sorts of questions about how it worked—I let the breath of new life found by my writing exhale all over our relationship.

"Well, aren't you just a bunch of sunshine?" Johan smiled at me from across the couch. We were sharing an evening pot of *glögg*, which was far and away the best part of the Svensk *jul*. I'd used my emergency-only credit card to get a couple extra items from City Gross that day. *Glögg* was worth a lifetime of credit card debt. I grinned at him over my warm cup.

"I know," I said. "I'm delightful, aren't I?"

"And this is all about the writing thing you're doing with Louise?"

"Well, sort of…" I briefly considered his feelings before confirming the inquiry outright. I didn't want him to think this project had a stronger influence on my mood than he did. You know boys. They always need to think they're the best thing you have going on.

"It's just that my job at the Crazies' was really getting me down before, and I couldn't pull myself out of it. It's hard for me to not have a job that means something to me, or to feel like I'm at least working toward something. I love writing, Johan. I love it. And this project is something that is my own. It makes me feel less immobile and trapped."

"You are feeling trapped, honnnnay?" Johan was on the ball at once. He scooted close to me on the couch, put his arm around me, and looked genuinely concerned. Oh Johan. Sometimes he was a complete dud, and other times he could be utterly sweet.

"Well," I giggled, "yeah, of course I am. I'm an adult who has to ask permission from her crazy employer to do anything, and then wait for her boyfriend to come pick her up every day. I'm not used to relying on people for every little thing. You know us Americans; we love our freedom."

Johan's eyes laughed at my feigned George W. Bush-style Texan drawl, but the rest of his face remained serious. "And do you think you'd feel less trapped if you had your own car to drive?" He gazed somewhere around my forehead while tucking a stray lock of hair behind my ear. "Would that help my little American feel free?"

"Well, of course it would," I said, practically laughing, "but the Waaras' won't even spring for my preferred type of cheese on their grocery list. I hardly think they're going to let me take over one of their precious antique station wagons."

"Ah, but I have an extra car."

"Johan, you have two cars. And one is in pieces."

"There is a third in my driveway."

He was referring to the tiny, old Volvo coupe he'd had me drive last weekend to pick up him and his drunken *julborders*. He must be kidding. That was someone else's car. And it was broken.

"It's fixed! But the guy who owns it is so old, and he's not expecting it back for weeks. You drive it for a while, and we'll decide what to do when I must return it."

And so he gave me a car. It was the most generous, if least ethical, thing anyone had done for me in this country. I was touched. Appropriately so, we then proceeded to have a really great night. It was just an ordinary Thursday, but it felt like one of our original nights of fun together. We listened to music, talked, and giggled, and Johan didn't even once look at his computer or turn on the TV.

It was almost midnight when we were stretched out on the couch together, talking softly, all warm and buzzy from the *glögg*. For the past couple of weeks we'd been in the habit of falling asleep with our heads on opposite ends of the couch. Tonight, we shared a pillow. I was scooping the last bits of *glögg*-soaked raisins and almonds from the bottom of my cup with a tiny spoon when Johan sat up and again turned on his concerned tone.

"I am so glad that writing make you happy, and I think you should keep doing it. But do you think maybe Louise isn't who you should have help you? Maybe you could do it on your own?"

"Johan, I wouldn't have the first clue how to do it on my own. Louise has all the right contacts in the publishing industry. I don't know which publications carry what type of content and who would be interested in me. Or how to reach the right people. And she speaks Swedish, so that's pretty helpful."

He didn't look convinced.

"Look Johan, I know Louise is a total bitch to Jakob. But she seems to like me, and I think this is going to be a good arrangement."

"So, do you know how you will be paid? Will Louise take some of the pay for setting it up? You trust she will just send you cash in the mail or something? You have no account here."

"Um…well, I hadn't really thought about the money. I guess being paid would be helpful, but it's not the only reason to have your work published."

"Nah…we don't do things for free here. You must be paid for your work. I feel…I just worry you may be taken advantage of. Or you will do all this for nothing."

"Why would you think that? Because you don't like Louise?"

Johan was visibly struggling with what he wanted to say. This was fairly astounding coming from this smooth-talking Svensk. He sighed.

"You are making reasons for her not getting back to you about your writing like she is so busy, but she seems to have plenty of time to talk to Annika about you.

"Annika?"

"*Jaaap*."

"That doesn't make any sense. Louise told me she barely knew Annika. She said she'd only met her a couple of times."

"Well," Johan was looking at his hands, "she met her again, I guess."

Clearly this information came from Annika, so I immediately dismissed it as biased. So what if Annika and Louise ran into each other? Why would I believe anything Annika said they'd talked about?

Johan said that Louise had told her about the writing project and made fun of me for thinking I was "some sort of writer."

"Annika said she thought your contrast of Tom Cruise and Swedes taking shoes off was kinda, you know, naïve, I guess she says?"

"She showed her my writing?" The *glögg* had already made my body warm, but now my face was burning hot.

"*Jaaap.*"

He also said that Louise had reported how irritated I'd been about Annika's constant texting while we were in Stockholm. I was in shock. How did this happen? Louise had asked me what Annika was like that weekend; she'd actually egged me on to say bad things about Johan's ex, but I honestly didn't know enough to report. Louise was obviously planning to tell her everything the entire time.

"She also asked me what it was like to be dating someone who was so poor," Johan said.

"What?"

"Louise told her that you came from a really poor family and had to work while you were in college. She said it was probably why you came here because you needed the work."

"Excuse me?"

What was it like to date a poor person? Wow. What an excellent priest. Shocking though it had been, the least Christian-sounding question I'd ever heard confirmed Louise's betrayal. Johan didn't even know she and I had talked about working during college. This had all been a ruse. Our friendship, the writing assignments—the whole point was to gather dirt on me for her friend's pleasure.

I cried.

Johan held me as my tears began to slowly drench the couch cushion. After all this, after getting my hopes up repeatedly about this place and these people, how else could I have reacted? I missed home. I missed my mom, and I missed my dad. I missed having people around me I understood and could trust. I missed normalcy. I missed Greg. Had he ever hurt me so badly? Maybe. I couldn't remember. All I could remember at that moment was that he made me feel so protected. He would have protected me from this.

But Greg wasn't there; Johan was. While he might have been betraying me as well, what with his various lengthy trips to attend to Annika's "glove box," and going off on drunken *julbords* to which I was not invited, I couldn't bring myself to care about those things. He was doing a satisfactory job of being there at that moment, and that was something.

Part of me wanted, between sobs, to explain that this sort of thing didn't happen to me. I was really nice and fun and had lots of friends and virtually no enemies, and where I came from people were fucking nice, dammit, and they didn't promise you the one thing that could redeem the terrible and irreversible decision you had made that resulted in all this loneliness and misery only to stab you in the back. But I couldn't talk. I couldn't manage it.

Thankfully, mercifully, Johan seemed to understand. He said nice things. He told me how sorry he was for telling me, but that he didn't want to see me taken advantage of. He said I was wonderful and kind and beautiful and how he didn't know how anyone could say anything bad about me. He reminded me that I had a car at my disposal now, so I could be more independent. He was actually very, very good. And I fell asleep next to him, finally exhausted of my tears, reorienting myself to the fact that Johan was what I had here, and he was kind to me, and I should be glad for him.

* * *

I continued to be glad for Johan. In the days that followed, he made an effort to keep up the pace of activity that I'd set during my brief period of rejuvenation. He took me to breakfast at the baguette place one morning, and actually took me to a movie—an American movie, no less, in a real movie theater in Helsingborg. I hadn't seen him so intent on pleasing me since we first met. It reminded me of Greg's complaint that I was too self-sufficient. He never felt like I really needed him enough, and that made him feel worthless.

So maybe he'd had a point, and this was what he meant. Never having been this helpless before, I'd never needed this kind of support. Letting Johan build me back up was actually delightful. Had I just learned how to let myself need someone, and to let that someone feel needed? It sure didn't feel good to me to need someone in that way, but it did seem to have a positive effect on Johan. I wondered if Greg could find happiness with this version of me who knew how to need someone. If I'd gotten low enough, maybe he could have played the role he'd always wanted in our relationship—the one picking me back up. I wondered if he'd get the chance to try, even as I giggled at one of Johan's jokes on the way home from the movies.

* * *

If my housework had been lackluster before the short-lived writing project brouhaha, it was now downright abysmal. I'd literally done nothing all day Friday. When the kids got home, I had a handful of DVDs from Johan's and asked them which one they wanted to watch with me. They decided on Michael Moore's documentary on American gun violence, *Bowling for Columbine*, and we all plopped down on the couch for two hours. I usually washed windows during this time slot.

What a terrific and terrible decision. Had I watched the film for the first time in the US, I would have loved it. And I did love it. But also, every scene made me groan and cover my eyes. The film was intended to be mortifying, to be sure, and I was mortified. Watching a native of my beloved Michigan expose all of our nation's dirty little secrets to the world felt like watching my own family appear on Jerry Springer. Even Oscoda, the neighboring town to my childhood home, made an embarrassing, trashy appearance.

"You lived there?" Lisbeth asked me. "Did you see guns?" She sounded urgently disturbed and frightened, as if this revelation might mean I had a gun on me at this very moment.

"No! I mean, I didn't live in that bowling alley. And not in Oscoda," I said, as if the 15 miles made any difference at this distance. And, in fact, I had actually been to the bowling ally featured in the film, but that was neither here nor there. Also, my dad owned about ten guns. They didn't need to know any of that.

"A lot of people do have guns in Michigan, but mostly for hunting and for sport."

"Sport?" Åke was always brief but poignant. "There are games you play with guns?"

"OK, let me clarify something first." At this point I was leaning forward on the couch, with the kids huddled around me like it was the weirdest story time ever. "I hate guns. I don't like touching them, I don't like being in the same house as them, and I don't like shooting them. But some people do. They put up targets in the woods, and they shoot at the targets. Or they go to shooting ranges and shoot at targets there. I know. It's strange, but it's pretty common."

"You've shot a gun then?" Pia almost seemed as interested as she was timid. That one had a wild streak in her.

"Yeah. I've shot a gun before. I think only once though. I didn't like it. Mostly because it was kind of…well, it hurt my hand for one thing, and then it was both boring and scary, if that makes any sense."

"It must be so scary to be in America. I don't think I want to go there ever." Lisbeth was dead serious. She'd also told me once that she wanted to learn about every part of a car and how each worked before learning how to drive one. Not a risk taker, that one.

I explained to them as best I could that one doesn't actually see guns on a daily basis in the US, and how the incidents of violence described in Michael Moore's film were isolated, and rare, when you considered the size of the country. In most places, it was really quite safe, I told them. Not as nauseatingly safe as this place, I didn't add, but safe.

Clearly, they did not believe me. That was OK though. I didn't really think any of the Waaras were America-bound anyway. The thing that really threw me for a loop was simply the fact that *Bowling for Columbine* existed in Sweden, and that people here had watched it. It's one thing to be within the confines of your huge, diverse nation and participate in a discussion about important domestic issues. It's an entirely different thing to watch the debate go on from the outside. A little bit of me wanted to place a call to my fellow Michigander Mr. Moore to say, "Psssst! They can all hear you out here! Keep it down!"

* * *

The kids had long ago left me to my thoughts on the couch, when a text woke me from my daze.

Come home soon as you can. Found song I think you like.

Based on the last time he found a song he thought I'd like, I was a bit skeptical, but the music quality didn't really matter. Johan had been thinking about me and had something to show me, and that was quite enough to get me through this evening's horseshit chores and get to the weekend.

I looked around me, and noticed I was the only one in within view on the second floor of the farmhouse. Pia was outside in the cat barn getting Joe and Agda ready to go on one of her calorie-burning walks, Åke was nowhere to be seen, and Lisbeth was in her room getting changed to go take care of the horses with me. Inger was in her office. I had just enough time to pull off a heist.

When you don't make enough money to feed yourself, and your host family has strongly suggested you live with someone who can't afford to feed you either, it leaves you with limited options. So I'd started stealing food from the Waaras. Really, they were supposed to be paying for all of my "living expenses," and since eating—in my mind—was inexorably linked to living, I was committing a justified crime. I'd only take a few pantry items at a time, however, as I had a feeling that Inger might disagree with my assessment of the food-napping situation were she to notice key items go missing in bulk. Each afternoon or evening, before leaving for Johan's, I'd find a moment to slink into the *kök* and collect a *potatis* or two, perhaps a can of tomato sauce or a half-empty jar of *lingonsylt.* I'd then rush down the basement stairs that led from the kitchen directly to my basement room where I still kept most of my things and pack the booty in my nightly bag for Johan's.

I'd never stolen food before. Actually, I'd never stolen anything before. I never had that awful childhood moment where your mom brings you back to the store to return the gum you naïvely shoplifted, and confess to the storeowner. I'd never been tempted to steal because—ironically, I noted now, given Louise's mockery of my socio-economic status—I'd been spoiled rotten my whole life. This explained why I wasn't a very good thief; the little prizes I brought over to Johan's weren't enough to really feed me in the evenings or all weekend. They were just tokens to alleviate my guilt while Johan fed me out of *kronor* he made fixing the 1.2 cars per month he seemed to average.

I was just stuffing the last to-be smuggled onion into my overnight bag when I heard a faint knock on my bedroom door. Obviously, I jumped, and my heart started racing.

"Ah? Yes?"

Inger was inside my room before the words were out of my mouth, and I struggled to stand, turn around and not stare at my backpack to scan for signs of damning evidence as she glided into the quiet, cold closet of a room.

"Natalie!" she said. "I see you have quite a number of personal items still arranged here in your room!"

Indeed, I did. My books were on the desk, my photos were scattered about. Although I was only here during the day, I still utilized the room as my personal space—the only personal space I really had left in the world, mind you. I did my laundry here, so my clothes mainly stayed here, and it was good to have a place to just sit down and take a load off in between chores sometimes. And anything could happen with Johan, really. I wasn't so bold as to just assume I really "lived" with him. I just "stayed" with him. Way different.

But Inger sought to change that.

"I wonder, darling, if we might discuss altering your living arrangement to better suit everyone," she said, large red smile in place. I had no idea what that sentence could possibly mean.

"Ah…what do you mean?" I asked.

"Well, you know how teenagers are, my dear, and Pia has gotten it into her head that she no longer wishes to sleep upstairs, sharing a hallway with her parents and brother. Ah HA! You must remember being a teenage girl, Natalie! You are nearly still one now!"

Right, I thought, *except if you're taking this conversation where I think it's going, you couldn't legally force a teenage girl to go live with the mechanic down the road for your own convenience.*

"Right, yeah," I said. "So, she wants a different room?"

"Well, naturally, she would like this room," Inger said, spreading her long arms into a large, sweeping, Vanna White-esque gesture. It was like she was showing off a new speedboat instead of a cement-walled servant's quarters. "And we do think it's a reasonable request since you are not really *using it*, and you are *so happy* to be staying with Johan."

Both of those were opinion statements.

"OK," I said. "I…I guess I understand that, but it is really nice—really nice, but really important too, I think, for me to have some space that belongs to me. I mean, I am enjoying my time with Johan, but we really have just started seeing each other. I feel like it's…I would really appreciate still having space available to me here."

"I must say I'm surprised!" Inger said sharply. "Are you and Johan not very much in love?"

Why? Why. Why did she need to ask me this? And then have the audacity to wait for a response?

"We're…we're quite happy." I guess I understood her confusion. Although Inger was a total nightmare to live with, she didn't know that. I'm sure she and her family were, to a certain degree, a little insulted by my tendency to spend every moment I could away from them. I suppose the idea that I was "very much in love" made that insult easier to bear. Otherwise, I was just choosing to shack up with the tattooed weirdo down the road to avoid them.

"But still, I feel," I continued, "that I'd like to continue to have a place here."

This, I could only assume, would be exactly how the "you should still pay for my groceries when I'm at Johan's" conversation would go. Inger was not having it.

"I think we can accommodate everyone," she said with a placating smile. "Natalie, if you'll plan to move your belongings up to Pia's room, I think everyone will be pleased."

Yes. Everyone would be pleased to have the awkward foreigner from the basement move up to the "residents" level. My room would be right between Jan and Åke's. I'd walk right past Inger's to get there. That's exactly the kind of private escape I needed.

"OK," I said. "Sure. Just…just let me know when she wants to move down."

And it was done. I was out.

16
Jul
Christmas

Winter is trying enough for one's self-esteem under normal circumstances, what with all the low energy and the getting chubby and the dry skin. Every year becomes a new struggle to find the right cold-weather jeans to properly contain the extra flab, and moisturizing multiple times a day to keep facial molting to a minimum. Add to this the inability to go anywhere or do anything potentially energizing, no means to seek out exercise (I officially could no longer afford Pia's classes), having no control over one's diet, and no access to a Clinique counter, and the equation added up to misery. I couldn't imagine how the Waara's former American employee had lost those alleged 10 pounds during her stay. There must have been a hunger strike involved.

It only took four days of housework, and Johan reverting slowly from his over-attentiveness to put me right back where I was before we left for Stockholm: spending evenings and weekends hating every bone-crushing moment of sitting on Johan's couch and vying with the computer and television for his attention. I can hear reasonable people reading this and saying, "Read a book! Learn to knit!" For the record, I did read books, but reading can only take up so much time per day. And at that point in life, I didn't even realize knitting was a thing. Whether I was being decidedly American or decidedly female or just plain spoiled made me self-conscious about my desire to whine; the truth was that I was all of those things, and they all rendered me decidedly bored.

We were having another round of Let's-Do-This versus Why-Do-You-Want-To-Do-That-It-Costs-Money.

"We don't do anything!" I whined, albeit flirtatiously. I certainly didn't want to turn Johan off by being a nag, but was beginning to seriously resent this "using my sexuality to fulfill basic needs" bullshit. Entertainment, by the way, was a basic need in my book.

"Honnney, we're going to *julbord* on Friday." He responded to my feigned smile with a genuine one. "And we just went to see Henrik. We should relax and enjoy ourselves!"

"We just went to see Henrik? That was three days ago! And the *julbord* is in another three days! And it's essentially a church potluck! Who counts sitting in someone's kitchen for an hour last week and going to a quiet buffet with strangers this weekend as a satisfying social calendar? That's insane! You're insane! You are completely batshit fucking boring and your life sucks!"

I didn't say that. I pleasantly agreed that I was looking forward to the *julbord* and was only sad that I didn't have a new book to read. I'd have to borrow one of Inger's the next day. Johan didn't have books. Ho hum. Back to mentally bashing my head against a wall.

December in Sweden was the reason I know about the term "agoraphobic." I looked it up precisely because I realized in a panic that whatever the opposite of claustrophobic was, I had it. All this open space. I'd look out Johan's or the Waaras' windows and realize the miles and miles of snow out there didn't add up to a fraction of the distance between myself and a human to whom I could relate. I adopted the term because I liked words and I liked naming things, particularly my state of mind. I knew, however, that I had the word's meaning totally misconstrued. It may be a fear of open spaces, but just like its closed-space partner, claustrophobia, it was meant to represent an abnormal, or irrational fear. Regrettably, there was nothing irrational about this. I could close my eyes and feel the weight of the empty space around me. I could feel every inch of the void that separated me from my family, from all of my friends, and also from the person I was used to being. I was boring here. I had no talents. I had nothing to contribute.

It was a late Friday morning at Johan's house. I didn't work, as it was the first day of my Christmas vacation, and we were going to meet the Waaras later at a *julbord* that would take place on the ferry to Denmark. Everyone was very excited about this *julbord* because it was on a boat, which was a very exotic place to eat a buffet. Johan and I were on the couch where we'd slept all night, too lazy to get our asses upstairs and sleep in a real bed. Again. We'd gotten off the couch to prepare our regular weekend breakfast of tomato slices and *knäckebröd* (I insisted on adding salt and oregano to my tomato, which Johan always reminded me was a waste of the expensive herbs he hadn't known he owned), but otherwise we hadn't moved.

At this point in our relationship we had firmly established couch positions: I would sit on the right-hand side of the couch, staring at the TV, "watching" a program of Johan's choosing that ranged from snowboard competitions to the Svensk news. Or *Alien vs. Predator*; Johan had that movie on DVD, and we watched it about once a week. Meanwhile, Johan would be engrossed in his laptop at the other end of the couch, keeping a constant vigil on his car stereo forums. He'd begin checking in during breakfast, and each day I was certain I could plan on falling sleep to the tick-tick-ticking of his keyboard that night.

Fuck me in the ear. I had to get out of there. If I didn't leave then, I feared I might petrify right there on the couch; I would spend the next sixteen days waiting out my life. I would never have another December as a bright and ambitious twenty-three-year-old woman, and I was spending it on a couch. For every second of complete stillness, the average worth of my existence was going down.

Life was a little worse now, I thought.

Wait a minute—just got even worse.

Yup. I definitely felt like more of a pathetic waste now than I did a minute ago.

I stood up. I was absolutely going to go somewhere. But where to go? I looked out the front window. White, snow-covered fields, as far as the eye could see. I looked out the back window. White, snow-covered fields, almost to the horizon. They were interrupted only by a sparse row of widely spaced houses, miles away. Even if I ran away, just put on my coat and left, where would I go? Nowhere I wanted to go was even remotely within reach. I could go out the door, start walking, and actually die of starvation or frostbite before I got anywhere desirable.

"What are you doing, honnnney?" Johan said without looking up from his screen.

Ah. Back to claustrophobic. Even him saying "honey" made me feel crowded. I've never let anyone call me that before. Had he even called anyone honey before? It was English; of course he hadn't. Or had he called Annika that? Why would he ever have used an English term of endearment? Had he just seen that on TV? Of course he had.

I did not respond.

"HUHNnnnnaaaayy?" Again, not looking up.

"I've got to go do something." He must have heard the desperation in my voice as I looked back and forth between the far-too-small house and the expanse through the window.

"Oh, come on, HUHNnnnnnaaaaayy, come sit. We're enjoying our day." Finally, but far too late, he looked up at me, his greasy, bleached hair all over the place. He gave me his best toothy grin followed by three air kisses, a favorite gesture of his. Smack, smack, smack. He smiled again, patted the couch next to him, and then went back to his computer screen. Still smiling.

Ugh.

"I'm going to the mall," I said, retreating upstairs to change my clothes for the first time in days.

"But you don't have any money to buy anything with," he generously reminded me. "What are you going to do there? It's just going to be a waste of petrol."

"I'm just going to walk around," I called back down the stairway. "It's not a waste, because I really need to just get some air and get out of here for awhile. Americans don't sit quite this still for quite this long. Americans go to the mall."

Dec 22, 2005

Here's the real predicament in our relationship:

I need him, but I am not in love with him. I like him a lot—I'd even admit to liking the idea of him being in love with me—but when it's time for me to go home, that is exactly what I will do, with no hesitation.

Maybe I could be in love with Johan at home, who knows? If I could be myself, and he could be himself, maybe it would work. But I can't really be myself here. Swedes may be able to speak basic English, but no one here understands nuance. They can't read my American body language, know my cultural expectations, or even sense what kind of person I am at a basic level. I'm not me here. And I know Johan would never be happy anywhere else. He can hardly emigrate off his couch. So I guess we're stuck.

Writing in my journal at the mall is so much better than writing on that couch. The air is moving here. I can smell hair products. I'm getting some *kaffe* now and going to browse...

Swedes are into Christmas, but in a different way than Americans are. It's possible that they are more obsessed with it, actually, but they are coy about their excitement. They channel it through their orderly rituals such as centering a single candle in each window of their houses and hiding anchovies in their scalloped potatoes.

Only three days before Christmas, the reserved buzz of yuletide cheer at the mall only underlined the differences between this Nordic twilight zone and home. The large shopping center was busy and neatly trimmed, with not even a hint of being fantastically gaudy or panic-stricken. Without the chaos, it just didn't feel like Christmas. Sigh. What I would have given to be accosted by a salesperson trying to rub lotion on me, or to trip over plastic Santas, or to feel the awkward guilt of passing by a Salvation Army ringer with no cash? Weird, the things you miss.

I had no real reason to be there. Johan was right; I had no money to spend. I had to use my forbidden credit card to buy myself a *kaffe*. But walking through the moderately paced, well-behaved crowds of people made me feel normal. If I didn't listen too carefully, if I blurred my vision and believed that it was mid-October rather than December twenty-second, I'd never know I was at a Svensk mall. If I didn't let my eye settle on the storefronts reading Din Sko and Hemtex, and only looked at the H&M and Esprit, I could have been in the US. It felt nice. It felt almost sentimental. But I definitely looked like an idiot, standing in the middle of a mall, squinting and blinking and smiling to myself.

And then, in the spirit of American, holiday-driven recklessness, I leaned in too close. I let my senses focus and my guard down at the first sign of comfort: *Skivlagret.* Literally, "The CD Store." I ducked inside to browse through the music, to run my fingertips over the familiar plastic squares, click, click, clicking through rows of them, one by one. It was always fun to pick up CDs, read their playlists and look at the pictures. I exclusively browsed for CDs I already owned, or had once but lost.

I had been in the store for ten minutes or so—I had already sifted through the limited Ben Folds Five offerings and was skimming my way through the much heartier Björk collection when the store became quiet enough for the overhead music to catch my awareness. The second Adam Duritz's voice slid into my ear I grinned with instant recognition.

You send your lover off to China, and you wait for her to call
You put your girl up on a pedestal, and you wait for her to fall.

This entire shop of Svensk strangers and I were midway through the title track of *Hard Candy.*

Oh Adam, I thought with a barely stifled grin, *halfway around the world, and you still can't lighten up.*

Greg and I loved Counting Crows. We thought of Adam Duritz as our goofy, overly emotional third wheel who just couldn't get his shit together with the ladies. It was the band we fell in love to. Adam's lyrics could be borderline adolescent and painfully redundant at times, but also beautifully earnest and terribly catchy.

What times we'd had together, Greg, Adam, and me. How many hours had we spent driving together from Michigan to Wisconsin to the Upper Peninsula to Niagara Falls to his serenade? We were always as high as the sunshine was bright, hands peacefully laced over the center console, with Counting Crows blabbing about Cadillac dreams and Elizabeth's bedtime. The amount of time the three of us had spent together was probably not measurable in hours; maybe days, but more likely weeks.

But damn, I thought, releasing myself from the memory's anti-gravity for a moment; Duritz was one reliably whiny sap. He was whiny in Michigan, and he was whiny in Sverige too, singing his familiar, wistful lyrics at me from the ceiling of the Skivlagret. I noted how much sadder his lonely lyrics were when there was no one there with me who knew them by heart. Our trio felt so off-kilter with just Adam and me in a whole continent of strangers.

Of course I'd stood there too long reminiscing. The song had changed, and while I knew what the next song would be, it still felt surprising to listen to Adam sing "American Girls" down at me, presumably the only American girl in this Svensk store. All of a sudden, it was happening; one pathetic, lovesick moron begat another. There I was, crying in the CD store.

I had never felt so alone. This pre-recorded voice came from a stranger who knew nothing of me or this place. And yet, at this moment, it was the only thing I had found in an entire continent to connect to, the only real piece of myself I recognized in months. Adam singing about "American girls" felt like someone pronouncing my name in a Midwestern accent for the first time since I'd left home. The full weight of my solitude struck my heart right in the spot I was hoping to superficially fill by visiting a mall right before Christmas.

To make things worse—as if I needed to make my own situation worse as I tried to discretely blot my tears on my sleeve while furiously flipping through CDs, aggressively pretending for would-be onlookers that I was browsing, not crying—I went ahead and wallowed in it. If Greg were there with me, I thought, there would be no need for tears. We'd be casually wandering around at opposite ends of the store, and when Counting Crows came on, we'd look up at each other from across the hedges of compact discs and smile before rolling our eyes. I'd make a point to slowly wander over to him and make a comment about Adam's melodrama, our old friend who had caught up with us at the mall to recount with us his last heartache.

"Geez, this guy just can't catch a break with the ladies, can he?" I'd say.

"Dude's never gonna learn," he'd reply as I passed behind him, off to comfortably browse through a new stack of CDs on the other side of the aisle.

For the second time that day, I had to get out. I mean really. I was crying in the mall. I bolted out of the store.

Where to go, where to go?

As if powerless against myself, I had to make one more stop on my dive to the bottom of the despair barrel. I went straight into a department store to find a fragrance counter where I promptly doused myself in Estee Lauder's Pleasures and shoved nearly the entire bottle of Pleasures for Men up my nose. That was us. That's what we smelled like together. And I knew that wherever Greg was, this was how he smelled right now. He never even left for the grocery store without a healthy fit of sprays of the light, only-slightly-spicy and just-a-tad sweet cologne. It was the kind of habit that would drive you mad if it didn't actually smell so awesome. He'd started buying the female counterpart of the fragrance for me almost immediately when we started dating. This was the smell of home. No one noticed as tears dribbled carelessly on the glass counter. There was nothing left to do but take a breath, straighten up, and walk away.

...It's not that I want him back. I just want to see him. I just want to call a time out and feel some sort of normalcy. I want him to know that I spent a half hour losing it in the middle of a mall because of him. It would make him feel good, I think. I'd probably leave out the cologne part though. That was kind of weird.

Maybe I should call him. Or not. I don't know. It would be different if I were in love with Johan. If that were true, I couldn't contact Greg because it would be a betrayal. I don't even know who I'd be betraying in this situation. Johan? Greg? Me? But someone, for sure. So I'll just...well...I don't have the first clue what I'll do.

Only eight months to go. My only choice is to make the most of it and make the most of Johan. I care about him, and more pressingly, I need him to make it through each day with a smidgen of sanity. And I really don't have a reason to go home right away anyway. No job. No money. No plan. I need a plan.

* * *

I was quiet on the way to the floating *julbord* to which we'd been invited by the Waaras. Well, they'd invited me to come. Inger asked if Johan might be interested in attending as well, and when he accepted, they were happy to pass my *julbord* ticket price onto him so he could pay for us both. As her cheapness was paralleled only by Johan's, I insisted on paying for mine, though I couldn't afford his too. Sorry, Mom and Dad. I was going to get you something cool from Sweden for Christmas, but instead I ate dinner one day.

The money didn't matter though. As we drove through the dark Sverige-scape to Helsingborg my mind was still in the music store, still shocked by my reaction and unable to shake it. You don't just have overwhelmingly strong feelings come roaring back from out of nowhere and just ignore them, right? They had to be indicative of something. Nothing mattered to me in the least at that moment beyond contemplating what those feelings could mean.

"Will you be spending Christmas with the Waaras?" Johan asked from the driver seat. I had zero information on my own holiday plans, including whether or not I had a choice in what my holiday plans might be. The question floated into the now-growing pile of my ennui.

"I don't know," I said. "I guess so. I mean, probably not though, because I won't be working and I'm never there when I'm not working."

"So you will be sitting at my house?"

I had no idea how that was supposed to translate. Did he mean "sitting at my house with me," or "sitting at my house while I do something else"?

"Um...I guess. You're probably having Christmas with your family, right?" Maybe I did care about my holiday plans. Or at least I felt like I should. Christmas was just a few days away. At the prospect of having another reason to feel sorry for myself, my interest was piqued.

"*Jaapp*," he gasped to the affirmative. "But ah...I can see if my dad would mind if I brought you along."

Wow. That was inviting.

"No," I said. "That's OK. I don't want to barge in on your family time. I don't want to be at the Waaras' either, to be honest. I'll just wait for you to come home and we'll do our own Christmas celebration."

"Is that what you want to do?"

To be clear: this was absolutely not what I wanted to do. I, like any normal human, didn't want to spend Christmas alone. I wanted Johan to have already cleared my presence at his Christmas gathering. I wanted him to have been hoping I'd agree to come with him. I wanted the Waaras to be assuming I'd be celebrating with them, as they had invited me to come live with them as a fucking family for a year. I wanted my sister and my mom and my dad to show up unexpectedly and all celebrate with me like the normal fucking people we are who give a shit about each other and like each other to feel included.

"Yeah," I said. "That's what I want."

The *julbord* was tolerable. No matter how at odds I felt with Johan, there was nothing like being around the Waaras to bond myself fiercely to him. We operated well as a couple in public, and we maintained polite conversation with Inger and Jan throughout the evening. I'd already attended a farmer's association *julbord* with the family earlier in the month, so we were fortunately beyond the perfunctory naming of and explaining each pile of herring-and-whatnot-sauce on my plate and could now chat about…you know, Svensk stuff. Jan got some car advice. Inger asked after our exciting week of relaxing and *fika* with Henrik and his wife. We all took exactly one shot of the traditional Svensk liquor, *snaps*, which sounds like "schnapps" but was way stronger and tasted like the space between your first and second toe. It was pleasant. The *julbord,* not the *snaps.*

I even saw Hanna, who acted very exited to see me and asked when I wanted to go out to her club with her. While the true answer was three months ago, I smiled and said, "Anytime!" knowing anytime would be never.

To my delight, however, at the end of the evening, Inger warmly asked if I would honor them with my presence on Christmas Eve, which was when they exchanged gifts. She had, in fact, been assuming I'd join all along. She insisted it was no imposition and the kids would be disappointed if I didn't come. Lisbeth, Åke, and Pia all smiled shyly in verification. I really liked those kids. I nearly cried, and accepted.

So I spent the next two days picking out my gifts for the kids and for Johan. I'm a bit of a Christmas nut, so I went all kinds of apeshit on my credit card. It was now officially costing me more money to work for the Waaras than I was making, but who could care? It was *jul!* So *God Jul* to us every one!

Johan, meanwhile, made arrangements for me to come over to his father's house on Christmas day. I knew it would be awkward as I'd be doing something rather intimate with his dad, younger sister, and her husband (apparently the older sister would be celebrating with the prodigal mother), knowing that I was going to forever be the very young, very blonde American he brought home that one time. But I was OK with that. It was a smidge better than waiting at home for him on Christmas.

Dec…something '05

I don't know the date. I know that it's after Christmas and before New Year's. I don't know what time it is. I know that Johan left to go pick up some CDs at Annika's at least one change in seating position, three e-mails, and a great deal of blog-reading ago. I'm guessing it's been around three hours. (Insert appropriate amount of suspicion that I'm pretending not to entertain here.) I'm thinking that makes it about midnight. And I'm betting it's around the twenty-eighth.

Christmas was great. Johan and I opened our stockings—mine from my mom that came in the mail just in time, and his from me. He was pretty gleeful about it, which made me really happy.

Mid-afternoon we went to his dad's. I was nervous. I was clearly invading their holiday. Would they speak Swedish the whole time and only allow me to come off as the quiet, smiling American bimbo who was replacing the ex-girlfriend priest they all loved? Worse, would they be forced to uncomfortably speak their second (or third) language at their own family gathering just to suit me, a virtual nobody to them? My very existence was bound to come off as rude.

Neither turned out to be the case. Johan's father, sister, and her husband were inclusive but not awkward. They spoke English to me, and Swedish to each other. They were kind, funny, warm, and sarcastic, just the people I would imagine his family to be.

And I even had a moment to demonstrate my non-bimboness! We were playing a board game, and Johan's sister was stumped on a question based on the Svensk word "entomologi." I chimed in that it looked like the same root word as "entomology," which is the study of insects. (As opposed to "etymology," I added to emphasize my smarty-pantsness, which is the study of words. Was that too much?) I was right. They were impressed.

So I felt like they had a good time, and I know I had a decent time, and they know I'm not a total idiot: Merry Christmas to me. And Johan got me a really great Christmas gift too—an MP3 player! It's so cool. He loaded it with music so I don't have to carry my computer from room to room with me when I'm cleaning at the Waaras', a habit that is, as he rightly pointed out, completely ridiculous.

Despite all that, I have been kind of obsessing about Greg. I don't know why. I suppose it's just that it's Christmas, and he was the last person who loved me in a certain way that I'm particularly missing right now. The be-all and end-all is that we didn't make it. We weren't happy. I chose my dignity and personal happiness over love. And look how personally happy I am with this dignified situation of shacking up with a mechanic I hardly know who might be screwing his ex-girlfriend right now.

It was New Year's Eve, and we had plans. Holy cow was I excited.

The prior week had been so dull that I begged Johan to take me to IKEA at one point specifically so we could scavenge the clearance room for his kitchen hinges. But tonight we were going out. I would wear something cute, I would drink lots of drink, and I would meet new, exiting people. Honestly, they didn't even need to be exciting. As long as they were humans I'd spent fewer than seven hundred hours with in the last four months, I was super pumped to be in their presence. I determined it was only proper for me to lower my standards for social interaction at this point.

In anticipation of this night of celebration and possible brush with normalcy, I was on Johan's phone with my mother, chatting away like a prom queen discussing her coiffure options for the big night. She was excited to hear me in such a state, I could tell. For more than a month, she'd been in the terrible position of knowing her daughter was miserable, while she was too far away to help. My mother, a perpetual fixer of messes (often mine), was for the first time only able to sit back and watch. This oasis of enthusiasm was as relieving to her as it was to me.

"Yes," I cheerily responded to her chirpy questions. "We are going to a...Moroccan's house? Johan? Moroccan?" I yelled out to him, as if he were any further away than the three yards between the couch and the kitchen, and as if he weren't hanging on our every word.

"Almost, hunaaay."

"Ah, he says almost...I don't know, Madagascan, maybe? What's close to Moroccan...? Oh...Hey, Johan, is it a moron we're going to see?"

I could see him smiling from behind the cupboard he was imagining himself to be "working on." No parts had been on clearance from IKEA for weeks, so he certainly wasn't making actual progress. He was clearly feeling cheerfully motivated due to his American lady love's elevated mood. Inspiring an even feigned sense of purpose in Johan was laudable, and I felt pleased all around.

Meanwhile, I was feeling like quite the worldly woman. Reporting to my mother that I would be attending a New Year's party at the home of someone of exotic ethnicity that possibly began with "M," while bringing my mysterious Svensk lover into our conversation, was just the thing to make her feel better about my dire circumstances. It was just the thing to make me feel better.

"Oh yes," I went on authoritatively, answering her question whether or not this was traditional New Year's drinking party. "I will most definitely be drinking myself silly tonight."

Johan happened to be walking through the living room just in time to smile sweetly at me and respond, "Oh no you won't, huhnaay. That will be me."

"Yeah, whatever," I teased him right back and got back to chatting with my mom. Minutes later we were saying our good-byes just as Johan was returning from upstairs.

"You know," he said casually. "I was quite serious."

"What?" I responded. "The Moroccan is seriously almost a moron?"

"No!" he laughed. "About the drinking! I will be the one drinking tonight."

Clearly, he was kidding. First of all, where I came from, there were no questions about who was drinking and who was driving. I was the girl, so I got the carriage. And even taking into account that I was living in a country with no appreciation for such chivalry, we had literally never been out drinking together before, and I was the new girl, the young one, the foreigner, the guest. It's a default rule, like the person with the next birthday goes first in any game without dice or alphabet tiles: common human courtesy insisted that Johan would be the first designated driver between the two of us. Especially after the recent drunken *julbord* incident. There was no way he was being serious.

Oh, but there was.

Apparently, Johan had been the designated driver last year while Annika had drunk herself silly. Consequently, it was his turn. His logic may have gotten lost in translation, but my indignation was blatantly universal. I made sure of it.

And thus, we had our first real fight. Over my right to get drunk. The Beastie Boys would have been proud of me. I won. Kind of. I won because Johan called the party host and secured a room for us and Ludde to stay in overnight, so we could bring him along and neither of us would have to restrain ourselves.

At this dinner party, to my delight, several new and interesting couples were in attendance, and we shared the most delicious meal I'd had in all of my time in Sverige. During this wonderful meal, I proceeded to accidentally get quite, quite, quite drunk. I had fairly clear memories of the meal itself, but everything was a little blurry from there. I remember being quite impressed by the variety of nationalities at the table, and while I was the only American, the foreign-ness of the others made me feel far less foreign than usual.

The most interesting woman was a tall, broad, gorgeous woman from Romania who had the most incredibly large mane of black curly hair I'd ever seen. She had come to Sverige as an au pair as well, and was now marrying the small, pale Svensk guy sitting beside her. She was so excited to be spending the rest of her days in this Scandinavian paradise. That had, apparently, been her goal all along. She'd come from a country where labor was hard, and jobs were scarce. Here, as soon as she started popping out babies, she'd be set for life. Johan, whose hand was already on my knee, gave me a little squeeze upon learning of their romantic, cross-cultural engagement. Yeah right, dude. Dream on.

That was all I could honestly report of the party. Although my drunkenness was truly accidental—between my lowered tolerance, my excitement, and my ongoing misunderstanding of Swedish alcohol content, I was doomed from the beginning—my only real memories between dinner and bed were of a seemingly fascinating conversation with a four-year-old and breaking the host family's shoe rack when I tried to sit on it. Johan later told me, in a tone of actual shame, that I was so drunk he couldn't even get me to walk from the house where we had dinner to the neighbor's where we were staying the night. Apparently, he'd tried to tow me through the snow on a sled, but I kept falling off. I'm quite sure this wasn't the image of his smart, sassy, young American girlfriend that he hoped to share with his friends. In fact, I knew it wasn't.

So there it was, my first genuine opportunity to have a long, engaging night of fun, and I'd gone and destroyed it for us both. I may have felt someone else had been to blame for everything else that had gone to shit here, but now I was faced with the aching truth that this was truly all my fault. All of it.

We didn't talk much on the way home the next day. I was hung over, and the snow was offensively bright as we traveled silently home. Johan and his smashed chunks of hair standing in all directions were unusually focused on driving.

"Did I throw up?" I asked, breaking the awkward silence. My reported behavior sounded distinctly puke-worthy, but my mouth seemed pleasantly tasteless.

"Ah…I think so," he replied, taking his eyes off the road to flash me his trademark smirk. "Some guy told me you did."

Fuck him, I thought. Some guy, somewhere, had told him I'd thrown up. Super nice.

A feeling of dread came over me as we drove closer and closer to familiar territory. Those ugly white and grey hills ahead were the ones across the field from Johan's—the ones where the horses lived. What was I dreading more, going back to shoveling their enormous shit in the freezing cold again in a week, or the eight days of couch-sitting and Swedish TV-watching between now and then? Ugh.

Nothing like loathing and shame to ring in the New Year. Welcome to 2006, Natalie.

17
Den Lägsta
The Bottom

"What are you still doing there?" perfectly sane and well-meaning people might have asked me at this point. Well, good question.

I was raised in a family where we fastened our seatbelts before the car was put into drive, and we followed through on all of our commitments. In my senior year of high school, I slipped during our overnight class lock-in, busted my left foot open, and had to get six stitches in my toe. The next day I woke up and played starting left forward in our regional finals soccer game. Left foot. Left forward. But I signed up to play soccer, so I finished it. I had two near-miss goals too.

I was that asshole in the yearbook who had two columns of extra-curriculars by my picture, excelled in all of them, had the most publications in the class literary journal, and the eleventh highest grade point average. OK, so my class wasn't really big enough for eleventh place to be that impressive, but point was, I was born and bred to accept challenges, be goal-oriented, and achieve success. One thing I never did was quit. So the question wasn't so much whether or not I knew this commitment had been a bad idea, it was whether or not I knew how quitting something worked.

Whenever I fantasized about leaving, I would become horrified by the quitting logistics. Our agreement was for me to stay a year, and Inger had paid me through February upon my arrival. Would I have to pay her back for two months? I had no money left. During my excitement-clouded contract negotiations, Inger and I agreed that we would split the cost of round-trip airfare for me in the form of me paying to get myself there, and her paying to get me home. (Yes, I could now see that this was a red flag.) If I were to cut out early, would she still hold up her end of this? It could conceivably cost me hundreds, maybe thousands of dollars to leave. Why was my dad right about everything? And how could I leave without admitting this to him?

Plus, what was I going to say to the Waaras? As a rule, I tried to circumvent having to tell people that they are unbearable, and I must therefore take leave of them. I'm really more of an "It's not you, it's me" type. As it stood, I had nothing to tell them. I had no job I wanted to get back to. I had no genuine family crisis. I had no idea what I'd do with myself when and if I returned to Michigan. I didn't even know what city I'd live in, or on what I'd base that decision. My only reason for leaving was that I didn't like these people or the job I'd said I would to do.

Plus, Johan had just gotten me a really nice Christmas gift. And given me a car to use. And he'd been feeding me and letting me live with him even though he'd never really invited me. How could I just say, "Thanks for all the room and board and gifts. I'm going back to America now"? If I'd felt prostitutey before, now I'd feel worse—like an ungrateful prostitute.

And then there was this:

It was a few days into 2006. Because New Year's Day was on a Sunday, everyone in the US would be going back to work on Monday or Tuesday. I was so jealous. I had to wait out another damn week. Not that I was excited to get back to the Waaras; I really just missed making a to-do list. I'd made it to Friday night, which I was celebrating by taking a shower. It was my big planned activity of the day. I was in the midst of soaping up when I noticed something suspicious. It appeared…it looked like…was this? I appeared to be leaking. From my breast. I rinsed off, I checked again. I checked both breasts. Both leaking. It would seem I was lactating.

Not a panicker by nature, I calmly assured myself this could be anything. Or nothing. I just needed to get out of this shower, do some research and find out what those anythings or nothings could include. There had to be myriad reasons for a young woman to have a little spontaneous lactation now and again, right? Myriad.

Hours later, I was still waiting to get my hands on Johan's computer (I absolutely was not bringing this information to him at this juncture), when my mind began to calmly sort out the possibilities before me. One was that this was no big deal. It was something that just happened sometimes, just not to me ever before, or to anyone I knew.

The other—the remote, ridiculous possibility—was that I was lactating for the reason one was, you know, supposed to lactate. I couldn't even bring myself to say the word. If that were true, then I would have to leave. Get to leave! Or, no. That would mean I couldn't leave, wouldn't it? I would be fleeing the country with someone's child—someone I had no intention of having a kids with, or any sort of future, or even a cat.

Historically, it certainly wasn't unheard of for a woman to have someone's baby and not tell him, but now, faced with even the remote possibility of considering such a thing, it seemed horridly immoral. Wouldn't that be tantamount to kidnapping?

Holy hell, Natalie. What kid? There was currently no kid to nap. There was a pending Google search and a weird showering experience. Calm down. Calm. Down.

Four hours later, I slipped into the bathroom to confirm it was still happening before pressuring Johan to give up the computer. It was, and I did. Unfortunately, I had limited time, and I knew I was going to have to spend as much time deleting my search history as I was actually researching. The result wasn't very helpful. Either I was experiencing an excess of nipple stimulation (something I believe I would have noticed), I had breast cancer (I was pretty confident that was a "no" as well), nothing was wrong with me, or nothing *serious* was wrong with me.

Nothing serious? What did that mean? What was serious? Was being—gulp—pregnant considered serious? Because it was feeling pretty fucking serious from where I was sitting. I couldn't even ascertain if leaky boob was even a symptom of pregnancy or not. The internet seemed mind-bogglingly void of this information. How did the internet not know? How was Johan asking for his computer back already? Delete, delete, delete.

It was 11 p.m. on a Friday. I had waited all day for Google to tell me my life wasn't over, and now I still didn't know for sure.

Holy hell. Holy hell.

* * *

I took twenty-four hours to decide what to do. The following evening, it was still happening, and I considered telling Johan. To prepare myself emotionally for this, I scootched over next to him on the couch, leaned on his shoulder, and tried to insert myself into whatever online activity he was involved with, only to find him chatting with Annika. He kept chatting with her, even though I was clearly peeping over his shoulder, which I guess was better than him trying to hide it.

"Ah, Annika is just feeling sad," Johan said. "I am just trying to make her feel better."

I suppose that was meant to make me feel better too, but what Johan didn't realize was that while my ability to speak Svenska was non-existent, I was literate enough to piece together what he was typing, which was something like this:

Annika: Today is really sad. There's nothing to do in this place. [Again, I think Annika and I might have actually had a lot in common.]

> Johan: Why did you move to such a town? You knew there wasn't anything to do there.
> Annika: I had to be close to the church. Too bad everyone at the church is old and they are the only ones here.
> Johan: Oh, don't be so sad. You want me to come over and make you feel better? ;-)
> Annika: :-)I think a visit from you and Ludde would definitely make the day better.
> Johan: You don't sound like you need a visit from Ludde. You want a visit from me. You sound like you need a good fuck to feel better.
> Annika: Nice offer. I think I know not to expect that.
> Johan: Maybe not, but you don't mind thinking it! You want to think about it some more? Maybe tell me what you'd like me to do to you?

Wasn't he sweet? Just another day of coming to the rescue of a damsel in distress with a little internet sex tease. It's really how every girl imagined her first pregnancy scare conversation beginning. I was oddly comforted by Annika's statement that she didn't expect him to follow through on his offer. What an adorably insensitive, technically faithful asshole.

What if Greg just walked through the door right now? I dared myself to wonder. That would be the ultimate Hollywood ending. I'd always needed a grand gesture from him! Something that said, "I know this is crazy and I'm going out on a limb, but I love you, and here I am." This could be his big chance. If he showed up and said he loved me and wanted me to come home, he would be my reason. It would be like that time when we'd first started seeing each other—was it two years ago now?—when he showed up to take me out and had decorated the entire interior of his huge Beauville van with hearts and streamers. I didn't even remember if we went anywhere or did anything, but I definitely remember sitting in the back of that dilapidated van and drinking wine and feeling like the luckiest girl in the world.

So it wasn't totally unlikely, I told myself. He was sort of the knight in shining armor type. Not really the "has a passport" type or the "can afford an international flight" type, but these were easily achievable things in my fantasy.

If this had happened with Greg, it would feel totally different, I thought, still leaning on Johan's shoulder, not even bothering to work on translating his sex chat anymore. I had planned to spend the rest of my life with him. We'd loved each other. If something like this were to happen with the right person at the wrong time it would be one thing, but with the wrong person altogether...I couldn't even finish the thought. I got up, walked into Johan's bathroom, closed the door, and began to cry my eyes out.

I was in there for a long time. Was it twenty minutes? Had it been two hours? I couldn't tell. Would Johan ever poke his head in and say, "Hey honey, what's wrong?" Did I want him to?

Yes. I wanted him to step up and be a man and make me feel better. But he wasn't going to. So I collected myself, wiped my tears, walked out of the bathroom and stood between him and ginormous television.

"Johan, I have to tell you something."

* * *

"I want to name it! I have a name! Let's name it—Moonbeam!"

So that wasn't the reaction I was expecting. After a tearful explanation to Johan about my horrifying symptom, we both dove back onto the internet together to see if we could find out more. It was too late to go to the *apotek* for a pregnancy test, and they'd all be closed tomorrow because it was a Sunday (really, Sverige? No one can go to a pharmacy on a Sunday?), so it was the best we could do.

Like before, we couldn't find anything definitive, but it was helpful to hear Johan say aloud what I'd been repeating to myself every minute and a half for the past 960 minutes-and-a-half.

"Natalie, it doesn't look like this is commonly meaning you are pregnant. I mean, I think we should be concerned and test it, but I'm not counting on this. But it's pretty fun to think about, *ja*?!"

OK, so that obviously not was I'd been thinking verbatim, but I was as relieved to hear his doubts as I was flabbergasted to hear his excitement. I mean really. The guy was on quite a tangent.

"You know, in Sweden, we get more than one year paid after having a baby," he said. "You will quit the Crazies, and you and Moonbeam just live here with me still making 70, 80 percent!"

"Johan," I said, laughing to underline how much that was not going to happen. "Legally, I make zero money from the Waaras, so 70 or 80 percent of that is still zero."

"Ah! *Ja,*" he said, quickly re-plotting the course of our imaginary future, "but I can take my father leave and still make money on the side, so we are fine! And you are always saying how you want to be doing more university."

"Well, yeah," I said, "but I'm planning to do that when I get home."

"Get home?" he said, sounding almost insulted. "Natalie, education is free here."

"Um, yeah, I keep hearing about that."

"But not just for citizens, you know," he went on. "If you lived here you could go to university and learn whatever you want for nothing. You know, you could still be done working for the Crazies whenever you want and go to school free. Why would you go back to America and pay so much?"

Interesting.

"Really," he continued. "If you hate working there, you should just not do it. You don't even need Moonbeam for that. It's not like they pay you so much."

More interesting.

"Yeah…" I began thoughtfully, grateful to be thinking about the next year of my life not including Swedish infant, "but if I didn't work there, I'd have to work somewhere, and I couldn't get a real job here. I'm not even here legally, apparently."

"Ah, there's nothing to worry about there. I will get more work when it is warm and we are fine for money. We would be good here." Johan turned to me and wrapped his arms around my shoulders. "Bah…you don't need to go home, not even when you are done with the Waaras. You don't want to miss me that much. And I know how much you would miss me." He grinned and made a silly face and squeezed me obnoxiously tight until I laughed so hard I lost my breath

I laughed because I wanted so much for this to be all a joke. It had to be.

* * *

The next day was my birthday. I turned twenty-four, and I received the best gift of my entire life. I got my period. I was so relieved, I spent most of the day genuinely relaxing, and even considering Johan's suggestion about going to college in Sweden.

I mean honestly, it was boring here, but going to school would at least make it worth my while. And what was grad school going to cost at home? Thirty grand? Forty? A couple years of boredom might actually be worth it. Plus, studying would actually be something to do, which could totally offset the boringness all together. It would also give me a real reason to quit. Could this actually work?

Oh, and PS on the whole leaky nipples thing: never did I uncover the mystery, and never did it happen again. Neither future doctor inquiries nor more extensive Googling—even years later when the internet became much more reliably sciencey—would point to anything definitive. While I'm not much of a supernaturalist, in this case I have settled on the diagnosis of having been visited by the Holy Spirit. Who, unfortunately, if we're going to stick with that theory, had one last message for me.

Sunday, January 8, 2006

Lise,

Thanks so much for the birthday card! It was absolutely adorable and totally made my day. How did the rest of the day go, you ask? Well...my mom and dad and sister each called, so that was nice. The kids all made me cards, and brought them over, which was nice too. No, I didn't get any presents from the Waaras, but I wasn't really expecting any. The kids just got me really cute Christmas presents, and remember how Inger already told me my pillow was my birthday present in like, October? Did I tell you about that? I probably forgot.

Anyway, you know how Inger, in addition to being a cult leader, is a Tempur-Pedic salesperson? It was around October-ish when Inger asked me if I'd ever slept on a Tempur-Pedic pillow. I told her I hadn't, so she gave me one of her pillows and told me to try it out. So I did. After the first night I told her it was amazing and thank you and tried to give it back, and she was like, "Oh no, dear! You must try it at least a week to really find the benefits!" Of course, she told me all the benefits too, in a really loud, enthusiastic voice and handed me a flyer that listed the benefits for good measure.

So a week later, she tries to sell me the thing. And it's like 1500kr. Do you know how much that is? Almost $200. It's also, like, half my month's pay. So, to summarize, this bitch was paying me what I didn't even yet realize was not even a living wage to clean her fucking house all day, and was trying to make money off me in my second month of service on top of that. She is so awesome. So when I politely declined the purchase, due to the fact that I couldn't even begin to afford it, she offered to give it to me as a gift. For my birthday and Christmas.

So anyway, Johan did make me coffee this morning and arranged our usual knäckebröd, cheese, and tomato breakfast. I'd gotten in the habit of doing this lately, mostly because I relish every opportunity to do something besides sit on the couch, and Johan relishes every chance to avoid leaving it. But I let him serve me today. Then we sat on the couch. We watched *Alien vs. Predator*. Then, two hours later, we watched it again. Really, it only made sense. We hadn't seen the movie since last weekend, when we only saw it two and half times. So we were due for a couple of rounds.

Now I guess we'll just ride out the rest of my birthday in peace. Which is fine...

So Johan hadn't made any special birthday plans for me. *Who cares, really?* I thought as I lay completely still on the couch, eyes closed, absorbed in the world my new MP3 player was piping into my brain. It'd been only two weeks since I'd been genuinely touched by that very gift, and I was far too elated about my regained sense of freedom and control over my future to care about non-existent birthday plans. In contrast to how genuinely trapped I might have been had the pregnancy scare panned out, I felt downright footloose. I could do anything I wanted with my life now. I could go to grad school in Sweden. I could go home. I wasn't going to make any more horrible decisions, that was for sure. Only good ones.

What would a good decision look like? Would I know it when it popped into my head? Or would I have to...sigh...carefully weigh some options or something?

I was listening in shuffle mode and mentally compiling a pros and cons list between going home and free grad school when I felt a slight pressure of something plopping upon my thigh. Curious as to what could have possibly motivated Johan to move in the slightest, I opened my eyes just enough to peep through the tiniest of slits.

There he was, my dear, devoted boyfriend, still apparently absorbed in something on TV, with his hands still positioned on his laptop's keyboard, with his pants unzipped and his flaccid penis flopped upon my leg. Just lying there.

Excuse me? Was that supposed to be funny? Or worse—sexy? Am I supposed to want to have sex with that? Should I take this as my cue to cease what I am doing and attend to that in some way? No. No way.

I closed my eyes again and prayed that the thing would disappear. And as I was waiting for it to sheepishly retreat, I realized this dick on my leg was the definitive mark on the "con" side of staying in Sweden. This dude was all I had. And this dude was a bad decision. I just couldn't stand it any longer. I couldn't stand waiting for a damn Svenska class to begin anymore either; I couldn't stand being a maid for another day or spending one more weekend of being bored to tears. Most of all, I couldn't stand the fact that I had every reason in the world to leave, but not a single reason to go home.

Getting this flaccid penis off of my thigh wasn't exactly a classy excuse to leave, but it sure was a powerful motivator.

Put it away.

Put it. Away.

I determined that I would listen to two more songs. When the songs were done, I would open my eyes. When I opened my eyes, the dick would be gone, and I would begin planning how to quit this mess.

* * *

It was decided the following Tuesday, and rather quickly, I might add.

I just needed to talk to Inger, I decided while mopping the kitchen. I needed to tell her that this situation was not working out for me. Maybe she'd suggest we try some different arrangement, and we'd give that a go for a while. Then, by February, I'd be able to say I'd given it my all and throw in the towel with dignity. After a day and a half of rehearsing how the conversation would go, I sloshed the mop into its bucket and marched down the stairs to Inger's office.

"Come in, dear!" Inger looked absolutely delighted to retract her pointer fingers from the keyboard and field my question or concern.

"Inger, do you have a minute? I need to talk."

"But of course, my dear!" Inger's red poof ushered me into the small room and onto the couch in the far corner. This was where her clients sat.

"Tell me, dear," she said from the armchair across from me. "What can I do for you?"

"Well," I began slowly, "I'm not completely happy with how things are going right now."

"And this trip has not been quite what you expected?" The crazy lady was learning toward me, her eyes as wide as they could go, nodding in agreement with herself before I'd even begun to respond. It felt like she'd been anticipating this conversation for some time. Here I'd been fretting over what to say, and all her lines seemed already rehearsed.

"Um, well no, but…"

"And you are missing your family?"

"Well…yes, of course I miss them."

"Then that is that! You want to go home! We will make arrangements!"

Wait. What? What had just happened?

"But Inger," I said, choking back tears of relief and confusion and a little bit of insult as well. "I made—I made a commitment to you and your family to work here for a year."

"Ah! But darling, your commitment must first be to yourself. Is that not true?"

"Well—"

"And you are much too bright and have too much in your life ahead of you to spend your days with our housework!"

"Yes, I guess, but—"

"I have thought this for some time, but it was my belief that your relationship with Johan had been keeping you here."

"Oh, ah..." Oh yeah, Johan. "Yeah, I suppose."

"I see." Inger's tone changed and a look of confusion came over her face. "You know, dear, if this is a matter of your love affair changing, and you'd like to resume staying in your room here, you must know you are welcome. Has something happened with Johan?"

How much would I pay for the words "love affair" to never come out of her big, red mouth again?

"Oh no," I said quickly. "Everything is fine with Johan."

"So do I misunderstand? Are you not wanting to go home?" Holy shit. No, no. Go back. Please don't stop firing me. If I answered incorrectly, would she make me stay?

"No," I said, "Johan is great, but honestly...I don't love him."

Yup, that's right, Inger. I don't love Johan. I'm just pretending to in order to not live with you and your crazy family. Judge me. She definitely looked like she was judging me.

"Actually," I continued, "I'm not completely sure that I'm not still in love with someone I left behind. I think I need to go home and see."

What did I just say? Did I mean that? Was I just trying to wiggle out of her judgmental stare? Or was I telling the truth?

"Well, as I said," she continued, "you are welcome to stay here or with Johan for the rest of your stay, and we have enjoyed you so much dear, but we cannot keep you from the things you are missing at your home."

Wow. Was that it? Did we just have that conversation? While I was somewhat mystified and totally elated, I felt compelled to explain to Inger that it was nothing she or anyone else had done that made me so ready to go home, and that I always intended to carry out my commitment. I babbled out some of these things in no particular order, but my head was swimming with completely other thoughts.

I was going home. Home. I was going home. And all I had to do was open my mouth. It had been that easy. I was going home. And was that true about Greg? Could it be? It had to be, right? But it couldn't be. The only way to find out was by going home, and that was exactly what I was about to do.

Inger could not start making plans quickly enough. It felt odd exiting her office fifteen minutes later to pick up where I'd left off on the mopping as she delved right into the process of finding me a return flight online. The only thing that slowed her down was to check certain dates and times and to ask if we'd be putting this on my credit card or if I'd like to give her cash for the transaction. I pulled myself out of my shocked haze do business.

"If you'll recall," I said awkwardly (what did I have to lose? I was leaving!), "we planned to split the travel costs. I paid for my flight here, and you said you'd pay for the flight back, right?"

Inger paused in the kitchen doorway. I think my case was upheld purely by her desire to expedite the transaction. She transitioned flawlessly into faux laughter and delight. "Oh! Of course, darling! Then I will proceed with the purchase. As we've paid you though the middle of February, I'll be putting you on a plane leaving thereabouts."

Sigh. Of course you would, bitch. Because the only thing more important to you than getting me out of your hair was not losing a *kronor* in the process, you cheap, maniacal witch who has fulfilled my greatest desire. Thank you.

18
I Limbo
In Limbo

Sigh. Two more digits.

9. 2.

Breath held.

Riiiing. Riiiing.

Although it had been just five months since I'd left the world I was now calling, it seemed impossible that Greg could be reached by dialing the same 'ol reliable number. Its familiarity was increased by the fact that before I cancelled my cellular contract to move to Sweden, my number had been almost identical to his—the consequence of having a family plan together, which we'd had for two years. Now, it was he alone at that area code and exchange, but those numbers still felt like home, even when preceded by a country code. Dialing it this way, on this aged landline in Inger's office, made it feel like I was playing pretend. Could it be real that I'd hear his voice coming through this old-fashioned telephone machine? Had he been this close the whole time?

I get existential when I'm nervous. And as Greg's phone continued to ring, I was terrified. Would he answer? Would he even want to talk to me? What would Johan think? I had serious concern over this, as if he were capable of knowing what I was up to in Inger's office, or as if he might care at all what kind of feelers I was putting out in preparation for going home.

It stopped ringing.

"Hello?"

"Hi."

Silence.

"Nat?"

"Hey." I had no doubt he heard everything in my voice with that one syllable: relief, fear, hope, joy, and desperately purposeful amnesia.

"How was your Christmas?" I asked, as if we had just a couple weeks of catching up to do.

"Oh, it was all right." I could hear it now too, all of the same things in his voice, especially the hope. And he was smiling. I could hear that too. "It was good. Got an ear infection."

I chuckled. "Did you get something for it?"

"Oh you know, sort of. Just a little QT. A few rubber Cokes."

"Rubber Cokes?"

"Yeah, Mom and Rachel made the trip down for a few days. We had a holiday."

I laughed, full on and loudly. There was nothing Greg liked more than creating confusion to set himself up for a goofy joke. I'd never known anyone like him before.

"Ah, for Christmas then. You got quality time and rubber Cokes for Christmas. Not the ear infection."

"No, it's just ringing. Not really doing anything about it. But Christmas was the shit."

Then we sat there, sharing a strikingly comfortable phone silence, holding onto each other's attention. I thought about his strong, solid torso, and how my short arms would just barely grace the bottom of his ribcage when wrapped around him. I could sense his long, dark brown bangs draping over his profile as he bowed his head to meet mine.

"Nat, are you OK?"

"Yeah," I said. "Yes." I felt more OK as I said this than I had since I'd left. Really, since before I'd left. "I mean, kind of. Not really. Things aren't good here. They're…really weird. But I'm OK now. I'm coming home."

* * *

Telling Johan was not my favorite. He was sad. I was sad because he could tell I wasn't actually sad. I told him the story of how it happened with the closest proximity to the truth possible without making him sadder.

For once, Johan's laptop sat idle on the coffee table as he sat dejectedly on the couch. He asked why I couldn't just quit the Waaras' and stay with him for a few months. Alas, I told him, the ticket was already booked. We had a month. And I'd be working throughout it.

"Isn't she horrid?" I commiserated, while actually being so, so thankful for both the haste with which Inger booked the ticket and the fact that continuing to work would give me something to do besides sit on this couch for the next month.

"Yes, she is terrible…terrible," he said sadly. "We haven't even had time to do everything yet."

My head cocked sharply to the side like a dog hearing a trigger word. It was all I could do to not break character and start laughing. We were going to do things? Like, later? Months into our relationship was when we were going to start doing things?

"Yeah…" I said, as if I knew exactly what he meant and totally agreed. Sure, he'd talked about taking me on a trip to London, and about the fun parties during the Svensk holiday of Midsommar, but somewhere between the IKEA clearance room and stealing cans of kidney beans, I'd realized that neither of those adventures were ever going to happen.

"*Ja*." Johan said. "And you know I spoke of my friends in Australia? They have been talking of inviting us down."

There was no downside to faking it, I decided. I could make it one more month. And playing pretend with Johan that we were very happy and would so miss each other would only make the time go by faster. I was in.

"Oh no!" I said excitedly. "Noooo! That would have been so much fun!" I leaned toward him on the couch, slid my arm behind his back, and rested my head affectionately on his arm. "What else would we have done?"

I was surprised how natural and not indescribably fake this felt. I did feel affection toward Johan, my strange, Eurotrash friend. I owed him a lot, and I cared for him. *This was a good plan*, I thought. *As long as he keeps his penis off my leg.*

We sat together and talked through our feelings, deep, true, and feigned alike. He told me how summer was the best time in Sverige, and how it was so unlucky that I had to come here in the winter when it was so dull.

"Midsommar is when Sweden is real Sweden," he said sadly. "We have so much celebration, and for me the cars are coming in more regularly, and there is more money to go around…"

He told me all about the holiday, and indeed it sounded like a good time. In fact, a small part of me even felt regretful that I'd miss it. But nothing could have convinced me to wait five more months to experience it. How in the world did these people live in a county that was fun once a year?

Johan and I came to the only conclusion there was to be had: that we would have a really great month together, and that would be that.

After a sufficient period of silence, I asked if I could use his laptop to write a few necessary emails to family and friends so preparations could begin.

Jan. 10, 2006

Dear Wonderful, Exciting, and Delightful Alisa,
Holy fucking shit. Start blowing up the balloons and rolling out the red carpet. I'm coming home, and I have no idea where I'm going to live, or what I'm going to do when I get there. Best prepare your couch. And your party shoes.

* * *

As I expected, continuing to work for the Waaras after my departure had been arranged was super weird. It was also weird that it had now been a week, and no one had mentioned it to me. Inger, Jan, the kids—they all treated me as if nothing had changed. Had Inger not told them? This was unclear. It was clear, however, that I would not be the one bringing it up. I'd just keep vacuuming, dusting, and laundering as if the whole thing was a secret I was quietly in on. Was it?

As I was wandering down the stairs one morning, about to begin the laundry, Pia was coming up. She wasn't feeling well and was home from school.

"Oh!" she quietly exclaimed upon seeing me. "The telephone is for you."

Excellent. My laundry plans were officially on hold.

"It is a man," Pia said, deeply intrigued as she turned to walk with me back down the stairs toward Inger's office. "Do you know who it is?"

I'd now called Greg three times from the Waaras. It was understandable that I'd be making more phone calls than usual now that I had all sorts of arrangements to make about my homecoming. Those arrangements had nothing whatsoever to do with my conversations with Greg, which centered on everything but concrete details, including where our relationship stood. We were just enjoying talking to each other.

"Yes," I said, smiling. "I know who it is."

"Will you be seeing him when you return home?" Pia's beautiful eyes were wider than normal with fascination. Pale from lack of sunlight, ten pounds heavier than I was when I arrived, and in my usual, desperately un-showered state, I could tell I was somehow a sort of romance goddess to her at that moment. I wanted to sit her down right there on the stairs to clarify to her that she should try very, very hard to never emulate any of this insanity, but there was no time for that. Greg was on the phone.

The drawback to our phone calls at Ödmjuk Gård was that each conversation had to be short and hushed. This time was no exception. There was so much we wanted to say, long soliloquies of where our hearts had traveled these many months, and where we found ourselves now, but the nature of talking in Inger's office relegated us to chatting about weekend plans (his) and football scores (also his). I told him I'd find some time to call him on Saturday when I wasn't working. I knew Johan had some car appointments, so the coast would be clear at some point. Greg didn't need to know I was calling from Johan's, and Johan didn't need to know either. I could make this transition painless on us all. I just matter-of-factly asked him to have an international calling card ready, and he agreed.

"So…was it someone important?" Pia was sitting outside the doorway when I left the office. Feeling exhilarated from the call and bursting to share, I sat down next to her.

"It is someone important," I smiled. "It's someone…yeah. He's important."

"Is he why you are going back?"

I wasn't about to tell Pia that her mother's misrepresentation of this entire deal had a lot more to do with it than Greg.

"Yeah," I said. "I think he really is. Or at least, the chance that he could be worth going back for is enough to back and find out."

"You are not going back to Johan's now before you leave?" She sounded happy about the suggestion that I might leave Johan, which took me by surprise. I knew they thought he was odd, but I'd always thought Pia found our relationship intriguing.

"Oh, I'll still stay with him," I said. "He and I are really good friends. We're really going to miss each other. It's nice that we have a few more weeks to hang out before I have to go."

"*Ja*, well…" Pia stood up a smiled as she started up the stairs. "He is lucky. We like having you."

It had never occurred to me that the non-Inger Waaras actually liked having me there. That was nice, but it was too late now. Besides, the explanation that Johan and I were good friends who would enjoy our last few weeks together before I went back to try and make things work with Greg sounded very logical. It felt like I had been making something up just then, but as Pia left me there at the bottom of the stairs, I realized I had just told the truth.

* * *

And so it was. On Saturday, Johan tore himself from his beloved couch and from our reenergized enjoyment of each other's company to go to work at the agreed-upon time. I said I was sad to see him go, hugged him, gave him a kiss, and then waited until his silver hatchback veered around the curve before digging out my calling card and calling Greg's number.

"Hi!" I said cheerfully. We were in the clear. We could talk. No one was around.

"Hey," he said. "I was just thinking about you. I'm really glad you called."

"Is this a good time to talk?" I said. It was four in the afternoon here, making it 10 a.m. in Michigan. I knew this was still a little early for Greg's taste, but I didn't have a lot of choice in the matter.

"Absolutely," he said. "How's it going?"

"Well, it's good, and I can talk for about an hour, but my calling card is going to run out any minute. Do you have your calling card ready to call me back? "

"Oh, yeah. Of course," he said. See? Always a gentlemen. "I just need to run to the corner and buy one. I'll call you back in ten."

Great. I gave him Johan's number, and then reminded him that I wasn't going to be able to talk after an hour from now. I had no explanation for this, and he didn't ask for one.

I couldn't even concentrate on filling the next ten minutes with any activity. I just sat with the phone in my hands. What would we talk about? What had he been doing these last several months? How much had he missed me? Had he been waiting for me to call him the whole time? What was going to happen when I got back? Would he pick me up from the airport?

The second ten minutes was a little more restless. I got out Johan's computer, checked my email, and wrote to Alisa about coming home details. She was offering to pick me up from the airport. I was almost ready to accept, but I'd need to get through this conversation with Greg first. If he were to offer, I would surely take him up on it. I hadn't mentioned much to her about he and I talking. I knew she'd be concerned about this, so I just neglected to mention it to her.

After a half hour had gone by, I began to be concerned. Should I call him back? I used Johan's phone to check the minutes on my card. Less than a minute. Then I fretted for the next ten minutes that Greg had tried to call while I was checking the minutes, and I'd missed him. That had to be it. Now, did I call him with my half a minute to say, "I'm sure you just called forty-five seconds ago exactly, but I messed it up, so call back now, I'm here!"? Or would that just risk another possible phone-call crossing?

My fretting reached maximum intensity when Johan, right on time for the very first time since I'd known him, pulled back into the driveway. Damn. He was going to be stinky and dirty though, I reminded myself. He'll probably want to shower.

Johan was stinky and dirty, but was just too happy to see me to pull himself away. Every minute he sat next to me, chattering away about something he'd heard on the radio made my stomach fill more and more with anxiety. This was not going to end well. He'd been home for a full twenty minutes—an hour and nineteen minutes since I'd called Greg—and had almost resolved to get himself in the shower when the phone rang.

I should have just jumped for it. I should have grabbed the phone and declared, "It's from America!" and pretended it was Alisa. But I froze. Johan casually got up, grabbed the phone from the dining room table where I'd left it, and answered it.

"Allo?" he said. There was a pause. Johan turned slowly and looked at me with one eyebrow raised. "Ah…*ja.* Natalie is here. May I ask who is calling her here?"

Fuck. Fuuuuuuuuuck.

"OK, Mr. 'A Friend' I will get her on the phone for you."

He then threw the phone onto the couch next to me, walked into the bathroom, and turned on the shower.

I took the phone into the kitchen for good measure.

"Greg?"

"Who was that?"

"I really can't talk anymore."

"Are you OK?"

"I'm fine, I just need to handle everything here carefully for these last couple of weeks. And I can't talk now."

"Nat?"

"Yes?"

"Everything is going to be OK when you get home. I love you."

I could hardly say good-bye. As soon as we hung up, I managed to condense what should have been a forty-five-minute crying spell into ninety seconds. He loved me. Alisa would be picking me up from the airport, but I'd gotten everything from that phone call I'd hoped to glean in the hour-long version I'd imagined. In ten minutes, when Johan was out of the shower, I was sitting on the couch with *Alien vs. Predator* in the DVD player, dinner on the stove, and cheerful questions about his car-fixing appointment. We never discussed it again.

I was surprised how swiftly Johan bounced back from this episode. Perhaps it felt to him much like reading his chats with Annika felt to me—unfortunate and bothersome, but really meaningless in the long run. We sat together on a couch that night, watched that ridiculous movie for the umpteenth time, did a couple of sudoku puzzles together, and the next morning, we ate *knäckebröd.* In accordance with our agreement, we were making the most of the time we had left.

* * *

My last day of work was on a Tuesday. The kids were off from school on some sort of holiday, so everyone was around as I brought my suitcase over to pack the last of my things that were still scattered around the room Pia never ended up taking over. I was deciding which of my books I'd just leave behind for Inger when there was a quiet tap at the door.

"Hi!" Lisbeth said in her quiet but upbeat voice.

"Hey, Lisbeth! Come on in!"

She gently stepped through the doorway, as if she were entering a new world, not the empty cellar bedroom that had been in her own home for her entire life.

"So…you are packing everything up?" This was the first time we'd acknowledged my leaving. My plane was due to take off in approximately twenty-four hours.

"Yup. I think I have everything, but I don't think I'm going to bring all of these books back. Would you read any of these?" I held up a couple of paperbacks for her to see as she awkwardly leaned against the table.

"Mmm…maybe."

"I'm really sorry I won't be able to help you with the horses anymore," I said.

"Jaaap! I know. But we may sell Mom's horse, and I don't know about Grölle," she said quietly. "I want to take a camp with him this summer, but I haven't ridden for so long. Maybe we don't need to take care of horses so much."

So *now* she decides to get rid of them. But I was glad for her. She'd told me once that Grölle was her best friend. That's probably not good when you're almost seventeen.

"I hope things keep getting better for you at school," I said. "It sounds like Beata might be a good friend for you." I was referencing the first girl I'd ever heard Lisbeth mention in casual conversation. She'd just begun to talk about her a few weeks ago, but the two had been eating lunch together at school. Maybe there was a path to social normalcy for Lisbeth.

"*Ja*…she's nice. Well, I like you being here," she said quickly. "We had a nice Halloween, and you were fun to be here."

With that, she turned on her heel and made for the door. That's what she came to say.

"Lisbeth," I called after her. She stopped in the doorway and turned around. "You're a lot of fun too. And I liked being here with you." She smiled, turned, and left.

Several minutes later, Inger popped in on me as well, but not to say sweet things about missing me. Rather, she asked if I'd seen the copy of her Miraculous Process text that she had definitely given me as a gift upon my arrival.

"I do believe it's been missing for some time, dear," she said in her darkly dreamy voice, "and they are not inexpensive, so I do hope you have an idea where it can be found."

Of course I had an idea where it could be found. It could be found in my suitcase, where I'd just packed it. It was an off-color souvenir to be sure, but it was the one I was most excited to take home. But alas. I wouldn't steal my gift back.

"Oh yeah," I said casually, "I think I may know where that is."

"Waaaaaaandaful!" Inger replied, pausing expectantly in the doorway, apparently waiting for me to reveal the magical book's hiding place. I waited as well, smile drawn.

"It might take me a minute to check a few spots," I finally said. "I'll be sure to leave it on the desk when I find it."

And she, like her daughter, turned and left, having heard what she'd come to my lair to hear. From beneath my packed clothes, I extracted the book, which was clearly designed to resemble the Bible, and I considered just how crappy a job Inger had done trying to convert me to Den Metod in the first place. *Zero evangelist points for you, lady,* I thought.

My official leaving of Ödmjuk Gård happened the next day. They didn't invite me over for dinner or for a family outing or anything of that nature. I was relieved. I was especially surprised, however, that no such offer came from Jan and Åke. There had to be some local castle or very steep cliff we hadn't explored yet. I supposed I had broken up the Adventure Team, however, and they had every right to feel bruised about it. But actually, to the contrary, Jan said over his *middag* on my last day, "It is no good that you are go before it is nice outside for the biking and the boat."

He seemed more sad than bitter, and I assumed both my being there and my leaving would go down as yet another grievance against his meddling wife. Inger had brought me there to help her son be less shy around girls and to give her husband a household companion. He had every right to feel weird about that.

As there were no formal farewells planned, Johan and I simply stopped by on our way to the airport, and we all stood awkwardly in the foyer exchanging goodbyes. It was like the world's most painful receiving line at history's most awkward wedding. I hugged them all, even Åke, who seemed like he might die of girl-touching when I went in for it.

Inger herself had only generic words of parting for me. After the others had said their casual, awkward goodbyes, and she took me by the shoulders to offer the household's official farewell statement.

"Oh, Natalie! It was so wonderful to have you with us, and you were soooooooo welcome here! We will write and take phone calls from you when you return home, so we may keep in contact with you forever!"

Big hugs, big red smiles, big waves, and I was gone. We would not write or take phone calls when I returned home, but then, those sentiments were no less true than the one she'd been repeating since the day I'd arrived, that I was sooooooo welcome there. What a bullshitter.

And then, Johan drove me to Helsingborg. He rode the ferry with me to Copenhagen and waited for me to check in at the airport. That process was quick, and my gate wasn't far away, according to the map we were standing in front of, but my flight didn't leave for and hour and a half. What were we going to do? Sit and talk? Make this weirdness last a second longer? Mmm…I was kind of hungry. I could see a café on the other side of security.

"I should get in line," I said, nodding at the super short and moderately paced security check queue.

"Ah…" Johan said sadly. He gently slipped his hand into mine and slid down into a seated position on the bench below the airport map. He so loved couch-similar objects. I sat down next to him and squeezed his hand.

"I mean, I could sit here for a minute, but that wouldn't change anything, right?" I asked honestly.

"Nah…" He looked down at our hands and shook his rumpled blonde head. "I am so sad for you to go, Natalie. I just think…" He stumbled to find the right words. "I just think what we could maybe have done if we had more time together. You don't even see how special you are to me. How no one else is so funny, so sarcastic, so full of words…I don't know how to find anyone after you."

Seriously, where was this guy a month ago? He's just spent three weeks with his car-greased hand down his pants watching snowboarding on TV for seven hours a day, and *now* suddenly he's the Svensk Antonio Banderas? I smiled, knowing at this point to take it all in with a grain of salt.

"I think you're the one who is underestimating himself, Johan," I said. "A week after I'm gone, you're going to forget I was even here."

He just looked down and shook his head.

"Listen," I said. "This is not a terrible way to end things, is it? Relationships never end on a good note. Either you break up because you're miserable, or you never break up and it ends when somebody dies. We're glad we were together, and we'll both miss each other—that's way better than those other options, right?"

He looked up and kissed me. It was a fine kiss, but I ended it quickly.

"Bye, Johan," I said sincerely. "Thank you—really, thank you for everything."

He said goodbye, and I turned away and walked toward the security check line. It was possibly the best feeling I had ever had. All that craziness was behind me. Everything good and familiar and possible was before me. It didn't occur to me until I was settling into my seat an hour later than I'd never looked back to see how long Johan stood there, waiting for me to make it through the line. Oops. I'd forgotten he was there.

Epilogue
June 2008

"I said, 'Breakdowns come and breakdowns go.
So what are you going to do about it?' That's what I'd like to know."
- Paul Simon, "Gumboots"

I was annoyed when I saw his truck pass me as I ran through the park, even more so when it slowed, turned right, and parked on the side of the road ahead. The fact that he was interrupting my excellent new running routine was enough to perturb me, but the sight of that truck really set my teeth into a clench. It had been a wedding present from my dad—the down payment had been, anyway—and now he was using it to move his things out of our house.

If I'd wanted to talk to Greg today, I wouldn't have texted him earlier to suggest he stop over to collect his things at the exact time I was going out. There didn't seem to be any avoiding him now; he was getting out of the truck, and I was running right toward him. As I approached, I recalculated the numbers I'd been reviewing every few days: it had now been sixteen days since we were supposed to have gotten married; that made it almost six weeks since he'd called it off; one year and two months since he'd proposed; five years since we'd first started dating. I couldn't make sense of it. Every time I added them up, it was like I was missing something.

"Hey."

He was waiting at the end of the sidewalk when I arrived, panting and sweating. He was smiling. Not a huge smile, but one that meant he was glad to see me. I couldn't for the life of me imagine why.

"Hi," I said between breaths, stopping on the sidewalk in front of him with my hand on my hips. "Did you get everything you needed?"

"Oh yeah," he said. "I'm on my way over to Steve's to hang out for a while. A few people are coming. Work's actually been crazy this week, so we're just going to chill. Nothing big."

Awesome. Good for you. It was annoying, but we did this now. We'd see each other in passing, and we'd catch up exclusively on the mundane details, like that was the thing we missed most about being together. He went on about orders at work, and softball league antics for a few minutes. Underneath his chattiness he actually seemed happy, which felt as insulting as it did genuinely pleasant.

Greg was electric to be around when he was up, and terrible when he was down. And he had been down increasingly often since we'd gotten engaged a year before. He'd begin so many days as if his goal was to make me feel terrible about one particular thing. He'd lay the groundwork in the morning. Then he'd drop subtle hints all day about whatever he was pissed about via email or over the phone. Then he'd come home, and we'd do the dance where I tried to keep him calm, and he tried to get me worked up. Sometimes I was careful enough, and nothing happened; other times there was the screaming and the swearing and the name-calling. Now, as we chatted, and he seemed happy, the leftover sense of relief that it was a good day for him still made me feel good.

Months prior, his dark outbursts were becoming more and more frequent as our wedding date approached—until they just stopped. That afternoon I came home after work to find him crying, telling me that we had fallen out of love with each other, something that was news to me. Apparently the discussion we'd had the night before about us getting help for whatever was going on hadn't done the trick. It turned out he didn't want help; he wanted out.

And now that we were here on the sidewalk chatting about his work drama, he'd gotten what he wanted. So he was happy.

"...so he won't take the phone call because he's afraid of talking to her, and we're all like, 'Alberto, she is one crazy bitch.' I mean, can you believe that? She called him at work from her husband's cell!"

"Wow," I replied flatly. "That poor guy. Well, anyway, I need to get back..."

I wanted to get out of there. Greg seemed like he was doing fine, but I was not. I'd just had my life torn apart, and this was not helping.

I turned to go.

"I went to see someone," Greg said.

I paused. That was not expected. I might have smiled. I might have been overcome with renewed hope, but instead, my gut was suddenly and sharply wound up like a coil. It had something to do with hope, but it was an angry, cautious brand of hope made possible by having recently sent forty-three apologetic thank you notes for wedding gifts requesting instructions on how to best refund the gift givers, not to mention having tearfully picked-up and paid for a custom-fitted wedding dress that would never be worn.

"Yeah?" I said quietly.

"Yeah," he continued. "I called around and found this guy who seems really…he seems like he could really help."

"And you went to see him."

"Yup."

"And how did it go?"

"Great, I mean, really great…" He explained that it went really, really well. Clearly, this counselor was triggering a surge of fresh-start feelings for Greg. He told me that the guy thought he might be depressed and told him his episode that led to our split was likely a mental breakdown. I don't think you're supposed to get jazzed about being told you'd suffered a mental breakdown, but Greg seemed to be pretty pumped up about it. Rather, he felt validated.

"So when are you going to go back?" I asked.

"Oh, I mean, some time," he said. "The thing is, he told me that…I don't know, you know how my schedule is. And there's this thing he has where he says pot is supposed to have some sort of effect on this, and he needs me to go a week without it before our next session. So…you know I had one scheduled, but then something came up, and then the next one was like…I don't know, he couldn't do it when I wanted to do it, so…some time. But I think it's going really well."

He was never going back. I had not seen him go an entire week without smoking weed for years. Maybe ever. Forty-eight hours would have been a challenge. I'd also never seen him finish a single thing he started. Maybe this time would be different. Maybe I'd be the thing that made him follow through. I'd have to just wait and see, but I wouldn't hold my breath.

"Well, good," I said. "I'm glad. I hope you go back soon." And I did.

I was turning again to leave, mainly because there just didn't seem like anything else to say. I was tired of talking. I was ready to start waiting and see if any of the talk panned out.

"Nat?"

I stopped and looked at him.

"I'll wait for you. For as long as you need."

Wait now. What? *He'll* wait for *me*?

While I was doing what? Trying to win back all the friends I'd given up because he didn't approve of them? Regaining the trust of the few people I had left after lying to them for years whenever he asked, making excuses for everything he did? Or would he wait for me to consider doing those things, but then realize going back to him was just easier? Probably that last one, since it's what I'd done every other time.

But I was tired of only having him left. I looked into his eyes, and for the first time I could see him trying to manipulate me. Like always, trying to convince me that that he was the faithful, patient lover, waiting out my dithering. It was so easy to forget whatever he'd done to make me leave, when he was so busy pointing out that I'd done the leaving, and the leaving was the true crime.

I had been waiting all this time for a crazy person to meet me halfway. For five years, no matter how far I walked toward him, he was actively stepping backward, constantly moving the goalposts to see if I could love him enough to keep trying. And now it was happening again, as if declaring he didn't love me three weeks before our wedding day had been just another minor step backward. Something I just needed time to get over.

I smiled. Not a huge smile, but it was a genuine one. The final number had just fallen into place. It had been two years and five months since I'd walked into Inger's office and told her I'd had enough. That was how long ago I'd learned what I was supposed to do here. Crazy people. They're all the same.

"You can wait if you want to," I said. "But I'm done waiting."

Greg watched me walk away from him. I could tell because I never heard a door shut, and the truck never started. I assumed he was watching because he took my response as a ruse. He was waiting for me to turn around, to wave, to do something to temper the finality of the word "done."

But I didn't. I was, in fact, completely shocked to find myself facing straight forward, not even tempted turn and look at him. It felt exactly like two years and four months ago when I'd walked away from Johan and Inger and a hundred meals of boiled *potatis* to board the plane in Copenhagen: like there was nothing behind me.

Svenska

apelsin	oranges
apotek	pharmacy
avdelning	ward
basar	bazaar
blandfärs	ground beef mixed with other meats
blodpudding	blood pudding
bror	brother
bröd	bread
bädd	bed
citronsås	lemon sauce
dillsås	dill sauce
Din Sko	A Swedish shoe retailer
doppigrytan	hot ham juice
dricka	drinks

eftermiddag	afternoon
Engelska	English
farbror	uncle
fika	a social gathering involving coffee
fisk	fish
fiskbullar	fishballs
fyllda ågghalvor	deviled eggs
glasrengöringsmedel	glass cleaner
glögg	mulled Christmas wine
God morgon!	Good morning!
grön ostsås	blue cheese sauce
gå och ligga	go lie down
gård	farm
Hemtex	Swedish home goods store
herrgårdsost	farmer's cheese
Hur mår du?	How are you?
ja	yes
Jul	Christmas
Julskinka	Christmas ham
Julbasar	Christmas bazar
julbord	buffet-style Christmas dinner

Juldagen	Christmas day
kavring	dense, seedy rye bread
kaffe	coffee
kokt rödkål	red cabbage
krona	Swedish currency
kronor	Swedish currency, plural
knäckebröd	crispbread
krök	bend
kvällsmat	dinner
kåldolmar	cabbage rolls
kök	kitchen
köttbullar	Swedish meatballs
Lutfisk	A Swedish delicacy, essentially rotten, gelatinous fisk
mat	food
matjes sill	a type of herring
med mycket kärlek	with much love
Metod	method; Den Metod: Inger's nickname for the Miraculous Process
moofin	muffin
middag	lunch
mjölk	milk
nej	no
och	and

ord	word
Ödmjuk Gård	Waara family farm, literally "Humble Farm"
Ost	cheese
Osthyvel	cheese slicer
potatis	potatoes
Potatis Korv	Christmas sausage
på	of, at, after, in
rågbröd	rye bread
rågkaka	soft, round disk of bread
sallad	lettuce
sillsallad	herring salad
sjukhus	hospital
sju	seven
skinka	ham
Skivlagret	Swedish CD retailer
Skåne	the southernmost county of Sweden
smör	butter
snaps	a Swedish liquor
socker	sugar
svamp	fungus
Svenska	Swedish (the language)

Svensk	A Swede, or something Swedish
Svenskar	Many Swedes
Sverige	Sweden
svettis	sweaty
timjan	thyme
tjugo	twenty
trampa	step
två	two
universitet	university
vetemjöl	flour
vitlöksås	garlic sauce
vänster	left
åkerjord	farmland

Acknowledgements

This book was nothing if not a group project. Years after coming home from Sweden, after repeatedly swearing my intentions to never revisit what had happened there, I flippantly suggested to my best friend that I might want to do some writing about it after all. That was when Alisa Bobzien showed up at my door with a binder that included every email we'd exchanged during the long-ago stay, saying, "I knew you were going to need these."

So it was truly her beautiful demonstration of faith in this story that launched *Swedish Lessons*. As big ideas sometimes do, the book quickly took on a life of its own, bringing together a loose association of acquaintances who thought they might want to join a writers' club. Though much more wine was drunk than chapters written between us, over the next several years these five women became my closest friends. They were the first readers, editors and critics of the book, but more importantly, they were the foundation upon which I rebuilt my life. Being a part of their weddings, pregnancies, careers, heartaches, adoptions, losses and triumphs has been the fuel that drove *Swedish Lessons* to completion. So to Rebecca Bischoff, Andrea Lawson, Suzy Goulart, Amy Watson and Alisa, thank you.

If my writing career began anywhere, it was not during my formal education, but when Robin Miner-Swartz hired me to write bar reviews for *The Lansing State Journal.* Robin not only took a chance on a 22-year-old dummy, but also gave me opportunities to write new and more challenging stories that would turn into the groundwork for a full-time freelance career. Robin also was the first person to read *Swedish Lessons* cover-to-cover – not once, but twice – and the feedback, edits and perspective she shared were invaluable. I owe her so much thanks, for her work on the book, and for being an all-around amazing example of how kindness and professionalism and generosity and wisdom can all somehow fit inside one person.

Sherrie Brindley was also an early and two-time reader of Swedish Lessons whose perspective and encouragement was incredibly helpful. More importantly, however, she has been a mentor of the highest order, first professionally, and then personally. It may have been my experience in Sweden that taught me how to walk away from things that were bad for me, but it was Sherrie who gave me the courage to do it a second time. For her ongoing friendship and life coaching, I am tearfully grateful.

Thank you as well to my parents and sister, Tim, Nancy and Brianna, who are generally discrete people, not given to over-sharing, but who let me be this way anyway. They have supported me when I was poor, loved me when I was (am) difficult, and still celebrate my successes with me as if I earned them myself. They are the kindest and best people I know, and how we are all related, I am not sure.

Finally, my biggest thanks belongs to the man who asked me out despite listening to a horrid, early first chapter of this book upon first meeting me, and married me three years later, not knowing if we'd ever get this thing out of our lives. Mike Vial is the bravest, smartest, most thoughtful man I've ever met. If *Swedish Lessons* makes anything clear, it's that I do not deserve him. That I have been allowed to share my life with a genuine rock star – who acts instead as if I am the rock star – is surely a crime against humanity or karma, and I'm sure I will suffer for it later. For putting up with this project for so long, for supporting me every day and constantly cheering me on, I owe him everything.

Let's not pretend I published this thing on my own either. I am so thankful to everyone who supported my crowdfunding campaign to make this book a reality. Your faith in me is undoubtedly misplaced, but all 188 of you have made a fan for life.

ABOUT THE AUTHOR

Natalie Burg is a freelance journalist with a passion for her home state of Michigan and for telling stories about growth and development. She lives in Ann Arbor with her husband, musician Mike Vial, and their silly, silly dog Lois. Learn more about Natalie and her work at natalieburg.com.

Made in the USA
Charleston, SC
02 October 2013